The Art of Light on Stage

The Art of Light on Stage is the first history of theatre lighting design to bring the story right up to date. In this extraordinary volume, award-winning designer Yaron Abulafia explores the poetics of light, charting the evolution of lighting design against the background of contemporary performance. The book looks at the material and the conceptual; the technological and the transcendental. Never before has theatre design been so vividly and excitingly illuminated.

The book examines the evolution of lighting design in contemporary theatre through an exploration of two fundamental issues:

1   What gave rise to the new directions in lighting design in contemporary theatre?
2   How can these new directions be viewed within the context of lighting design history?

The study then focuses on the phenomenological and semiotic aspects of the medium of light – the role of light as a performer, as the medium of visual perception and as a stimulus for imaginative representations – in selected contemporary theatre productions by Robert Wilson, Romeo Castellucci, Heiner Goebbels, Jossi Wieler and David Zinder.

This ground-breaking book is required reading for anyone concerned with the future of performance.

Yaron Abulafia is an internationally respected and critically acclaimed artist-in-light, whose stirring work has appeared in some of the most familiar European and North American dance and theatre companies including Nederlands Dans Theater, the English National Ballet, Rambert, Staatsballett Berlin, Ballet BC (Vancouver) and the Hungarian State Theatre of Cluj (Romania) – to mention but a few. This book is based upon his PhD research at the University of Groningen in the Netherlands.

The Art of Light on Stage

Lighting in contemporary theatre

Yaron Abulafia

Routledge
Taylor & Francis Group

LONDON AND NEW YORK

First published 2016
by Routledge
2 Park Square, Milton Park, Abingdon, Oxon OX14 4RN

and by Routledge
711 Third Avenue, New York, NY 10017

Routledge is an imprint of the Taylor & Francis Group, an informa business

British Library Cataloguing-in-Publication Data
A catalogue record for this book is available from the British Library

Library of Congress Cataloguing-in-Publication Data
Abulafia, Yaron.
The art of light on stage : lighting in contemporary theatre / Yaron Abulafia.
pages cm
Includes bibliographical references and index.
1. Stage lighting. I. Title.
PN2091.E4A28 2015
792.02'5—dc23
2015005884

ISBN: 978-1-138-91365-3 (hbk)
ISBN: 978-1-138-91368-4 (pbk)
ISBN: 978-1-315-69130-5 (ebk)

Typeset in Garamond
by Swales & Willis Ltd, Exeter, Devon, UK

To my lovely wife Manja, my parents Raphael and Sarah,
my children Emanuel, Noam and Itamar and my brother Eyal,
without whom this book would have
been completed three years earlier.

Nevertheless,

I wouldn't change a thing . . .

Contents

Figures

Foreword

Light becomes a sign and instantly receives meaning thanks to the surface that catches it, and the shadows created by everything that eludes it.

This is why every phenomenon can be said to be light, and where there's light there is fire.

On the boards of a stage this law is raised to a higher power, because every aesthetic gesture has been chosen by someone. I myself, for example, working with beams of light, move them as though I was directing the leading actors.

Just like the latter, they enter the stage, say what they have to say in the time they've been given, and exit. The light that I respect is not functional, but illuminates itself in a tautological blaze. If light is a sign, my work consists in ensuring that this sign signifies, engraving itself on the spectator.

Romeo Castellucci

La luce è significata dalla superficie che la raccoglie e anche dall'ombra prodotta da ciò che la sfugge.

Per questo si può dire che ogni fenomeno è luce e dove c'è luce c'è un incendio.

Questa legge è elevata a potenza sulle tavole di un palcoscenico perché ogni gesto estetico è stato scelto da qualcuno. Io, per esempio, quando muovo dei fasci di luce lavoro come con degli attori protagonisti.

Come loro anch'essi entrano in scena, dicono quello che devono dire nel tempo prestabilito, escono di scena. La luce che rispetto non è quella funzionale ma quella che illumina se stessa come in un rogo tautologico. Se la luce è un segno il mio lavoro è quello di fare in modo che questo segno segni.

Romeo Castellucci

Acknowledgements

This project would not have been completed without the help of many. I am very grateful to Barend van Heusden, my PhD supervisor at the University of Groningen, whose dedication and guidance were exceptionally enlightening and inspiring for the research on which this book is based. Hans van Maanen from the University of Groningen and Heiner Goebbels from the University of Giessen have provided me with extremely valuable guidance for which I am indebted.

For three years, my research has been generously supported by an Ubbo Emmius PhD Scholarship, for which I owe my gratitude to the Institute for Cultural Research at the University of Groningen. I would also like to thank the Frank Mohr Institute, the Hanze University of Applied Science Groningen, and Petri Leijdekkers, Gusta Lebbink, Ton Mars and Leo Delfgaauw in particular, for awarding me a scholarship that made it possible to start this PhD research.

This book would not have been brought to press without the long-time support of Talia Rodgers and Routledge, and the valuable advice of Pamela Howard, Freddie Rokem, David Zinder, Miriam Guretzki, Ben-Tzion Munitz, as well as Kees Vuyk, Stijn Bussels, Nick Moran, Andrew Nisbet and Hansjorg Schmidt, who read various chapters and gave me valuable feedback during the writing process. This book was printed in full-colour with the generous support of ROBE. I would like to express my gratitude in particular to ROBE CEO, Josef Valchář; thanks also to Jiří Baroš and the ROBE team in the UK.

I would like to extend my gratitude to the theatre directors, choreographers and designers, visual artists and photographers, opera and theatre companies, museums, university libraries, and archives who responded with kindness to my requests for artworks for publication in this book. In particular, I would like to thank Clifford Allen and the Watermill Center, Tanja Mlaker and the Dutch National Opera, Dani Redler and the Stage Lighting Museum at Hod Hasharon in Israel, the Edward Gordon Craig Estate, van Abbemuseum Eindhoven, Studio Olafur Eliasson, Anthony McCall, István Biró, Arno Declair, Christophe Raynaud de Lage, Klaus Lefebvre and Kiryl Synkou for their generosity and kind assistance.

I offer thanks to Naomi Paz who began proofreading the manuscript and to Tal Haran for the final proofreading and improvement with useful suggestions. I would like to thank Nick Brock for his help in finalizing the manuscript and preparing the book for publication, and also Brent Waterhouse for translating Romeo Castellucci's Foreword. Thanks to Ira Avneri, Dina Konson, Louis Jansen and Declan Randel for their help with the preparations for publishing this book.

Writing this book was hugely inspired by years of artistic collaboration with choreographers and directors, designers and composers, performing artists and technicians while working together on productions around the world — many thanks to you all. I would also like to thank my former students in the Theatre School of Amsterdam and in other institutions I visited as a lecturer, whose enthusiasm and questions inspired me to reflect on the role of light in contemporary theatre and spurred me on to complete the writing of this book.

And last but not least, my deep gratitude to Manja, my love, whose patience and care knew no boundaries while caring also for Emanuel, Noam and Itamar — without her, this book would not have been written at all.

Introduction

I like to work with light in a way that respects the light bulb as a sculpture, or that is able to develop the force of a light itself as an artistic force, which means that I have to work with light from the very beginning, from the very first rehearsal I have the light, because otherwise whenever an element comes late in the process, it will be not only not so important, it will also be only illustrative.

(Heiner Goebbels in an interview with John Tusa,
Broadcast BBC Radio 3, 3 March 2003)

. . . light is not an afterthought.
It's something that's architectural,
it's structure,
it's thought about from the beginning,
it's part of the book,
it's like an actor.
So it's not a decoration.

(Robert Wilson in an interview with John Bell,
Theater Week, 3 January 1994)

The context

Since the 1960s, we have witnessed an increasing fascination with and development of the visual dimension in western theatre, through experiments with interdisciplinary forms and new technologies, changes in the position of the performers and the addressees, the function of space, and the relationship between theatrical *representation* (based on verisimilitude) and *presentation*.[1] This shift has caused scholars to move away from theories of literature (e.g. hermeneutics and structuralism) towards the rather performance-oriented semiotics of theatre and, later, towards phenomenology and cognitive science. The decline in the hierarchy whereby the text lost its dominance over the other media paved the way for the emergence of contemporary post-dramatic theatre. Although I am aware that some theatre scholars prefer relating to theatre as such as a 'medium', composed of a certain number of elements (one of which is light), in this study I choose to refer to light as a medium in itself. Considering it a *medium* rather than a theatrical element, I side with those theatre scholars (such as Hans-Thies Lehmann) who have argued that in contemporary theatre the individual media of the performance tend towards a greater autonomy of expression. Since this notion is more thoroughly elaborated in the third chapter of the study, in this introduction I shall offer only a brief description of some of these tendencies and characteristics of contemporary theatre.

In contemporary theatre the text is often 'disturbed'. It tends to become fragmented, which also affects the relations between the text and the other media. The manifold ways in which the various media in contemporary theatre are used – occasionally taking separate or even contrasting directions – inevitably lead to a mutual reflection of one medium upon the other. Multi-channelling of information sets the relationships between the media in a constant, unstable movement and uncertainty with regard to possible meanings. This tendency is stimulated by the 'openness' of the post-dramatic text, which Lehmann characterized as a *'linguistic landscape'* (Lehmann, 2006). Theatre texts by Heiner Müller, Robert Wilson, Elfriede Jelinek, Bernard-Marie Koltès and Sara Kane, for example, demonstrate how language is used as a material, to weave *landscapes of ideas* with atmospheres and suggestive meanings. The 'rhizome-like' nature of the text stands in opposition to the 19th-century conventions of linear narrative, causal logic and probability of events.[2] If the text employs any characters at all, they seem to be more the *agents or deliverers of themes*, lacking the psychological profiles of fictive characters. As Elinor Fuchs stated in her book *The Death of Character* (1996), the psychological dimension that had been so central in the 19th century theatre has progressively lost much of its importance since the rise of Modernism. Replacing a character with an ambiguous entity or persona can bring the performer's own expressive individuality and presence, even corporeal qualities, to the fore. Furthermore, the body of the performer may become *an arena for human experience 'beyond drama'*, a body that, by being aestheticized, turns anonymous. The works of acclaimed theatre-maker Alain Platel and the company *les Ballets C de la B*, for example, clearly feature this tendency. On actors in the contemporary theatre Lehmann writes: "They act out their own corporeal logic within a given framework: hidden impulses, energy dynamics and mechanics of body and motorics. Thus, it is problematic to see them as agents of a discourse of a director who remains external to them" (Lehmann 2006, 32).

Since the decline of post-modernist thinking, the arts have mainly evolved conceptually, and no new innovative aesthetics have emerged. A major change occurred in how we think about and approach art. "The idea becomes a machine that makes the art", noted Sol LeWitt (1965). Hans Belting mentions conceptual artist Joseph Kosuth, who contended, in *Art after Philosophy* (1969), that art has become an analytical proposition, a critical practice that deals with *the nature of art* and no longer with producing new art (Belting 2003, 117). In the words of Danto (1998, 47), "Art has come to its end by becoming something else, namely philosophy". In view of this tendency to philosophize art, then, the major artistic progress in the past century occurred in the work on the image. Innovative and radical artists, questioning what the function of the image is in the arts, brought about Light Art, among other movements, and influenced the aesthetics of contemporary theatre and of theatre lighting in particular (Weibel 2006, 95–6).

That being so, theatre performances have also evolved into more suggestive and conceptually elaborate works which, accordingly, required theatre studies to reassess the new interrelation between the theatrical event and the audience, against the background of phenomenological experience and the negotiation of meaning. Since the contemporary arts, and theatre in particular, leave a degree of openness in the work that the addressees are invited to explore, the 'success' of the process depends on the effort the addressees are prepared to make. In contemporary (post-dramatic) theatre, therefore, the reception process becomes more complex and potentially confrontational for the spectators. The 'open text' allows for more playfulness and drift between associations that arise in the interpretation process; although, the negotiation of meaning can also fail. In the 19th-century Theatre of Realism, for example, the chance of such 'failure' was significantly lower because of the dramatic paradigm of the performance, the idea that the meaning was encoded in the play, and that the spectator's role was to decode its meaning. By contrast, and most significantly, in contemporary works the spectators construct their respective meanings individually – there is no 'hidden meaning' that they must decode or unfold in the performance. Edward Braun quotes theatre director Vsevolod Meyerhold:

> Your imagination is activated, your fantasy stimulated, and a whole chorus of associations is set off. A multitude of accumulated associations gives birth to new worlds – whole films which have never got beyond the cutting room. You can no longer distinguish between what the director is responsible for and what is inspired by the associations which have invaded your imagination.
>
> (Braun 1995, 318–19)

The questions

This book explores and discusses the evolution of lighting design against the background of developments within contemporary theatre, briefly outlined above. It will be argued that in contemporary theatre both the representational possibilities and the artistic potential of the medium of light have grown significantly. This evolution of lighting design has aesthetic, phenomenological, semiotic and poetic dimensions that resulted from new ways in which artists devised light in the theatre.

For the sake of clarity, I note that the terms *aesthetics* and *poetics* are highly concrete and not interchangeable in my discussion of theatre lighting: the former refers to the level of stimuli, visual perception and the materiality of the artefact (the light-image); while the latter refers to the creative ways by which some elements that are identified by the addressee as signs of light become part of the experience of the piece and the establishment of *imaginative representations*. I use the term 'representation' here to refer to the work of the theatre-makers who create an aesthetic experience and trigger the imagination of the addressee. When watching theatre, people engage emotionally and conceptually with the environmental stimuli that they register, and choose for themselves what they find to be significant. I use the concept of *imaginative representation* to refer to this work by the audience. I thus refer to the cognitive work done by the addressees, what Merlin Donald coined as the "cognitive engineering" of an experience (Donald 2006, 4). The representation of the theatre-maker becomes the imaginative representation of the audience. The *phenomenological* dimension is the conscious experience of our environment, as we subjectively grasp it. It refers to *the experience of things* as we assimilate them through our perception, imagination, memory, thoughts, desires and emotions. The *semiotic* dimension relates to the process of meaning-making, conceived either as human communication, according to Ferdinand de Saussure or as signification, according to Charles Sanders Peirce. Further elaboration upon these aspects is provided in the theoretical framework of this study (Chapter 3).

I examine the evolution of lighting design in contemporary theatre by engaging with two main questions. The answers to these questions encompass both a theoretical reflection and an interpretative analysis:

1   What caused the new directions in lighting design in contemporary theatre?
2   How can these new directions in lighting design be characterized in comparison to the use of light in earlier periods?

Following a chronological historical path, the study discusses the evolution of the medium of light in the theatre, especially from the end-19th century up to the 21st century. The aesthetics, the phenomenological experience, the semiotics and the poetics of light are analysed in relation to the development of lighting technologies. The study then focuses on the phenomenological and semiotic aspects of the medium of light in contemporary theatre. It does not offer a panoramic view of the many new formal characteristics one encounters in contemporary theatre performances; rather, it illuminates the function of lighting as a cogent force in the performance, the rising autonomy of light and its relation to other performative media, and the new themes and concepts from which contemporary lighting design derives its meaning.

Main themes and objectives

In the first chapter, "Towering figures in the history of theatre lighting design", I focus on how the medium of light was regarded by different theatre-makers since the late 19th century and how the available technologies of artificial lighting influenced the creation of visual experiences and imaginative representations with light in the theatre. Wherever possible, I present evidence of the spectators' reception and their imaginative representations. I consider the artistic function of artificial theatre lighting as 'design' only from the period in which effective control systems were invented and used for modifying light distribution during the performance, beginning with gas lighting systems. Writing about the history of lighting design is problematized through the perspective of light vis-à-vis the text, and the experience offered by the lighting to the spectator. With this in mind I address the works of lighting designers and theatre historians and theoreticians such as Adolphe Appia, Edward Gordon Craig, David Belasco, Allardyce Nicoll, Gösta M. Bergman, Christopher Innes, Richard C. Beacham, Arnold Aronson, Christopher Baugh, Joselin McKinney and Philip Butterworth, Oscar G. Brockett, Margaret Mitchell and Linda Hardberger, and Scott Palmer – to name but a few.

In Chapter 2, "Light Art: The rising autonomy of artificial light", I examine the use of artificial light in the visual arts, especially in regard to the phenomenological, semiotic and poetic dimensions of light, while seeking similarities or equivalences with light as it is used in the contemporary theatre. Individual visual artists, whose creative work is characterized by their use of light as the main 'material' in the piece, are presented in this chapter with reference to their conceptual frameworks. The technological, aesthetic and conceptual developments that led to the movement of Light Art have extended our thinking regarding the ability of light to act upon or influence the theatrical event and its degree of autonomy. Photographic documentation of selected works of Light Art will be included and analysed in relation to the artists' artistic visions.

The third chapter, "Theoretical framework", elaborates the theoretical grounds on which this book is based, using the complementary perspectives of semiotics, phenomenology, and cognitive and neural sciences, with a focus on the study of art. This chapter will establish a theoretical background for the development of a new conceptual framework for the analysis of lighting design in contemporary theatre. I will, for the semiotics, address the central notions of Ferdinand de Saussure, Charles S. Peirce, Umberto Eco, Keir Elam, Erika Fischer-Lichte, and the critique of structuralist semiotics by Jacques Derrida, Roland Barthes, Michel Foucault, Régis Debray, Willmar Sauter and Bert O. States. In the field of phenomenology I will address studies by Maurice Merleau-Ponty, Patrice Pavis, Hans-Georg Gadamer, Paul Ricoeur, Herbert Blau and Maaike Bleeker. On art in a cognitive and neural sciences context, the work of Ernst Cassirer, Merlin Donald, Steven Pinker, Robert L. Solso, Richard Palmer, Giacomo Rizzolatti and Corrado Sinigaglia will be discussed.

Chapter 4, "A new conceptual framework for the analysis of light", introduces an approach for the integrated analysis of the aesthetics, the phenomenological experience, the semiotics and the poetics of light. This study is the first of its kind in this field and a pioneering endeavour in demonstrating the usefulness of the approach through the in-depth-analysis of a number of contemporary theatre performances. Taking a theoretical stand as my point of departure, I set out to present a new, scholarly approach that is intended to expand the awareness, and enrich the discussion of the various dimensions of light in contemporary theatre by theatre-makers, critics, scholars and students.

In the next five chapters, I undertake an analysis of the lighting design used in five contemporary performances:

Madama Butterfly – directed by Robert Wilson/written by Giacomo Puccini

On the Concept of the Face, Regarding the Son of God – by Romeo Castellucci

Stifters Dinge – by Heiner Goebbels

Rechnitz – directed by Jossi Wieler/written by Elfriede Jelinek

Peer Gynt – directed by David Zinder/written by Henrik Ibsen

Madama Butterfly is the only opera production that I analyse, and it will serve as an example of the work of one of the greatest and most innovative theatre-makers of the 20th and 21st centuries, Robert Wilson. He designed the light for this performance together with his long-time collaborator and light designer, Heinrich Brunke.

On the Concept of the Face, Regarding the Son of God presents a visually-based, state-of-the-art theatre production almost devoid of verbal text, and based on the evocative images that characterize Romeo Castellucci's work. Castellucci himself designed the light and scenography for this performance.

Heiner Goebbels' performative installation *Stifters Dinge* is a 'no-man show', in which he takes to the extreme Gordon Craig's notion of the exclusion of the performer ('Über-Marionette'), thus exploring the boundaries of music theatre and re-establishing inter-activity among the different media in the theatre striving for polyphonic expression. Klaus Grünberg designed the light, scenography and video for this production.

The performance *Rechnitz* introduces a provocative, yet highly detailed and intelligent staging of Elfriede Jelinek's literary work on a theatre stage. In this performance, there are no characters, no dramatic conflict and no motivation to act – indeed this exemplifies the 'death of a character' as a phenomenon. Prominent opera and theatre director Jossi Wieler staged an extremely rich, poetic and elaborate literary text, with subtle light design by acclaimed designer Max Keller.

The *Peer Gynt* production features the appropriation of this dramatic poem into a contemporary theatre performance, in a radical adaptation by director David Zinder and tantalizing scenography by Miriam Guretzki. Since I myself designed the light for this production, the chapter comprises insights into the creative process combined with references to the experience and meaning of light, following the structure of the conceptual framework.

These chapters on state-of-the-art productions, which provide an analysis and interpretation partly based on professional insights, present vivid examples of the new directions that the medium of light has taken in contemporary theatre. In each of these chapters, I first present a general introduction to the performance, leading to a detailed analysis of the lighting and its interaction with other media in the performance.[3] In each chapter the analysis of the aesthetics, the experience and meaning of light in a performance is followed by an examination of *the visual dramaturgy of light*, as embodied in that performance. Some of these performance analyses include interviews with the theatre-makers – directors and lighting designers. They obviously reflect my own reception 'work' and imaginative representation, and do not seek to 'decode' the intention of the theatre-makers. My goal is not to compare the designers' and directors' conceptual understanding of their production with my own informed interpretation, but rather to propose and demonstrate the usefulness of a method for the analysis of the experience and meaning of light.

Motivation and goal

The art of light in the theatre has not as yet been researched systematically either from phenomenological, or from semiotic or poetic perspectives. No new literature on this particular subject has been published for more than a century. In fact, with the exception of Adolphe Appia's writings on the poetic role of theatre lighting from the end of the 19th century, there are no analytical and/or philosophic works on the subject. It is quite surprising that while our thinking about theatre and performance has taken giant steps since then, and theatre lighting technologies have developed enormously, until now no one has written critically about this topic. This book is, in fact, the first of its kind to deal with the art of light on stage from these perspectives.

Almost all of the books on theatre lighting that have been written over the past thirty or so years concentrate on technology and/or the history of the medium, while lacking reference to the phenomenological and semiotic function of lighting design.[4] The few books that do refer to semiotics and lighting – among them Erika Fischer-Lichte's *The Semiotics of Theater* (1992) and Scott Palmer's *Light* (2013) – devote little attention to the semiotics of theatre lighting. Many other books on lighting, scenography and stage technology, such as *Theatre, Performance and Technology: the Development of Scenography in the Twentieth Century* (2005) by Christopher Baugh or *The Cambridge Introduction to Scenography* (2009) by McKinney and Butterworth, provide concise references to developments in the theatre over the past three decades. Other books on scenography address the adaptation of studies of semiotics and phenomenology to the analysis of the theatrical event, but make no reference to the field of lighting design in contemporary theatre. The books I mentioned mainly deal with lighting conventions that were introduced with the advent of Realism in the theatre at the end of the 19th century (!) and might still prevail in mainstream theatre today – i.e. theatre lighting as illustrative support for the text.

This, then, is the major innovation of the present study – offering a unique, systematic exploration, from historical as well as aesthetic, phenomenological, semiotic and poetic perspectives of the functions of light in contemporary theatre.

On a more personal note, this study would never have been written had it not been for profound experiences I had in the theatre a few years ago (during the study of MFA Scenography in the Netherlands) while watching numerous performances of Europe's most innovative contemporary theatre-makers. At the time, my background as a professional lighting designer and young scholar did not suffice to enable me to interpret what I had experienced; and, moreover, I had questions about how I would have designed such a performance myself. The experimental characteristics of these performances were unfamiliar to me, and the lighting design in particular was the catalyst that prompted me to begin a systematic exploration of the issues that I was to raise in this book. I hope this study, expanding the parameters of theoretical research on theatre lighting, will benefit theatre practitioners – designers, directors, choreographers and critics – as well as theatre scholars and students, helping them to understand the most recent developments in the medium of light as well as their origins in theatre history, art philosophy and technology. With this study, I aim at reinforcing the bond between the study of art and light on stage.

Notes

1 Much work has been published recently on visuality in the context of the contemporary theatre performance – by Maaike Bleeker, Arthur Holmberg, Joe Kelleher, Hans-Thies Lehmann, Patrice Pavis, Nicholas Ridout, to mention but a few.
2 The term 'rhizome', as coined by Gilles Deleuze and Felix Guattari (1983; 1987) with reference to media theory and their critique of the field of hermeneutics, is a philosophical concept by which the structure of an artefact can be approached in a non-dialectical and non-hierarchical mode. The authors distinguish between the linear and consequential model ('the tree') that became a dominant convention in western thought, and the simultaneous movement in multiple directions that characterizes the rhizome. Rhizome is an organization of conjunctions between different points and it has no clear structure. Theoretically, according to Deleuze and Guattari, at any point in the rhizome something else can appear, other than its origin. So, there are neither beginnings nor ends, but just voyages through 'middles'. The fact of being subjected to a 'plethora' of new media has modified our cognitive capacities in the contemporary culture, note Deleuze and Guattari. Following one continuous course of related events now seems to be insufficiently engaging. Instead, we are accustomed to be simultaneously triggered by multiple stimuli and events, and to perceive our conglomerated environment as a 'collage'.
3 We often encounter in the theatre light-effects or projected still images that can be produced by either conventional lamps and automated moving lights (using glass gobo, for example) or by a video beamer. If a beamer is used to distribute a static image, or to merely emit light that is not a film, I will regard the element as light and analyse it. If the projection is a film, it is beyond the scope of this study.
4 Among the recent and older works on the process of lighting design and its aesthetics, I address: Max Keller's *Light Fantastic: the Art and Design of Stage Lighting* (2010), Linda Essig's *Lighting and the Design Idea* (2005), Richard Pilbrow's *Stage Lighting Design: The Art, the Craft, the Life* (1997), Richard H. Palmer's *The Lighting Art: the Aesthetics of Stage Lighting Design* (1994), Frederick Bentham's *The Art of Stage Lighting* (1980) and Stanley McCandless' *A Method of Lighting the Stage* (1932).

References

Belting, H., *Art History after Modernism*, translated by Caroline Saltzwedel and Mitch Cohen with additional translation by Kenneth Northcott, Chicago: University of Chicago Press, 2003.

Bergman, G. M., *Lighting in the Theatre*, Stockholm: Almqvist & Wiksell International, 1977.

Bolter, J. D. and Grusin, R., *Remediation: Understanding New Media*, 1st edition, Cambridge, MA: MIT Press, 2000.

Braun, E., *Meyerhold: A Revolution in Theatre*, 2nd edition, London: Methuen, 1995.

Danto, A. C. *After the End of Art: Contemporary Art and the Pale of History*, Princeton, NJ: Princeton University Press, 1998.

Debray, R., *Transmitting Culture*, translated by Eric Rauth, New York: Columbia University Press, 2000.

Debray, R., *Media Manifestos, on the Technological Transmission of Cultural Forms*, translated by Eric Rauth, London: Verso, 1996.

Deleuze, G., and Guattari, F., *A Thousand Plateaus: Capitalism and Schizophrenia*, Minneapolis, MN: University of Minnesota Press, 1987.

Deleuze, G., and Guattari, F., *On the Line*, translated by John Johnston, New York: Semiotext(e), 1983.

Donald, M., "Art and Cognitive Evolution", in *The Artful Mind, Cognitive Science and the Riddle of Human Creativity*, edited by Mark Turner, New York: Oxford University Press, 2006.

Eco, U., *The Limits of Interpretation*, Bloomington and Indianapolis, IN: Indiana University Press, 1990.

Eco, U., *The Open Work*, translated by Anna Cancogni, with an introduction by David Robey, London: Hutchinson Radius, 1989.

Fischer-Lichte, E., *The Semiotics of Theatre*, translated by Jeremy Gaines and Doris L. Jones, Bloomington and Indianapolis, IN: Indiana University Press, 1992.

Fuchs, E., *The Death of Character: Perspectives on Theatre after Modernism*, Bloomington and Indianapolis, IN: Indiana University Press, 1996.

Lehmann, H. T., *Postdramatic Theatre*, translated and foreword by K. Jürs-Munby, London: Routledge Press, 2006.

Ricoeur, P., "Mimesis and Representation", in *A Ricoeur Reader*, edited by M. J. Valdes, Toronto: Toronto University Press, 1991.

Ricoeur, P., "What is a Text? Explanation and Understanding", in *Hermeneutics and Human Sciences*, Cambridge: Cambridge University Press, 1981.

Szondi, P., *Theory of Modern Drama*, edited and translated by M. Hays, foreword by J. Schulte-Sasse, Minneapolis, MN: University of Minnesota Press, 1987.

Weibel, P., "The Development of Light Art", in *Light Art from Artificial Light, Light as a Medium in the 20th and 21st Century Art*, edited by Peter Weibel and Gregor Jansen, Ostfildern, Germany: Hatje Cantz, 2006.

Interviews

Heiner Goebbels: Heiner Goebbels in an interview with John Tusa.

Robert Wilson: An interview with Robert Wilson about his opera production of *Madama Butterfly* by Giacomo Puccini, De Nederlandse Opera, Amsterdam 2003. A DVD recording by Opus Arte 2005.

Robert Wilson: Robert Wilson in an interview with John Bell, *Theater Week*, 3 January 1994.

Chapter 1

Towering figures in the history of theatre lighting design

Light in the theatre has developed tremendously, perhaps more than any other medium, since the time of Greek theatre.[1] Especially since the Renaissance, theatre lighting techniques have increasingly evolved. Yet, systems for gas and electric lighting were increasingly introduced in the theatre only at the beginning and the end of the 19th century respectively, and these, for the first time in history, allowed for the effective control and modified distribution of light throughout the performance. This feature, in particular, was revolutionary since it linked light with *the dimension of time* and later enabled theatre-makers to begin pondering *the artistic function* of light within a *practice of design*. The ability to adjust lighting intensity at will provided theatre artists with the new capacity to control the visual organization of the dramatic space.

In the history of western theatre, the development of light as a theatrical medium was closely related to technological inventions. Often the introduction of new lighting technologies for public and industrial use, such as gaslight and electric lighting, was followed by the adaptation of these technologies in the theatre. There were a few cases, however, in which lighting technology was invented especially to answer the demands of theatre-makers, ballet masters or managers, and later of lighting designers. The numerous outbreaks of fire in Renaissance and Baroque theatres, much more common and disastrous in the 19th century, were usually caused by inflammable scenery catching fire and make it clear that the lighting was often unsafe and did not as yet meet the needs of the theatre.

With new technologies becoming available throughout the history of theatre, artists were gradually and increasingly able to change the perceptual features of expressive visual effects. Later technological developments enabled artists to realize their contemporary ideals of beauty on stage by the use of light, and to increase the effects that light had on the experience of the spectators. Inventions enriched the palettes of light designers – or stage painters and technicians in earlier periods – with which they could illuminate the stage, represent ideas, or influence the way the spectator perceived, felt toward, and interpreted a performance. Since control systems enabled lighting to change in time and tremendously modify the perception of space, the complexity of this work was acknowledged and resulted in a production demand to entrust the creation of light to dedicated artists. This resulted in the establishment of a new theatrical profession – that of 'lighting designer'.

There are numerous elaborate historical studies on the development of theatre technology and lighting in particular that provide excellent in-depth investigations, among them books by Allardyce Nicoll (1961), Gösta M. Bergman (1977) and, more recently, by Christopher Baugh (2005), Arnold Aronson (2008), Joslin McKinney and Philip Butterworth (2010), Oscar G. Brockett, Margaret Mitchell and Linda Hardberger (2010) and Scott Palmer (2013). It is not my purpose to introduce one more myself. Rather, this historical chapter provides a context and background for the discussion, later in this book, of new tendencies of lighting design in state-of-the-art contemporary theatre — emphasizing the *experience* and *meaning*, and the rising *autonomy* of light in contemporary performances.

In my writing about the development of the poetic dimension in light design I will refer to the work of influential pioneer lighting designers and theatre-makers from the *fin de siècle* to the contemporary 'post-dramatic' theatre. I will concentrate on how the medium of light was regarded by different towering artists; what function(s) it played in the performance, and how technological developments created new possibilities for artistic expression. In this chapter I will follow light on its path to becoming a fundamental element and cogent force in the creative process and the 'sculptor 'of the spatial dimension in the perception of the addressees and performers alike. This chapter also elaborates upon influential ideas in modernist and postmodernist art that inspired innovators in light design – one of them being the distancing oneself from a verisimilar representation of reality.

While touching upon the aesthetic conventions of light that were common in different periods since the late 19th century, I focus on light's position in relation to the text, on the visual experience that artificial light offered the spectator (phenomenology), and on the ways in which light represented ideas or concepts (semiotics and poetics). Some artists have sought to stimulate the emotions and the imagination of the spectators by means of new spectacular, ever-brighter lighting technologies (Aronson 2008, 33), or used light to arouse the emotions of the performers, as David Belasco did. Others have examined the interrelations among the media in the performance, sometimes replacing one medium with another and 'staging' expressive light instead of a human performer (Svoboda's *Das Rheingold*, Geneva, 1977). When possible, I present evidence of audience reception in conjunction with drawings and photos. The historical research thus focuses on how light affected the spectators emotionally and/or contributed to the understanding of the piece.

In this chapter, I will address both the writings and the artistic work of selected pioneers in the history of theatre lighting design, and concentrate on their poetic approach to the role of light in relation to a representation of reality based on verisimilitude and to the changing position of light with regard to the written/verbal text. Many others deserve to be mentioned, of course, but this would exceed the scope of this chapter, which aims to provide an historical and conceptual context for the discussion of the new trends and rising autonomy of light in contemporary theatre.

Before proceeding with the historical overview, note should be made concerning my use of the terms 'realism', 'representation' and 'mimesis', in line with the introduction to this book. In *On Realism and Art* (1921), Roman Jakobson argues that the term 'realism' has been used uncritically since the mid-to-late 19th century, narrowing its definition as a result of the associating with the familiar art movement of Realism. Since then, realism has been affiliated with a very particular aesthetics based on the similarity of art to day-to-day reality.

However, there is another definition of the concept of 'realism' that was neglected according to Jakobson. Art has always been *realistic*. Realism is more of a reflective quality of the contemporary spirit through the arts. Views and experiences, expressed by artists through their work, were continually a *reference to reality*. As such, the arts have always been facing, and were part of, cultural changes in the course of history, demanding the occasional renewal of aesthetics. In the mid-19th century, the tendency was to represent reality through the formal characteristics of contemporary reality. This was the artists' *contemporary reference to their reality*. Since then, art movements have also maintained the quality of 'realism', be they abstract painting or post-dramatic theatre. Referring to 'realism' through the mere perspective of verisimilitude, of visual likeness to reality alone, would prove to be misleading. Instead, 'realism' should be discussed in terms of quality, and the relation between the work and its aesthetic and poetic contexts.

The addressees are invited to accept a new aesthetics as more appropriate for representing the human position in the universe, according to the reality of their time. To use Jakobson's words: "I rebel against a given artistic code and view its deformation as a more accurate rendition of reality" (Jakobson 1921).

Mimesis, the imitation of human action, in line with Jakobson's approach, has no fixed 'form'. Mimesis is, rather, a dynamic element in the process of representation. It can indicate, to a certain extent, how artists and audience perceive art in relation to a certain culture in a given period of time. Understanding 'mimesis' in this sense ascertains the validity of the concept for any period and liberates us from the traditional association between realism and representation based on verisimilitude.

Sir Henry Irving (1838–1905)

Theatre director Henry Irving, actor and manager of the Lyceum Theatre in London from 1878 until 1899, was one of the most innovative shaping figures of both the late Romantic theatre and the early theatre of Realism. During his term at the Lyceum, the introduction of gas lighting, followed by the progression to electric light, constituted a whole new theatrical element to be explored. This went far beyond the well-awaited brighter intensity, the availability of safer instruments and the controlled distribution of light. This was, in fact, a wholly new artistic tool for the directors, with which they could shape the visibility of the stage (and auditorium) with greater freedom than ever before (Nicoll 1961, 195). The Lyceum Theatre was the first in London to dim its houselights during the performance, as early as 1892 (Palmer 2013, 174). By so doing, the atmosphere on the stage and the spectators' attention were both enhanced (Innes 1998, 20). For the perfecting of the performance, Irving used to dim the lights during transitions and, with the help of almost 100 stagehands, perform quick changes of highly elaborate scenery (Palmer 2013, 35). Darkening the auditorium during performances helped him to selectively highlight details out of the darkness and creating illusionary and atmospheric spaces on stage. Following the late Romantic tradition, Irving attributed great importance to the atmospheric unity of scenery and costume as well as to rhythm in acting and movement. As Allardyce Nicoll writes, "The main tendencies of nineteenth-century scenic art may be summed up in the words spectacular and antiquarian" (Nicoll 1961, 190). Theatre houses took pride in presenting seemingly accurate replicas of history, as the following leaflet preface to *The Merchant of Venice* (Princess Theatre, 1850) states:

> The costumes and customs are represented as existing about the year 1600, when Shakespeare wrote the play. The dresses are chiefly selected from a work by Cesare Vecellio, entitled *"Degli Habiti Antichi e Moderni di diverse Parti del Mondo* [sic.]. In Venetia, 1590"*: as well as from other sources to be found in the British Museum.
>
> (quoted in Nicoll 1961, 191)

The preface reflects some of the theatrical conventions of the period, while obliquely indicating the expectations and high esteem of the theatre public for scenic illustration of the text. In relation to the text, the design practice fulfilled an 'archaeological' mission and remained loyal to the aesthetics of the historical period in which the play was written.[2] Moreover, the often-spectacular scenery was to decorate and 'glorify' the dramatic text, as Irving stated in 1886: "The first duty of anyone who mounts a piece is to produce a beautiful and pleasing effect" (Finkel 1996, 83). In order to reach a high degree of *beauty based on observation of reality*, Irving hired leading contemporary painters to decorate his stage. Painting was still the main medium by which to construct the stage image; only occasionally were minor parts of the scenery three-dimensional, giving the impression of a three-dimensional painting (McKinney and Butterworth 2010, 86).

The shortcomings of illumination capacities prior to the invention of electric lighting influenced the development of design conventions, acting style and limited range for actors' mise-en-scène (mainly downstage) since the earlier theatre of the Renaissance. Before long, the reforms in stage lighting enhanced acting in deeper stage areas and hastened the replacement of previous theatrical conventions such as painted flats and wings by a new aesthetics of Realism, in which new materials and stage machinery were used (Nicoll 1961, 199–200).

After Irving had mastered the techniques and possibilities of directional lighting (using the limelight), he skilfully lit all of his performances. In a conversation with Ben-Tzion Munitz, he notes that "Irving's innovations and contributions to stage lighting are associated with gas lighting rather than electric lighting. In fact, he tried to resist the transition to electric lighting". Bram Stoker, who was Irving's business director and assistant for many years, wrote that Irving's light designs incorporated different elements, for which he used a large number of gas jets and powerful limelights with various lenses. Through the use of these lighting sources, Irving was able to divide the stage into separate illumination areas, thereby selecting where to use more light on stage and where less; where to use colours and which ones, etc. On Irving's method, Stoker wrote: "open limes, 'spot lights' of varying focus and intensity, lights so constructed as to cover a certain amount of space, and so on" (quoted in Bergman 1977, 301). New features such as increased intensity, control capacities and enhanced optics of theatre lighting enabled not only the illumination of stage areas more distant from the audience, but also differentiation of stage areas through various intensities of light. Bright light also influenced other theatrical elements, including scenery, acting, costumes, movement on the stage and makeup – to mention but a few.

In addition, Irving renewed the use of footlights that had ruled since 1589. He separated the lamps into group sockets, enabling illumination of different stage areas instead of all areas at once. Each group of lamps had a particular colour and when several groups were used simultaneously the mixture of colours blended into a new one, similar to the now-common use of RGB LED mixing (for example, Blue and Red lights create magenta, Red and Green lights generate yellow, and so on). Using this system, Irving could create a different look for each stage area, in terms of both colour and intensity. Although not the first to use coloured footlights, he was a pioneer in successfully dividing and illuminating stage areas differently, rather than as one homogeneous unit. To quote Stoker once more: "He has noticed that nature seldom shows broad effect with an equality of light. There are shadows here and there, or places where, through occasional aerial density, the light is unevenly distributed. This makes great variety of effect, and such, of course, he wanted to reproduce" (quoted in Bergman 1977, 302).

With the introduction of gaslight, and later electric lighting, the consumption of brilliant light had increased significantly (Palmer 2013, 174). Irving, by contrast, valued the importance of shadows as an integral part of light design that can contribute to *the imitation of light as perceived in nature*. Shadows were a necessary, vital and valuable element in the composition of light since, in their absence, the image appeared unnatural, symmetrically and evenly lit. By using directional light and high intensities (limelights), the shadows of illuminated objects also emerged more clearly in space. Stoker reports: "In fact, darkness was found to be, when under control, as important a factor in effect as light" (Stoker 1911, 907).

In view of his efforts to imitate reality and to counter disbelief, the colours previously used in Romantic theatre proved to be too saturated and dominant. Influenced by the tendencies of late Romanticism and Realism, Irving refined the tonality and saturation of colour filters of light, in order to imbue the representation of nature in the theatre with perceptual features closer to those of reality. "He had transparent lacquers applied to the glasses of the limelights and, when electric light came in, to the bulbs of the electric lights, and thus produced effects of colour both of intensity and delicacy up to then unknown" (Stoker 1911, 302).

"At the time that the preparation of the lighting of a theatrical production was a marginal activity, Irving used to conduct long extensive (and consequently expensive) rehearsals devoted to lighting", and, according to Munitz, "these would sometimes take whole nights, and were held without actors but with the participation of his 30 gasmen and 8 lime operators". Like a painter, he created light with greater freedom, asymmetrically and unevenly, to depict a space with a diversity of colours, weights and tonality that together composed complex light-images. Undeniably, Irving did not completely dispose of the symmetric lighting system that English theatre had inherited and practiced since the Renaissance, and which some major North American and British companies still maintain today. However, he often added to it other powerful lighting sources (limelights) and, through his novel way of composing light and shade in space, with colour mixing, one might say that Irving paved the way for the innovative ideas that Adolphe Appia and Edward Gordon Craig were soon to introduce.

David Belasco (1853–1931)

David Belasco, an American director, playwright, actor and manager, was another of the pioneers in light design around the end of the 19th century. He devoted many years to experimentation with different lighting sources and optical apparatuses, seeking the specific qualities and light-effects he envisaged for every production. His search for verisimilitude to nature was extreme, as Louis Hartmann, the technical director, notes in his book *Theatre Lighting: A Manual of the Stage Switchboard* (1930). Breaking away from the long tradition of painted flats, Belasco sought to intensify the characteristic of 'Realism' in his theatre, using scenery built of genuine materials such as wooden and plaster walls (Palmer 1998, 169). To increase the sensation of 'the real', he also used live animals in farmyard scenes, and included the cooking of real food on the stage so that the aromas would spread to the auditorium during the performance (Nicoll 1961, 198–9). However, according to Belasco, no element in the theatre was as powerful as light in the creation of atmosphere, without which a scene would fail to evoke the intended moods and feelings. Metaphorically, Belasco notes: "Lights are to drama what music is to the lyrics of a song. No other factor that enters into the production of a play is so effective in conveying its mood and feeling. They are as essential to every work of dramatic art as blood is to life" (Belasco 1919, 56).

Belasco considered light to be one of the most important media in the theatre, to such a degree that he usually designed light for new productions even before allowing the actors to step onto the stage. Hartmann writes the following about the methodology:

> It took some time to light any sort of a scene; but detail work consumed the major portion of it; and hours would slip by while we experimented on some effect that appeared simple enough after we had perfected it. Mr. Belasco would generally begin before bringing the players on the stage by getting the scene lighted. The lights were graduated and balanced so the setting had the proper effect for the time of the action. If the scene was illuminated so that it had the proper atmosphere, it was generally found, when the players were brought on the stage, that their faces were too dark.
>
> (Hartmann 1930, 19)

When necessary, Belasco carefully increased light intensities to provide sufficient illumination of the actors' facial expressions, using various lighting sources other than the footlights. The inevitable side-effect of footlights was that, apart from its unnatural angle, it produced vast illumination and shadows cast by the actors on the overhead borders and flattened the plasticity of the performers and the scenery. Moreover, the footlights illuminated, and cast the shadows of, the actors and the scenery from the floor-level upward and so, the inverse relation between light and shade made any object look strange, differently than its look in nature. Belasco, therefore, increased the intensity of lighting elements that were already working in the light-image (lighting state), and so retained the atmosphere he desired, but with a slightly greater brightness. As early as 1879, in the performance of *The Passion Play* in San Francisco, Belasco had made up his mind to entirely eliminate footlights from the lighting system of the theatre.

In his book *The Theatre through its Stage Door* (1919), Belasco refers to "the use of color [sic.] and light to communicate to audiences the underlying symbolism of a play". Light supports the play by creating a 'believable' – or at least acceptable – atmosphere fit for the fictive space of the scene (Belasco 1919, 180). The spell of atmospheric light, which is experienced by spectators sensually – not only intellectually – is the domain of lighting. This is a highly interesting observation because, prior to all of his contemporaries, Belasco was already reflecting upon the corporeal experience of light in line with later phenomenological approaches and discoveries in the neurosciences. The experience of light in our cognition happens simultaneously on both the corporeal and the semiotic levels. I will address this subject later, as part of the theoretical framework of this study.

Much has been written about the impact of atmospheric light on the spectator, but Belasco seems to be the pioneer theatre-maker in writing about the emotional influence that light has on the performers. For the first time, Belasco draws our attention to cognitive aspects of performing theatre, one of which relates to the way the performers as human beings are affected by light. Light is capable of evoking subconscious emotional reactions in the performers, independently of their intellectual approach to the roles they play. Belasco, thus, used light as means by which to shape and unify the acting and the scene as a whole. He writes: "Light has a psychological effect which perhaps he [the actor] is not able to understand or explain, but he feels it instantly and responds to it, and then the audience just as quickly responds to him" (Belasco 1919, 74).

Adolphe Appia (1862–1928)

Adolphe Appia is one of the most innovative figures in the history of modern theatre. As a young musician and architect, Appia noticed and critically pointed out an aesthetic disharmony in the visual dimension of theatre and opera around the end of the 19th century. His influential theoretical work foresaw the necessity to fundamentally renew the theatrical traditions of the 19th century and paved the way for modern theatre. The unconventional ideas that Appia advanced covered a broad range of subjects, and led to calls for reforms in all the theatrical media. In view of the scope of this chapter, however, I concentrate here on Appia's writings that are relevant to the aesthetics and poetics of light and the relation between light, music and the written/verbal text.

One cannot elaborate upon Appia's critical, even rebellious perspectives on the theatre around the *fin de siècle* without discussing their origins; namely, the impressions that Richard Wagner's opera performances made on him. Appia was an unreserved admirer of Wagner and considered him to be the most accomplished composer of music-drama because, more than anyone else, Wagner had succeeded in interweaving the music and the libretto so as to create a powerful intimacy and symbiotic connections. However, watching the performances of music-drama at the Festspielhaus in Bayreuth, directed by Wagner himself, proved to be a highly disappointing experience for Appia.[3] Frustrated, he argued that Wagner's visual representation was based on a "compromise between the music and the actor, between the art of sound and rhythm and the art of plastic and dramatic movement", and failed to realize the great dramatic potential of the visual dimension that the music deserved (quoted in McKinney and Butterworth 2010, 10). The performances suffered from a lack of expressiveness in the singers' movement on stage, the use of space was not imaginative enough, and the overall impression was monotonous (Beacham 1989, 9).

Actually, both as a director and as a librettist, Wagner cared little for the scenic elements in his operas, arguing that the spatial design should provide merely "an unobtrusive practical background and framework" (Beacham 1989, 13). By employing the old aesthetics of painted illusionary depth and the pretence of verisimilitude on backdrops and wings, Wagner preserved the long tradition that prevailed on most theatre stages right up to the end of the 19th century. The two-dimensional flatness of the painting contrasted with the real three-dimensional plasticity of the human body. Appia shared Wagner's idea that music is the driving force and the *'soul' of the drama*. However, he took issue with Wagner concerning the formal characteristics of the set. The Wagnerian design was based upon three categories:

1   *Painting*: two-dimensional, colour painted.
2   *'Aufstellung'*: the few plastic, three-dimensional objects in the scenery.
3   *Lighting*: genuine artificial light produced by gas and electric sources.

The music has an overall mediating effect: it modifies, suspends and accelerates the sense of passing time, spatial dimensions emerge and metamorphose due to its acoustic influence, and it leads the narrative, with the libretto being an inseparable part of the musical composition. The musical score and the verbal text share in the creation of atmosphere, emotional expression and suggestive meaning. Therefore, Appia claimed, the director-designer is expected to strengthen the already-existing musicality of the opera by extracting corresponding 'musical qualities' from within the three-dimensional space — the space should become a visual embodiment of music-drama (Figure 1.1). Appia notes:

> The musical score is the sole interpreter for the director: whatever Wagner has added to it is irrelevant . . . his manuscript contains by definition the theatrical form, i.e. its projection in space; therefore any additional remarks on his part are superfluous, even contradictory to the aesthetic truth of an artistic work. Wagner's scenic descriptions in his libretto have no organic relationship with his poetic-musical text.
>
> (Appia 1924, 374–5)

In his most influential published work, *Die Musik und die Inszenierung* (1899), Appia criticizes an aesthetic dissonance in Wagner's staging of his own operas. In particular, he reflects upon the ideological incoherence deriving from staging live performers against the background of flat backdrop and wings. The result seemed both artificial and pretentious. The coexistence of real performers, lively, dynamic and three-dimensional, next to an artificially painted (imitation of) reality resulted in disharmony. In their book *Adolphe Appia 1862–1928: Actor–Space–Light*, Bablet and Bablet quote Appia as follows: "Our stage-directors have long sacrificed the living bodily appearance of the actor to the lifeless fictions of painting. It is obvious that, subjected to the tyranny of painting, the human body has not been able to develop its means of expression normally" (Bablet and Bablet 1982, 58). Thus, the only genuine element on the stage, the human performer, was aesthetically detached from its 'habitat'. For example, one can imagine how the relative proportions of the performers and perspective-based painting were constantly in conflict, depending on the position of the performer next to the painting. Increasing the level of light intensities in the theatre extenuated this aesthetic contrast even more, meaning that the difference in plasticity was noticed all the more clearly.

Appia, however, was not in favour of a strengthening of verisimilitude in the theatre. In fact, even Naturalism, pre-eminent in accurately imitating the perceptual features of reality, failed to do so convincingly. In *Looking into the Abyss*, Aronson notes that "Whereas a naturalistic set was a physical manifestation of a psychological and sociological study, the new, modern décor was the spiritual essence of an object — scenery as Platonic shadows" (Aronson 2008, 17). In his writing, Appia explicitly advocates a

Figure 1.1 Adolphe Appia, a design for the opera *Parsifal*, music and libretto by R. Wagner, Act I, scene one (the sacred forest), 1896, courtesy of the Swiss Theatre Collection Berne

break away from the fiction of Naturalism towards a more holistic, architectonic design, using a geometric aesthetics that stems from the music, and treating theatre space as a platform for dramatic action. The spatial dimension should not be a materialized replica of the real world; rather, its formalism (i.e. the symbolic and stylized outlook of the production) should enhance the presence of the performers in the space and support them in representing their innermost mental states. Accordingly, the space of the new theatre will better suit the *'musical movement'* of the performers and the *'rhythmic architecture'* of the music (Figure 1.2).

Goldman and Sprinchorn shed some light on the aesthetics of theatre in Appia's days, pointing to the fact that contemporary theatre directors used decoration arbitrarily (Goldman and Sprinchorn 1988, 379). Creating a design exclusively for a specific production was not very customary at the time. In fact, the norm in late 19th-century European theatre houses was that one and the same setting might also be reused by different productions dealing with a similar theme. This type of economy led to a lack of connection between the visual and musical aspects of music-drama performances, lessening the potential to achieve harmonious expression between music, libretto, scenery and acting. Ideally, Appia argued, the harmonious composition of all the components in a performance should elicit a spiritual experience. Light plays a major role in interrelating the media and uniting their unique ways of expression. In *La Gymnastique Rythmique et le Théâtre* (1911) Appia writes:

> Thus the all-powerful light, supple to the music, will be united with it; light without which there is no plasticity; light which fills the room with brightness and moving shadows; which falls in placid drops or which blazes forth in coloured, live beams. And bodies, basking in its animating atmosphere, will find themselves in it and greet the Music of Space.
>
> (Appia 1911, 438)

The much-needed reforms that Appia wished to introduce were intended to repair two fundamental defects (Beacham 1989, 21–3). The first was that, since the Renaissance, the western visual arts and theatre had been dominated by a strict set of aesthetic conventions. The neoclassical interpretation of Aristotle's *Poetics* and the concept of 'mimesis' proved quite limiting for the making of a more symbolic and suggestive theatre that would depart from the aesthetics of Realism. Thus, the increasing interest in Ancient Greek literature, especially in the 18th century by the French neoclassicists, had established the association between 'mimesis' and verisimilitude, following the Aristotelian ideal of the three unities of time, space and action. Likewise, patrons who owned or supported theatre companies highly appreciated and encouraged them to integrate the trendy perspective paintings in their sceneries. They helped to maintain the painted representation of space according to the latest academic ideals of beauty in painting. Appia's first goal, therefore, was to liberate the theatre from the narrow horizon of older conventions of representation.

Furthermore, his second aim was to overcome the gap between the *'meaningful expression'* rendered by the *creative artist* (composer-dramatist, librettist or playwright) within the written work, and its eventual theatrical realization on stage, as a complementary element. Appia declared that theatre would develop to become a genuine art-form only if it were able to demonstrate its capacity to faithfully express the intentions of

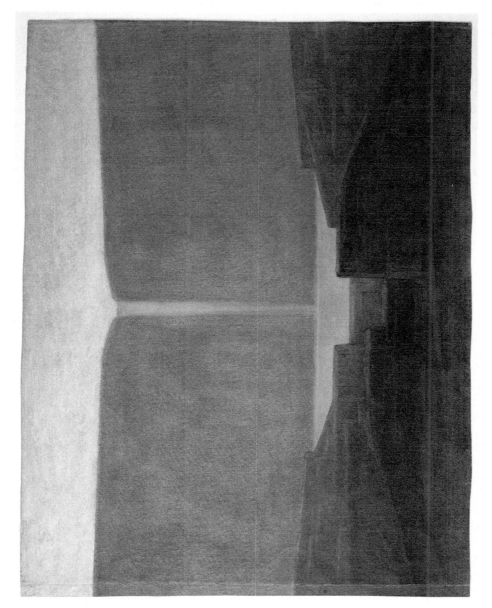

Figure 1.2 Adolphe Appia, *La Cascade (The Waterfall)*, 1909, courtesy of the Swiss Theatre Collection Berne

the creative artist. This was not yet the situation with regard to light and setting. He believed that a meaningful expression of light and space could be reached in spatial settings, comprising three-dimensional abstract geometric objects, that would be metaphorically equivalent to musical qualities (Goldman and Sprinchorn 1988, 379). His alternative formalistic aesthetics was inspired by the classicist mode, using ideal forms, overt structures and rigid proportions that were restrained to 'minimalist' formal expression, similar to Craig's aesthetics to a certain extent. 'Rhythmic Spaces', Appia called them, since these spaces contained a prominent visual rhythm of horizontal and vertical lines within geometric objects. The spaces enabled a clear potential for movement patterns of both performers and light, inviting light and shade to complement one another (Figures 1.3 and 1.4).

Appia classified light into three categories (Appia 1899, 81):

1   *Painted light:* the two-dimensional painted imitation of light that Appia repudiated.
2   *General Light:* the diffused and soft illumination of the stage, simultaneous and symmetrical from various directions and sources ('Helligkeit').
3   *Creative/Formative Light:* directional and concentrated light beams highlighting performers and other three-dimensional objects, casting their clear shadows in the space and creating contrast between light, shade and background ('Gestaltendes Licht').

The first and second categories of light were known and had been available since the theatre of the Renaissance, but the technology that would allow generating *creative/formative light* was still missing. Creative light was a valuable means to unify the human bodies with their environment, by directing the light onto the body and casting its shadow in the space. Prior to the invention of limelight that dominated later 19th-century English theatre and the electric arch that was very popular in the continent before the introduction of effective electric lighting, the archaic symmetrical lighting systems were incapable of producing any expressive light. Now, however, powerful lighting sources became available and could be moved around the stage by stagehands. Light could become active, and correspond to the musical qualities. Among the new possibilities for 'live' changes were: repositioning the lighting fixture, focusing its beam, blending or replacing colours and resizing illumination fields using early unrefined zoom lenses.

Appia devotes a large part of his innovative writing to the growing poetic role of light in the future. This new role would surely influence the role of other media in the performance, affect both visual and textual dramaturgy, and most importantly – call for a re-examination of the perception and reception of light by the addressees. In this respect, Appia suggested that it is light's exclusive role to unify the entire scene and to emphasize the plasticity of the performers and their space, but also to change the ways in which spectators perceive every object in the performance. Light is atmospheric. It is capable of representing both the internal domain of (fictive) emotions and thoughts, and the external dimensions of space and time. In the essay *Eurhythmics and Light* (1912), Appia remarks: "We shall learn that, merely 'to make visible', is not to light in this sense at all, and that, on the contrary, in order to be creative or plastic, light must be an atmosphere, a luminous atmosphere" (Aronson 2008, 34). Appia's major contribution should, nevertheless, be contextualized with regard to the emergence of new lighting

Figure 1.3 Adolphe Appia, *Scherzo*, 1910, courtesy of the Swiss Theatre Collection Berne

Figure 1.4 Adolphe Appia, *Clair de Lune*, 1909, courtesy of the Swiss Theatre Collection Berne

capacities and control systems for electric lighting – both resulted in a reconsideration of light's artistic function within the theatre (Palmer 2013, 78).

Only after receiving international recognition did Appia finally have the opportunity to explore his ideas empirically, after years of anticipation, and to stage a production of *Tristan and Isolde* (Milan, 1923). "Darkness and light have in the course of the drama the same importance as a musical motif", he notes (Bergman 1977, 327). Scott Palmer writes: "In previous eras, shadows were a necessary by-product of light that needed to be accommodated. Appia's vision placed light and shadow, and its movement over time, as central to the dramatic experience" (Palmer 2013, 87). The light directed the gaze of the spectators from one object to another in a quite empty space.

Appia thus opposed the aesthetics of Naturalism and gradually omitted most elements illustrating the narrative in favour of a more holistic and atmospheric 'rhythmic space', 'animated' through the use of light. His sets for the Wagnerian operas at the end of the 19th century, however, were not entirely devoid of architectural references to the fictive space of the narrative; e.g. Tristan's castle in *Tristan and Isolde*, and the hall of pillars representing the forest in *Parsifal* (Figure 1.1). In his later work in Hellerau, he eliminated such narrative associations in favour of more holistic architectural arrangements of platforms, stairs, curtains and other three-dimensional objects. This was a crucial change that echoed shifting perspectives on the world around us at the beginning of the 20th century. His newly envisaged ideas regarding the aesthetics and poetics of light and space made him undoubtedly one of the most inspiring pioneers of modern theatre and light design.

Edward Gordon Craig (1872–1966)

> I wish to remove **the Word** with its **Dogma** but to leave **Sound**, or the voiced beauty of the soul. I wish to remove **the Actor** with his **Personality** but to leave **the Chorus of masked figures**. I wish to remove **the Pictorial Scene** but to leave in its place **the Architectonic Scene**
> (Edward Gordon Craig, 1908–10; all emphases are in the original text).[4]

Brought up by the leading British actress of the time – his mother Ellen Terry, and with Henry Irving, the actor and manager of the Lyceum Theatre in London, as his mentor, Edward Gordon Craig was destined to diverge from the 19th-century Victorian theatre traditions. He introduced new and all-embracing ideas that were meant to overhaul the conventions of the former theatre of Realism; ideas that were driven by a modernized concept of drama and its staging. 'The theatre of the future', as he referred to it, was to evoke in the audience a spiritual elevation. Craig tried to restore a sense of religious and holistic feeling towards the theatre, as it had been experienced by the Ancient Greek, the Japanese and, to a certain extent, the theatre-spectators of the Middle Ages (Innes 1998, 120).

For Craig, the most stimulating creative force in his new visionary theatre was *movement*. Metamorphoses of space and body, with the change of coloured light, brought about a vibrant harmony between the various theatrical components, more than had been accomplished ever before (Bergman 1977, 330–1). Symbolic choreography - patterned movement and stylized gestures - was surrounded by geometric architectural scenery in order to attain visual simplicity, and this became part of Craig's unique theatrical signature. The total dismissal of an aesthetics of Realism led him to search for simpler characteristics of symbolism in earlier theatre forms, and to explore the traditions of Ancient Greek theatre and Japanese No-theatre. As Nicoll writes, "For those falsities [i.e. realism – my addition Y.A.], he would substitute symbolic form, and in order to cast out the trivialities he would make the theatre once more a temple" (Nicoll 1961, 203). In those early theatre styles the use of masks and puppets provided a restrained and calm expression that fascinated Craig. In addition, this kind of visual representation kept a distance from the perceptual features of reality, which modern art movements developed to the extreme. Likewise, theatre-makers sought alternative forms of expression that would be closer to the 'sublime', to the essence of ideas beyond their materialized forms.

An acclaimed actor in his own right, Craig acknowledged that actors' egos occasionally lead them into over-acting that disrupts an accurate execution of their designated role and orchestrated actions (McKinney and Butterworth 2009, 19–20). Craig aimed to distil from the performance of the actor the very essence of the human condition – attaining what he called *noble artificiality* (Craig 1911).[5] Consequently, he introduced the ambiguous term 'Über-Marionette'. It has long been under scholarly debate as to whether Craig actually advocated the exclusion of the living actor in favour of large marionettes, or the concealing of the actors inside a marionette-like costume (Le Boeuf 2010, 102–14). In his most controversial and groundbreaking publication *The Actor and the Über-Marionette* (first published in the magazine *The Mask*, edited by Craig himself, 1908), he explains: "The über-marionette will not compete with life – rather it will go beyond it. Its ideal will not be the flesh and blood but rather the body in trance – it will aim to clothe itself with a death-like beauty while exhaling a living spirit" (Craig 1911, 259).

Similarly, Craig's scenographies did not 'compete with life' either, but constituted instead a multifunctional and three-dimensional dynamic space with suggestive qualities that dismissed verisimilitude to realistic environments. Craig, like Appia, rejected the aesthetics of the theatre of Realism and repudiated, in particular, its fabricated two-dimensional illusionistic paintings. His tendency to favour geometric spatial abstraction arose from his artistic aspirations to develop *a new art of theatre* and to fundamentally reform all the aspects of the theatrical event - not merely its design. Craig's system of mobile 'screens', stretched canvases on wooden frames that could easily change position and angle, and thus allowed to create different variations of stage compositions, was patented in 1910 after years of experimentation (McKinney and Butterworth 2009, 20). This type of scenery was made for and dependent upon (coloured) light and shade. The aesthetics of theatre that Craig envisaged, well ahead of his time, did not relate to technological innovations only, but also to the traditional hierarchy of media in the theatre:

> The decoration is simplified in that, above all, the changes of light, refracting against the various volumes, give expressiveness to the décor. By these simplifications one seems to achieve 'une fluctuation musicale du décor' which, in time, links the décor to the changes of the drama. Hitherto, the decorations, which have been made by painters, or so-called painters, have been immobile "rags" suspended around a mobile action. It is desirable that the décor, mobile as the sound, elucidates the phases of the drama in the same way as the music accompanies and underlines all movements, just as it develops in pace with the drama.[6]

Nevertheless, for Craig, scenography did not solely result from the interpretation of the text. In fact, he occasionally disregarded the concrete text of the play he was working with, and re-used elements or even complete sceneries from different earlier productions in other, later productions. In his essay *Postmodern Design*, Aronson notes that the innovative idea of three-dimensional design with spatial unity:

> . . . was a response to the fragmentary nature of much nineteenth-century Romantic design in which coordination among the visual elements was sporadic and haphazard. The disunity of design in the nineteenth-century, however, was simply the result of contemporary stage practice rather than the result of any consciously thought-out aesthetic.
>
> (Aronson 2008, 17)

However, in Craig's case, the choice to employ a 'ready-made' scenography was resolute. The freedom and autonomy that Craig provided for light and scenography, in loose relation to the particular qualities of the written text, are crucial aspects for the later discussion of contemporary theatre. His ideas concerning the role the visual dimension could play in theatre, independently from the (dramatic) text, were in fact ahead of his time. Light and shade gained prominence in characterising and metamorphosing space and developed a simultaneously orchestrated score of looks. Indeed, Craig disregarded the theatrical convention by which the text is the driving force of the performance. The spiritual and ritual aspects of theatre performance interested him more than illustrating the text. In *On the Art of Theatre*, Craig writes the following on the relation between the visual and textual:

> We are to accept it that the play still retains some value for us, and we are not going to waste that; our aim is to increase it. Therefore it is, as I say, the production of general and broad effects appealing to the eye which will add a value to that which has already been made valuable by the great poet.
>
> (Craig 1912, 21–2)

In the majority of his drawings, Craig presents gigantic spaces with sharp angles and geometric compositions that often include a shaft of directional light contrasting with the gloomy surroundings. Using light, he aimed at creating the impression that space was monumental and had no boundaries of height and depth. In Figure 1.5, for example, a small individual at the back of the stage is standing enclosed between gigantic pillars. The qualities of the space and its atmosphere were of greater priority to him than the visibility of the individuals on stage. Both the expressive contrast of light and shade and the dimensions of the massive shapes appearing in his sketches were utopian in nature, since the existing means at the end of the 19th century could not yet produce these qualities. Craig's series of illuminated staircases demonstrate his fascination with the magic of light that creates 'drama' and with light's capacity to perform by itself. He notes: "I believe in the time when we shall be able to create works of art in the theatre without the written play, without the use of actors" (Palmer 2013, 100).

Craig's advanced and pioneering ideology was highly metaphorical and inspiring, yet too far ahead of its time for realization in the theatre. Critics and theatre practitioners frequently labelled him as an impractical mystic and claimed that his theories of space

Figure 1.5 Edward Gordon Craig, *Stage scene design for Hamlet*, c. 1910, from *A Second Portfolio of Etchings*. Graphic Arts Division, Department of Rare Books and Special Collections, Princeton University Library. Publication is with the kind permission of the Edward Gordon Craig Estate

were unrealizable. The following report by René Piot, after visiting Craig and observing the fully illuminated model-box of his famous scenic screens, provides a first-hand impression of one of his contemporaries on his work:

> Craig wants his scenery to move like sound, to refine certain moments in the play just as music follows and heightens all its movements; he wants it to advance with the play . . . I don't know how far this idea can be put into practice; but the idea itself is first-class, and if it were carried out it would revolutionise the art of scene-designing; for there has always been an antagonism between the movement of the plot and the immobility of the scenery; if the scene could change in harmony with the development of the plot, this would provide an entirely new sources of expression.
>
> (Craig 1911, viii)

Craig tirelessly experimented with lighting effects using coloured slides and patterned illumination, shadowing of plants in front of lamp lenses, lighting through semi transparent curtains, lamps with numerous reflectors that throw light irregularly, in order to separate areas on the stage – to mention but a few of his explorations (Bergman 1977, 336–7). Recalling Appia's idea of 'creative light', Craig created a sense of musicality, rhythm and mobility within the space, by the use of light. He changed the look of the performers throughout the performance, representing the emotions and moods of the fictive characters according to the dramatic situation. His work with light was extraordinary for the period. The dominance of light in his sketches indicates Craig's divesting from the performers something of the emotional affect they were otherwise to create. It reflects his approach to the new theatre as an all-encompassing artist who uses the performers as just one performative element among others, granting light a dominant role that rivals the performer's work in attracting the spectators' attention. In *Dido and Aeneas* by Purcell – Craig's first production as a director (1900) – he composed a metamorphosis of 'creative', colourful and directional light concomitant with that of the narrative. In a review of the performance a critic wrote: "The real triumph of the setting was, however, in the use of light and shade; it was as carefully considered as in a wood engraving, and added immeasurably to the tragic simplicity of the whole performance" (Palmer 2013, 95). Before the last scene, for example, when Dido mourns Aeneas, Craig illuminated the actress with a strong light from above, casting long shadows beneath her eyebrows, nose and chin. By choosing this unnatural lighting angle, he created a strong contrast between the illuminated and shadowed parts, thus distorting the actress's face.

The following quote from Craig reveals how he envisaged a scene for Bach's *Matthew's Passion* – his final work, which was planned but never staged. How intensive and dynamic the description of the scene is, and how overwhelmingly charged, Baroque-like, the image is – as if he aspired to represent the evanescent sublime by light:

> . . . great flights of steps, crowds of moving figures, crowds that opened up as a single figure ascended to his destruction, figures wandering in darkness, shafts of light appearing as great chords brought them forth, pink skies turning to blue, then to purple and indigo, against which solitary figures stood out in gold.
>
> (Craig 1968, 115)

Long past his own lifetime, the great merit of Craig's inspiring theories persists in stimulating generations of theatre-makers to rethink fundamental ideas concerning the art of theatre, rather than providing a pragmatic program for the theatre of the future (Innes 1998, 5–6). His modernized perspectives on theatre as a venue for communion and spiritual elevation, where all the media work together in a non-hierarchical symbiotic connection, have remained highly relevant for many avant-garde artists, postmodern and contemporary theatre-makers. Light, in particular, has become a primary poetic element, a rising and highly expressive medium.

Light and the Theatre of the Symbolists

In contrast to the ethos of mainstream realism, the theory of the Theatre of Symbolism already began to develop in Paris in the late 1880s, through the work of poets, painters and theorists who expressed their contempt for the 'copying of reality' and stood against the ideals of Realism and Naturalism (Bergman 1977, 311). Taking the first steps to create a Theatre of Symbolism in the 1890s, they desired to escape day-to-day reality and 'dive into' the depths of the human soul to explore dreams, hallucinations, fantasy and mysticism. In the Symbolist manifesto, published in 1886, Jean Moréas wrote the following: "Ainsi, dans cet art, les tableaux de la nature, les actions des humains, tous les phénomènes concrets ne sauraient se manifester eux-mêmes; ce sont là des apparences sensibles destinées à représenter leurs affinités ésotériques avec des Idées primordiales" ("In this art, scenes from nature, human activities, and all other real world phenomena will not be described for their own sake; here, they are perceptible surfaces created to represent their esoteric affinities with the primordial ideals") (Moréas, 1886).[7]

At the same time, the scientific and artistic interest in the phenomenon of synaesthesia (the exchange of impressions between the sensory modalities) was growing. Speculations on synaesthesia and on the analogous sensorial effects of different art disciplines on the addressees, the relationship between colour and music in particular, have continued to fascinate many visual artists around the emergence of Modernism – Richard Wagner, Wassily Kandinsky (1866–1944) and Charles Baudelaire (1821–67) were among the prominent artists who explored synaesthesia throughout their creative work. Appia's and Kandinsky's concepts of 'Rhythmical Space' and 'The Piano Metaphor', respectively, also reflect the influence of early studies on multisensory crossings and the interchanging of stimuli between different senses in the brain.[8]

Light, colour and projections had a major role in the development of the new Theatre of Symbolism. At the same time, it was the development of electric lighting especially that brought about new possibilities for artistic expression. Unfortunately, the Parisian symbolist Théâtre d'Art and Théâtre de l'Oeuvre left little record of the exact use of lighting during the performances at the beginning of the 1890s, or on how successful they were in realizing their ideas. We do know, however, that semi-transparent veils and painted tulles with light behind them were used as if to de-materialize the appearance of the scenery and the actors. (Bergman 1977, 312–13).

American dancer and choreographer Loïe Fuller (1862–1928) made her debut in Paris in 1892–3 with her *Serpentine Dance* (Palmer 2013, 149 and Bergman 1977, 315). The spectacle consisted mostly in quick circular and sinusoidal movements of the body and a costume, made of huge pieces of bright silk attached to the hands, in tune with projections of changing coloured lighting sources. The complex light design by Fuller herself was to complement the beauty of her solo performance. Her costume reflected intense and colourful light onto the bewitched audience. Documentation confirms that a large team of electricians, usually ranging in number between 14 and 38, used mobile electric arc lamps and limelight to follow the movement and highlight specific areas on Fuller and her surroundings. Fearful of artistic theft, Fuller forbade anyone in her productions to write down the orchestration of the lighting changes, and these had to be memorized, and operated to great precision by the electricians.

In 1917, the Italian futurist painter and clothing designer Giacomo Balla (1871–1958) presented the first world-premiere of live *colour music* performance. This was an innovative work that featured the musical score of *Feu d'artifice* (1908) by Igor Stravinsky (1882–1971), and although it was produced by Sergei P. Diaghilev's Ballets Russes, ironically, the performance included no dancers (Baugh 2005, 122). The scenery, owing its metamorphoses to light and shadow, was composed of large three-dimensional geometric bodies that were partly translucent, and which, through the use of backlighting, appeared radiant. The light modified the space by changing its colours and illuminating the geometric bodies in different ways, generating shadows and reflections that varied the spatial characteristics.

This audio-visual spectacle lasted five minutes, with no human performer participating in it. Balla created forty-nine light images with distinctive characteristics, but used some of them more than once. Controlling this lighting system was still a complex task at the time and a new custom-made lighting console with switches had to be constructed in order to regulate all the dimmers and lamps. The utopian idea of a visual theatre of the future, governed by images rather than words, was also shared by other artists of the post-First World War period, including Oskar Schlemmer (1888–1943). As Schlemmer argued wishfully: "It would be probable that the theatre designer would, in future, develop a range of optical phenomena and **then** [sic] seek out the poet and dramatist who would provide an appropriate language of words and musical sound" (Baugh 2005, 123).

Wassily Kandinsky was one of the visual artists whose body of work, perhaps more intensely than other artists, had continuously questioned the interrelation of light and colour with music, and the exchangeability of stimuli between the senses. Kandinsky is known as a painter but his work also includes theatrical work. It was after watching Wagner's opera *Lohengrin* (in 1896) that Kandinsky began to conceive of painting as an art-form that might have a similar influence on its addressees as that of music (Zimmermann 2006, 18–19). He was intrigued by the phenomenon and explored it in his paintings, stage compositions and theoretical writings (especially in his essay *Concerning the Spiritual in Art and Painting in Particular*, 1912). In this essay, Kandinsky elaborates upon the experience of colour and its effect on the perception and the psyche. In his later theory of *synaesthesia*, Kandinsky used musical terminology that included rhythms, mathematical structures, repetition and movement (of colours in the space) to elucidate his ideas regarding the process of visually perceiving a painting. He considered colour, including light, as a means to generate a direct emotional influence on the human soul by orchestrating colours in harmony, like playing a keyboard (*the piano metaphor*). Symbolically, he described the viewing experience as follows: a spectator's soul is like a piano with its many strings and the eye is the hammer, while the artist, who suggests a visual stimulation, is the hand that makes the spectator's soul tremble.

Interestingly, concerning the theatrical collective of media, Kandinsky stressed the importance of maintaining *the separate expressions of the art-forms* (music-colour-light). His goal was to conjoin colour movements with musical and rhythmical dance movements, and to form a new symbolic theatre of the future. Nevertheless, he argued that each medium should retain its strength and uniqueness in harmonious cooperation – or even in disharmony and dissonance with the others – and had to keep functioning 'autonomously'. In *Der Blaue Reiter Almanach* (1912) Kandinsky describes in great detail a visionary stage composition for colour, movement and sound that he named *The Yellow Sound*. Almost as a protagonist, the yellow light attempts to enter a blue environment (McKinney and Butterworth 2010, 179). The performance eventually remained unrealized:

> Beams of light in glaring colours drop in rapid changes from all sides (blue, red, violet, green) and alternate several times. All these beams melt in the middle, where they are mixed. All is motionless. The giants are almost invisible. Suddenly all colours disappear. For a moment everything is black. Then a matt, yellow light filters down over the stage, becoming by degrees increasingly intense, until the whole stage is glaringly lemon yellow.
>
> (Baugh 2005, 121)

As a visual artist who experimented with the perception and reception of light in space and time, Kandinsky was a pioneer in his advocating further autonomous, unique expression of each medium in the theatre. His prophetic ideas have remained relevant and provided inspiration for additional developments in contemporary theatre.

Bertolt Brecht (1898–1956)

Much has been written about the revolutionary theatre of Bertolt Brecht and his far-reaching contribution to the emergence of new perspectives on modern theatre, its social function, and the collective theatre-making process, all requiring exploration of new aesthetics and poetics. In the context of this chapter, however, I examine what innovative role light played in the dramaturgy of Brechtian theatre. Before turning to light in particular, let us elaborate upon a few aspects of Brecht's poetic theories.

Brecht's work indicates a break from a long-established theatrical tradition of Neoclassicism followed by Social Realism. According to David Barnett, the urge to create a new kind of theatre arose in Brecht as a response to the Naturalist movement which represented the world as a venue with determinate conditions that gave rise to inevitable actions, and failed to attend to contemporary forces acting in the world and to contribute to socio-cultural change. The changes Brecht experienced bore the necessity to reconsider and 'modernize' the dramatic paradigm and give the spectator a different position and responsibility with regard to the work of theatre (Barnett 2008, 212–13). According to the dramaturgy of this new theatre, light was destined to play a major role - through a new mimetic approach that was more suitable for the representation of modern reality.

Since the 17th century, the neoclassicist interpretation of Aristotle's *Poetics* had dominated the tradition of western theatre, an interpretation from which Brecht estranged himself. Aristotle, however, did not concentrate on the staging of drama but proposed, instead, the canons of writing tragedies. For centuries, the *Poetics* was read as though Aristotle had advocated the imitation of life on stage with a large measure of verisimilitude, while the imitation ('mimesis') he refers to was, in fact, of human thinking through *actions*. The sensorial was ranked lower than the logos. In this respect, Aronson notes that ancient Greek culture cherished poetry as an elevated form of *logos*, as opposed to the *sensuous* visual arts. Among the liberal arts and sciences one could find oratory, history, tragedy, comedy, choral song and dance, and astronomy (Aronson 2008, 2–3). The dramatic style, culminating in Realism and later in Naturalism, gradually and increasingly paid much attention to visual imitation of 'copied' reality as identically as possible.

Brecht distinguished his theatre from earlier styles in 19th- and 20th-century mainstream western theatre, which he termed 'dramatic'. Whereas the 'dramatic' play was, and still is, dependent on the phenomenon of fiction, and based upon the illusory portrayal of metonymy-like microcosms with characters acting in a dense timeframe and space, Brecht's texts tended to the epic qualities of theatre while questioning virtually all the conventions of dramatic theatre, in all its media. Yet, much of German theatre in the early decades of the 20th century was still dominated by the Wagnerian concept of the *'Gesamtkunstwerk'*, the total work of art, which unites music, poetry (dramatic text), scenery, dance and other media (Leach 2004, 115). This notion encouraged the *unified expression* of the media with *mythical qualities* and *overwhelming intensity*, to evolve in *one direction of meaning*, following the *music*. As the work of Brecht developed, it seemed to revolt against these precepts.

Brecht stated that his goal was to create a *'theatre of the scientific age'* that would keep the spectators intellectually and critically engaged while watching the performance. The complex of various media left a degree of openness and even contradictions for the addressees to reconsider and settle – each medium maintaining its integrity and unique form of expression (Palmer 2013, 136). Brecht was particularly interested in the rational balancing of the audience's emotional involvement and their empathizing with fictive characters, as opposed to most of the 19th-century Theatre of Realism (e.g. Ibsen, Chekhov). Bergman writes:

> The break-through of functionalism and the German movement Die neue Sachlichkeit around 1930 brought to the fore, in dramatic art, an anti-romantic social trend, which penetrated also outside Germany, e.g. in Sweden with several settings with a strong social and political involvement. White light was here employed – even before Brecht point light, provocative striking power.
>
> (Bergman 1977, 378–9)

And so, light was to harshly expose the course of actions on stage and lead to an immediate impression concerning the artificiality of the presentation. Brecht used the German term *'Verfremdung'* ('de-familiarization' or 'alienation') to reflect the aesthetic distance taken from the representation of the world based on verisimilitude, in order to see it afresh (Leach 2004, 118; and McKinney and Butterworth 2010, 50–1). A pragmatic dimension was created in the distance between the representation (performance) and life outside the theatre, between the actor and the character, and between the sign and 'the signified'. Contributing to the discourse on semiotics and theatre, the dichotomy of sign and signified in Brecht's theatre was particularly favoured by Roland Barthes.

Brecht's epic texts, as opposed to Wagner's mythological fiction of transcendent realities, were grounded in the historicized earthly world and resisted escapism into theatrical illusion. At times, the performers addressed the audience, breaking the 'fourth wall' between the stage and auditorium. Performers occasionally spoke about their characters in the third person and even switched characters with one another. Speech and movement in space were systematically separated and orchestrated as part of the dramaturgy. Consequently, one's potential of immersing oneself with the performance was often disturbed, and the work seemed to be the 'presentation' rather than the 'representation' of the narrative. The reporting way in which the text was delivered, shifting between the 'voice' of the character imitated by the performer and the voice of the performer as a reference to the character, also helped in keeping the addressees attentive and analytical. Brechtian actors 'demonstrated' actions and recited text, but as the agents of a director and without an emotional involvement that might seem to originate from the fictive character; an emotional expression, for instance, could instead be the result of the performer's interpretation: "Do you speak passionately? Not unless there is a particular point to be made by it, and even then you may preface your apparent increase in emotion by acknowledging that 'he got really cross'. Do you 'lose yourself' in the performance? Of course not" (Leach 2004, 121). The shifting perspectives within the performance brought about a diversity of acting hues and theatrical styles, exchanging speech with song, and often creating ironic interrelations between the text and the image, music or movement. As Joslin McKinney and Philip Butterworth write: "Rather than a fused and harmonious presentation of text, actor, scene and music, the effect was one of multiple viewpoints. Brecht called this the 'separation of the elements'" (McKinney and Butterworth 2010, 51).

As a fundamental medium in the production, scenography was to develop during the rehearsal process, in close relationship with the acting. Brecht preferred to begin rehearsing without any concrete idea about scenery and to work in close relationship with his long-time collaborator Casper Neher in the rehearsal room, letting the space evolve simultaneously with the performers who were to inhabit it. Occasionally, Neher's expressive sketches were accepted as proposals for direction and indicated acting style in addition to scenography. Robert Leach writes, for instance, about the first production of *Mother Courage and Her Children* that "The production also used projections – pictures and texts – which referred to the great events like war and strikes going on beyond the particular story being told, but affecting its events. The setting, projections, and so on were designed" – according to Brecht – "[not] to help the spectator, but to block him; they prevent his complete empathy, interrupt his being automatically carried away" (Leach 2004, 124). Barnett also suggests that "the principle of interruption is central to Brecht's theatre as it promotes the readjustments of perception and an acknowledgment that nothing is necessarily as it seems" (Barnett 2008, 215).

By exposing the technical environment of the stage that is commonly hidden, the scenography also manifested forms of *interrupting* fictive representation of the space. The composition of scenographic elements rejected any pretence of fictive space, *demonstrating* the use of the stage as a spatial platform for theatrical presentation. "To him, scenery should merely suggest the location of the action or comment on it. It should never seek to give the illusion of a place in its entirety but should undercut the sense of permanence and unchangeability" (Brockett, Mitchell and Hardberger 2010, 279). As Wilhelm Hortmann notes: "Neher's stages no longer hid but demonstrated the theatre's mechanics" (Hortmann 2008, 286). The spectator becomes aware of the fact that, as Bergman quotes Brecht, "the designer has built up a stage; he is given the means to see in another way than he does outside the theatre" (Bergman 1977, 391). And so, as McKinney and

Butterworth note, the stage pointed to "a conscious theatricality where spectators were always aware of the context of the theatre" (McKinney and Butterworth 2010, 44). The image was intended to comment, challenge and encourage the addressees to entertain reflective views on image and text as well as on the world of reality beyond the theatre.

Light contributed to the V-effect ('*Verfremdung*') in various ways. Since the early 1920s, Brecht and Neher rejected trends of theatre lighting that prevailed in the theatre of Realism as well as the theatre of Naturalism, but also effects of Expressionist art and stage design – among them, "the tightly focused, steeply angled light sources and the use in the theatre of fashionable filmic dramatic shadows" (Baugh 2005, 76). Next came the deliberate *exposure of the lighting devices* – a deviation from the tradition of bourgeois theatres that was nothing less than radical. In the production of *The Threepenny Opera* (1928), for example, lighting equipment was intentionally fixed in positions visible to the spectators, the musicians were on stage near the performers and scenery changes were performed (in full-light) in front of the spectators (Brockett, Mitchell and Hardberger 2010, 279). In the Zurich production of *Mr. Puntila and his Servant Matti* (1948), symbols of sun, moon and clouds were hung in the back of the scenery 'like the hanging signs for pubs and shops', and were illuminated in the different scenes according to their relevance to the narrative (Palmer 2013, 134). The signification of time was created, in a similar way to that of Elizabethan theatre, mainly by the performers, the text or through an object; thus a candle, for example, represented night-time on the Elizabethan stage. Brecht states that no coloured lighting was used and powerful lighting was evenly distributed on stage. Occasionally, however, this restriction was eased and shades of slightly coloured light were added, with the invention of a filters technique that offered a broad variety of pale tints. Martin Esslin describes lighting style, advocated by Brecht, as presenting the action under "unvarying and glaring clarity (even in scenes taking place at night, when the fact will have to be indicated by properties such as lamps or candles)" (Esslin 1987, 77). Light takes no part in the creation of atmosphere, or in supporting an illusion of time and place. It is informative, straightforward, acting as a clarification of the space. Erika Fischer-Lichte states that:

> Brecht was determined to remove the sign system of light altogether from his theatrical code. Light was to be used merely in its practical function and to illuminate the stage space completely and evenly. When light was eliminated as a system that generates meaning, the fact of its elimination advanced to be the status of a sign which was capable of signifying in a special way Brecht's rejection of atmospheric bourgeois theatre.
>
> (Fischer-Lichte 1992, 114)

Beyond its functioning as mere illumination, light assisted in eliminating any impression of verisimilitude in the scenography and avoiding the creation of captivating atmospheric looks on stage, both of which were familiar conventions in dramatic theatre. It played a role in 'energising the public', to use Brecht's words. The side-effect of high light intensity was the 'V-effect' of estrangement or alienation, as if the light ignored the emotional expression of the performance, and avoided giving any interpretive reflection upon it. In fact, this withdrawal from all reference to emotion played a part in *holding back the rise of emotion*, in favour of the critical reception and intellectual spectatorship that Brecht wished to promote in his 'theatre of the scientific age'. Palmer quotes Brecht remarking (around 1940): "a half-lit stage coupled with completely dark-ened auditorium makes the spectator less level-headed by preventing him from observ-ing his neighbour and in turn hiding from his neighbour's eyes" (Palmer 2013, 135).

This transitory phase of 'muting' the medium was an important step in the evolv-ing function of light in the theatre. Looking at the history of theatre lighting, it seems that 'development had run full circle' – as if we had returned to the symmetric and even illumination of the Renaissance stage, only with much brighter intensities and the ability to modify light distribution throughout the performance (Bergman 1977, 380). The liberation of light from its illustrative or supportive position with regard to the narrative began with Brecht's theatre and later gradually evolved in contemporary post-dramatic theatre. The role that light played in Brecht's dramaturgy was highly influential in the aesthetics and the poetics of German theatre and has been ever since, inspiring the succeeding generation of European directors in Germany, such as Jürgen Gosch, Dimiter Gotscheff and Luk Perceval, among others. The loosening of the connection between light and text and fiction, and the idea that various performative media can concurrently develop their expressive potential to its fullest resulted in more autonomy and new possibilities for the medium of light.

Josef Svoboda (1920–2002)

> Scenery by means of lighting rather than paint is the future, because the individual artist can do exactly what he wants and then have it projected, thereby really con-veying the artist's signature and possessing quality.
>
> (Josef Svoboda, in Burian 1983, 81)

Josef Svoboda was one of the most celebrated lighting designers and scenographers of recent decades, whose work has deeply influenced the aesthetics and poetics of the theatre since the mid-20th century. Jarka Burian refers to Svoboda as an heir to Adolphe Appia and Gordon Craig, as well as a developer of Futurism, Constructivism and Bauhaus in ide-ology and practice (Burian 1983, 4). He was educated as an architect, and his stage design reflects elaborate formalist tendencies and accentuation of materiality, and three-dimen-sional (occasionally dynamic) abstract or geometric elements. In his work he opposed the naturalist approach of accurately depicting reality, as he notes: "I'm not interested in making a burning bush or an erupting volcano on stage, in creating an illusion of reality, but in acknowledging the reality of theatrical elements, which can be transformed non-materially into almost anything. I've called them 'space in space'" (Svoboda 1993, 18). In some productions (*The Seagull* 1960, for example) the intangibility and suggestiveness of light fascinated Svoboda even more than matter, in terms of "portraying the unpor-trayable" (Albertová, 2008, 95). He sought to unfold the dramatic action and the *inner essence of drama*, creating metamorphoses of the stage space through a poetic use of light, stage machinery and kinetic elements. The synthesis of diverse elements embodied the 'psycho-plasticity' of the space, i.e. "a dramatic space which Svoboda describes as "elastic in its scope and alterable in its quality" (quoted in McKinney and Butterworth 2010, 72). Baugh explains that the distance Svoboda kept in his scenographic work from the perceptual features of reality, and the enhancement of technological 'fingerprints' on the aesthetics of space, were in favour of a more 'futuristic' character:

... Svoboda's belief that the stage should use technologies to retain a sense of *distance from representation*. In other words he consciously used the strangeness, the mystery of effects and their frequently complex technologies to keep the scenography on the level of the inner feelings and meaning of the play.

(Baugh 2005, 88; emphasis added)

The 'representation' mentioned by Baugh is, I believe, the representation of reality based on verisimilitude. In Svoboda's design, verisimilitude was replaced by highly synthetic and somewhat 'sterile' images, fabricated by the most cutting-edge materials and visual technologies. He was thrilled to experiment with and adopt new technologies when these could carry out an effect that seemed to be dramaturgically driven, while simultaneously reflecting the contemporary experience of humanity. "The material has to speak", Svoboda states in the biographical film *Theatre Svoboda* by his grandson, Jakub Hejna (2011). The possibly alienating environments of sophisticated machinery and computer-like imagery, with either graphic or geometric qualities, provided a powerful and evocative, even immersive surrounding within which human actors played. In a number of productions Svoboda even incorporated mirrors and magnifying lenses to distort the actors' images while they moved behind these lenses. The new aesthetics of Svoboda's scenography did not derive from the availability of new technologies. Rather, it echoes parallel developments that occurred in the visual arts with the rising dominance of multimedia. The aesthetic and poetic dimensions in his work reflect the postmodern explorations regarding representation of the human condition in accordance with the state-of-the-art philosophy and changing cultural climate after the Second World War.

Light, projection and scenography were so strongly engaged with each other that the discussions of light and space could hardly be separated.[9] Svoboda's use of expressive ('creative/formative') light and his elaboration of the kinetic and plastic qualities that comprise a three-dimensional space can be traced back to Appia's and Craig's ideas (McKinney and Butterworth 2010, 65). Even more than Craig, Svoboda succeeded in mobilizing and vitalizing scenography and employed it as a counterpoint to the activity of individual performers, whether through optic-visual means or structural-physical movements (Baugh 2005, 84). Maintaining a strong connection between the singularity of the scenography and the inner qualities and content of the play in each particular production was more important for Svoboda than it was for Craig (see earlier on Craig's use of the same set for multiple plays). Svoboda sought to refer to the locus of underlying emotions and ideas *within the drama, but to expand on them in scope and effect*. Like Appia, Svoboda's ambition was *to embody the essence of the text in a composition of light* that changed over time, and to affect the spectators' spatial perception by means of light – even when the scenography had been otherwise perceived as static. He acknowledged the enormous potency of light to engage the scenography in a visual dynamism, without dependence on architectonic dynamism. To do so, he frequently used low-voltage lighting with a thin haze to make the light-beams seem solid, as well as slide projections or mirror plates to reflect light on, or away from, parts of the scenography.

In the Wiesbaden-Cologne production (1967) of Wagner's *Tristan and Isolde*, for instance, Svoboda created three main scenographic/lighting elements with which he represented all the locations in the opera: a large downward spiral construction at centre

Figure 1.6 Josef Svoboda, *Tristan and Isolde*, Wiesbaden–Cologne, 1967. Courtesy of the Josef Svovoda Estate/Sarka Hejnova

stage for the actors to walk on; a new cyclorama made of dense cotton cords that could receive and reflect light and projections; and special lighting effects. Svoboda's premise for the performance was: "The whole opera is marked by its end – there is no solution except death, it's inevitable. And the spiral embodies this. It creates a meeting point and a point of no escape" (Burian 1983, 41).

Abstract images of sails were projected on the cords-cyclorama, to suggest various locations on the ship where the first act takes place. In the later acts, coloured light was projected onto the cords, establishing atmosphere and representing the inner world or emotional state of the characters. To accentuate the climax of the opera with a special lighting effect, Svoboda used the low-voltage lamps inside the spiral, facing upward (Figure 1.6). These lamps shone from the bottom of the spiral like a light tunnel, as a rising pillar or an inverted shower of light – a lighting effect which, as Burian notes, "enclosed the lovers to convey the burning intensity of their passion". In order to intensify the impression of this effect, theatre technicians sprayed aerosol oil droplets in the air for 10–15 minutes to generate a haze through an electrical process before the lamps were switched on.

Light thus appeared to be a mass of concrete material with a three-dimensional presence, and it could emerge in the midst of the spiral, or vanish, at will. This light, which was invented by Svoboda and has carried his name ever since, is one of the few examples of a lighting technology that was invented especially to answer the unique needs of theatre-makers in devising special effects. Such inventions helped artists to create extraordinary visual effects by means of which representations of reality were achieved solely through the use of light.

For a different production of *Tristan and Isolde*, this time in Bayreuth (1974), Svoboda developed a more abstract imagery of light and projection on cords for each scene. The original idea was, in Svoboda's own words, to metaphorically *"enter into the score"*. Practically, by projecting pointillist images, coloured lights and textures, the atmospheric space suggested a tangible expression for the psyches of the characters. Burian describes the Bayreuth production as follows:

> In Act 1, for example, a strange, eclipse-like effect of darkness at noon occurred after Tristan and Isolde drank the potion. They were then isolated in a pool of the deepest blue light imaginable, illuminated by what appeared to be moonlight against the ghostly white sail behind them. In Act 2, probably the most successful in creating the desired effect, a dappled, autumnal, shimmering light on the cords and the floor established the real world. Then the lighting faded more abstract, muted colors and projected forms that blended into increasingly dark brown hues until the critical moment deep in the love scene. At this point, a midnight blue was injected into the total picture, evolving toward a virtual blackout with occasional subtle shifts of abstract projected images.
>
> (Burian 1983, 45–6)

In Act 3 of that same production, Svoboda cast a shadow of a tree with a wide trunk and foliage onto the cords. The suggestion of a tree was sufficient for the spectators to establish its existence in their perception, although they could not see the actual tree. Metamorphosing scenography by means of light, or rather, in this case, of shadow, was one of the keystones and suggestive qualities of Svoboda's work. Like the actor,

Figure 1.7 Josef Svoboda, *Tristan and Isolde*, Bayreuth, 1974. Courtesy of the Josef Svovoda Estate/Sarka Hejnova

he argued, scenography should be able to undergo transformations during the perfor-mance, in response to the flow of the action, as a kinetic place of performance. This could be achieved either by an actual physical change in the decor, or by means of light, projection or special devices like mirrors, which alter the perceptual features of the set. Bergman quotes from a conversation that Svoboda had with Burian: "I don't want a static picture, but something that evolves, that has movement, not necessarily physical movement, of course, but a setting that is dynamic, capable of expressing changing rela-tionships, feelings, moods, perhaps only by lighting, during the course of the action" (Bergman 1977, 385).

Another innovative use of light was in the 1977 Geneva cycle of Wagner's *Der Ring des Nibelungen*, a production in which Svoboda assigned a completely new poetic role to light. In *Das Rheingold*, Svoboda replaced Erda, the goddess of Wisdom, Fate and Earth, when she first appears in the opera, by a seemingly solid beam of light emanating from the upstage area and focused upward. The performers referred to the light as if it was Erda, while the actress/singer who sang Erda's libretto remained offstage. Her voice was assigned to this shaft of light, delivering the lyrics without any corporeal appearance of the singer herself (Burian 1983, 85). The separation of the voice from its creator, in favour of the visual effect of light, had a tremendous dramaturgical, sensational and even acoustic impact. On a narrative-related context, one can consider the *representa-tion of God or the Divine* using light, as a reference to the long tradition in medieval art. Alternatively, from an aesthetic and poetic perspective, one can associate the *light as performer* with fundamental ideas of Light Art. Several visual artists have employed the medium of light as their main agency, as the core of the artistic experience within works of Light Art. This will be the subject of the following chapter. I will discuss the work of a few visual artists for whom artificial light became the main medium of work and the main 'material' to construct the experience of the addressee with. I will not make the case for an explicit influence of Light Art on theatre design. However, it is self-evident that light designers and scenographers are inspired by this art movement and occasion-ally make reference to works of light artists.

Having the human performer replaced on stage by a light-beam in Svoboda's pro-duction (Geneva 1977), and the detachment of the voice from the human body and the stage image, would seem to showcase the emergence of what Lehmann calls *the dilemma with the actor's position in the contemporary theatre* and a theatre of *stage poetry*.

Conclusion

The works and ideas of the towering figures in the history of late 19th- and 20th-century theatre lighting design discussed in this chapter reflect the fundamental devel-opments in the artistic function of light during this relatively short period. Light's potential as a poetic and autonomous force arose within the performance, evolving into a semiotic and poetic element in its own right. For the creation of a new aesthet-ics, the availability of new lighting technology was essential, of course, but the influ-ences of the visual arts, in addition to the philosophical discourse on Modernism and Postmodernism, also inspired artists to ponder upon 'the theatre of the future'. Since Appia and Craig, we have witnessed a growing estrangement from a representation of reality based on verisimilitude, in favour of a more holistic approach to space in which light has a dominant creative role. The position of the written text with regard to the image was reconsidered.[10] In the work of the Symbolists and postmodern theatre designers – among them Josef Svoboda – the presence of stage technology, lighting and projections and the enhanced sense of materiality, were reflected upon explicitly. The visual dimension of the performance occasionally became highly dominant, immersive and, some would even say, extravagant.

Notes

1 To clarify, I differentiate in this book between '*light*' and '*lighting*'. *Light* is what the designer creates and characterizes in order to influence the way that spectators perceive. *Lighting*, on the other hand, is the technology involved in this process – the devices, lamps, projectors and optical systems that designers use – in order to design light in the theatre.

2 As noted in the introductory chapter, I use the term 'aesthetics' in relation to the perceptual features, the formal aspects of the performance that are perceived by the addressee. Consistently, the aesthetics of any representation relates to perception and not to the semiosis, or meaning-making process that is generated by the performance.

3 Appia watched in Bayreuth Wagner's productions of *Parsifal* in 1882, *Tristan und Isolde* in 1886, and *Die Meistersinger* in 1888, but found the visual interpretation to the music-drama to be dissapointedly literal.

4 E.G. Craig, *Daybook 1, 1908–10*, pp. 79 and 77, in C. Innes, *Edward Gordon Craig, A Vision of Theatre*, 2nd edition, Harwood Academic Publishers, the Gordon and Breach Publishing Group, 1998, p. 121.

5 E.G. Craig, "The Actor and the Über-Marionette" (1911) in *Theatre and Performance Design: A Reader in Scenography*, edited by J. Collins and A. Nisbet, London: Routledge 2010, p. 258.

6 R.M. Mouduès and J. Rouché, *Revue d'histoire du théâtre*, III, 1958, p. 313, in G.M. Bergman, *Lighting in the Theatre*, Stockholm: Almqvist &Wiksell International, 1977, p. 338.

7 J. Moréas, *The Symbolist Manifesto* ('*Le Symbolisme*'), in *Le Figaro*, 18 September 1886.

8 For more on Appia and his notion of 'Rhythmic Space' see earlier in this chapter, and find more on Kandinsky's 'Piano Metaphor' later in this chapter.

9 In regard to Svoboda's work, I shall not elaborate here on his *Laterna Magica* theatre, because in this kind of performance film was more dominant in the creation of optical illusions and visual imagery, than the lighting. I consider film projections to be an emerging medium in the theatre and not always in the scope of light. A collage of real occurrences on stage together with the film projections was the fundamental effect that this theatre presented. Therefore, I prefer to demonstrate Svoboda's use of light by means of examples that are more explicit and connected to light itself rather than to film projections.

10 Since I have already addressed the subject in the Introduction, I mention it here without elaboration.

References

Albertová, H., *Josef Svoboda, Scenographer*, Prague: Theatre Institute Prague, 2008.

Appia, A., *Die Muzik und die Inszenierung,* Berlin 1899.

Appia, A., *La Gymnastique Rythmique et le Théâtre, Der Rythmus, Ein Jahrbuch der Bildungsanstalt Jacques-Dalcroze,* Dresden: Hellerau, 1911.

Appia, A., *Theatrical Experiences and Personal Investigations*, unpublished essay of about 1924, translated by Walther Volbach, the Appia Collection, Beinecke Library, Yale University, pp. 374–5 of the typescript.

Aronson, A., *Looking into the Abyss: Essays on Scenography*, Ann Arbor, MI: The University of Michigan Press, 4th edition, 2008, (1st edition 2005).

Ashby, C., *Classical Greek Theatre, New Views on an Old Subject*, Iowa City, IA: University of Iowa Press, 1999.

Auerbach, E., *Mimesis, the Representation of Reality in Western Literature*, Garden City, NY: Doubleday Anchor Books, Doubleday & Company, Inc., 1957.

Bablet, D. and Bablet, M.L., *Adolphe Appia 1862–1928: Actor–Space–Light*, Zurich: Pro Helvetia, London: John Calder (Publishers) Ltd and New York: Riverrun Press, 1982.

Banham, M., *The Cambridge Guide to Theatre*, first published in 1988 as *The Cambridge Guide to World Theatre*, new edition, Cambridge: Cambridge University Press, 2000.

Barnett, D., *Naturalism, Expressionism and Brecht*, in *A History of German Theatre*, edited by Simon Williams and Maik Hamburger, Cambridge and New York: Cambridge University Press, 2008.

Baugh, C., *Theatre, Performance and Technology: The Development of Scenography in the Twentieth Century*, New York: Palgrave Macmillan, 2005.

Baugh, C., "Brecht and Stage Design", in *The Cambridge Companion to Brecht*, edited. by Peter Thompson and Glendyr Sacks, Cambridge: Cambridge University Press, 1994.

Beacham, R. C., *Adolphe Appia: Texts on Theatre*, first edition, London: Routledge, 1993.

Beacham, R. C., *Adolphe Appia: Theatre Artist*, Cambridge, New York, Melbourne and Sydney: Cambridge University Press, 1989 (first published 1987).

Belasco, D., *The Theatre Through Its Stage Door*, New York and London: Harper & Brothers, 1919.

Bergman, G. M., *Lighting in the Theatre*, Stockholm: Almqvist & Wiksell International, 1977.

Brockett, O. G., Mitchell, M. and Hardberger, L., *Making the Scene: A History of Stage Design and Technology in Europe and the United States*, San Antonio, TX: Tobin Theatre Arts Fund, 2012 (first published 2010) .

Brown, B., *The History of Lighting* in *Motion Picture and Video Lighting*, 2nd edition, Oxford: Focal Press-Elsevier, 2008.

Burian, J., *Svoboda: Wagner, Josef Svoboda's Scenography for Richard Wagner's Opera*, Middletown, CT: Wesleyan University Press, 1983.

Burian, J., *The Scenography of Josef Svoboda*, Middletown, CT: Wesleyan University Press, 1971.

Collins, J. and Nisbet, A., *Theatre and Performance Design: A Reader in Scenography*, Abingdon and New York: Routledge, 2010.

Craig, E. G., *On the Art of Theatre*, London: Heinemann, 1911; reprinted by Mercury Books, 1962.

Craig, E. G., "The Actor and the Über-Marionette" (1911) in *Theatre and Performance Design: A Reader in Scenography*, edited by J. Collins. and A. Nisbet, Routledge, Abingdon and New York: Routledge, 2010.

Craig, E. C., *Gordon Craig, The Story of his Life*, London: Knopf Inc., 1968.

Diderot, D., *Oeuvres complètes*, vol. VII, Paris, 1875.

Donald, M., "Art and Cognitive Evolution", in *The Artful Mind, Cognitive Science and the Riddle of Human Creativity,* edited by Mark Turner, New York: Oxford University Press, 2006.

Esslin, M., *The Field of Drama: How the Signs of Drama Create Meaning on Stage and Screen*, New York: Methuen, 1987.

Finkel, A., *Romantic Stages, Set and Costume Design in Victorian England*, Jefferson, NC and London: McFarland & Company Inc., Publishers, 1996.

Fischer-Lichte, E., *The Semiotics of Theater*, translated by Jeremy Gaines and Doris L. Jones, Bloomington and Indianapolis, IN: Indiana University Press, 1992.

Flecknoe, R., *A Discourse of the English Stage*, 1660, in P. Penzel, *Theatre Lighting Before Electricity*, Middletown, CT: Wesleyan University Press, 1978.

Goldman, A. and Sprinchorn, E., "The Staging of *Tristan and Isolde* by Appia", in *Wagner on Music and Drama: A Compendium of Richard Wagner's Prose Works*, New York: Da Capo Press, 1988.

Hartmann, L., *Theatre Lighting: A Manual of the Stage Switchboard*, New York and London: D. Appleton and Company, 1930.

Hejna, J., *Theatre Svoboda*, a film by Jacub Hejna, Endorfilm s.r.o., The Czech Television, Jakub Hejna – Joung Film, 2011

Hewitt, B., *The Renaissance Stage: Documents of Serlio, Sabbattini and Furttenbach*, Miami, FL: University of Miami Press, 1958.

Hortmann, W., "Revolutions in Scenography on the German Stage in the Twentieth Century", in *A History of German Theatre*, edited by Simon Williams and Maik Hamburger, Cambridge: Cambridge University Press, 2008.

Innes, C., *Edward Gordon Craig, A Vision of Theatre*, 2nd edition, Harwood Academic Publishers, The Gordon and Breach Publishing Group, 1998.

Innes, C., *Edward Gordon Craig*, in the series: *Directors in Perspective*, Cambridge: Cambridge University Press, 1983.

Jakobson, R., *On Realism and Art*, 1921, collected in *Readings in Russian Poetics: Formalist and Structuralist Views*, edited by Ladislav Matejka and Krystyna Pomorska, Cambridge, MA: MIT Press, 1971.

Kandinsky, W., *Concerning the Spiritual in Art and Painting in Particular*, 1912; reprinted New York 1947.

Kuritz, P., *The Making of Theatre History*, Englewood Cliffs, NJ: Prentice Hall, 1988.

Leach, R., *Makers of Modern Theatre: An Introduction*, Abingdon and New York: Routledge, 2004.

Le Bœuf, P., "On the Nature of Edward Gordon Craig's Über-Marionette", *New Theatre Quarterly*, 26, 102–14, 2010.

Lee, B.H., "Pierre Patte, Late 18th Century Lighting Innovator", *Theatre Survey*, 15, 177–83, doi: 10.1017/S0040557400006281, published online 7 July, 2009.

Lehmann, H. T., *Postdramatic Theatre*, translated and foreword by K. Jürs-Munby, Abingdon and New York: Routledge, 2006.

McKinney, J. and Butterworth, P., *The Cambridge Introduction to Scenography*, 2nd edition, Cambridge: Cambridge University Press, 2010 (1st edition 2009).

Mascart, E., *Rapport sur l'éclairage des théâtres, Revue d'histoire du théâtre*, Paris, 1955.

Mouduès, R. M. and Rouché, J., *Revue d'histoire du théâtre*, III, 1958, p. 313, in G. M. Bergman, *Lighting in the Theatre*, Stockholm: Almqvist & Wiksell International, 1977.

Nicoll, A., *The Development of the Theatre: A Study of Theatrial Art from the Beginnings to the Present Day*, London, Toronto, Wellington and Sydney: George G. Harrap & Company Ltd, 4th edition 1958; reprinted 1959, 1961.

Noverre, J. G., *Lettres sur la danse*, Paris, 1760.

Palmer, H. R., *The Lighting Art: The Aesthetics of Stage Lighting Design*, 2nd edition, Upper Saddle River, NJ: Prentice-Hall, Inc.

Palmer, S., *Light, Readings in Theatre Practice*, Basingstoke, UK: Palgrave Macmillan, 2013.

Penzel, P., *Theatre Lighting Before Electricity*, Middletown, CT: Wesleyan University Press, 1978.

Pilbrow, R., *Stage Lighting Design: the Art, the Craft, the Life*, London: Nick Hern Books, 1997.

Popper, F., "Light Kinetics", in *Light Art from Artificial Light, Light as a Medium in the 20th and 21st century Art*, edited by Peter Weibel and Gregor Jansen, Ostfildern, Germany: Hatje Cantz, 2006.

Pyne, W. H., *Wine and Walnuts; or After Dinner Chit-Chat*, vol. I, printed by A. & R. Spottiswoode, New Street Square, London, 1823, pp. 289-90. http://www.archive.org/stream/wineandwalnutsor01pyneuoft#page/n3/mode/2up (last accessed 8 June 2011).

Ricoeur, P., *What is a Text? Explanation and Understanding* in *Hermeneutics and Human Sciences*, Cambridge: Cambridge University Press, 1981.

Schivelbusch, W., *Disenchanted Night: the Industrialization of Light in the Nineteenth Century*, Berkeley, CA: University of California Press, 1988.

Spolsky, E., *Word vs Image: Cognitive Hunger in Shakespeare's England*, Basingstoke, UK: Palgrave Macmillan, 2007.

Stoker, B., "Irving and Stage Lighting", *Nineteenth Century and After*, vol. LXIX, January–June 1911, London.

Svoboda, J., *The Secrets of Theatrical Space*, edited and translated by Jarka Burian, Tonbridge, UK: Applause, 1993.

The New York Times, *Amusements: The Theatrical Week*, a review on Irving's performance of 'Faust', 8 November, 1887. http://query.nytimes.com/mem/archive-free/pdf?res=F00E1EF73F5F10738DDDAF0994DA405B8085F0D3 (last accessed 8 June 2011).

Vasari, G., *Vite de piu eccelenti pittori, scultori ed architetti*, Parte Terza, Primo Volume. Bologna, 1678.

Zimmermann, R., "Early Imprints and Influences", in *Kandinsky, The Path to Abstraction*, edited by Hartwig Fischer and Sean Rainbird, London: Tate Publishing, 2006.

Chapter 2

Light Art

The rising autonomy of artificial light

> The theatre, the world of appearances, is digging its own grave when it tries for verisimilitude; the same applies to the mime, who forgets that his chief characteristic is his artificiality. The medium of every art is artificial, and every art gains from recognition and acceptance of its medium.
>
> (Oskar Schlemmer, quoted in Tut Schlemmer 1990, 126)

Ever since Greek Antiquity, theatre has been a complex multidisciplinary art-form in which a variety of cultural traditions were appropriated and renewed according to contemporary worldviews, employing the aesthetics of other art-forms – among them poetry and literature, visual arts, architecture, and eventually cinema. Throughout the history of theatre, painters have decorated theatre stages, superseded by an increasing number of architects and visual artists in the 20th and 21st centuries. Since the 1960s, Performance Art and Happenings have led to new views on theatricality and spectatorship, and have explored the (diffuse) boundaries between art and daily life. These experimental art-forms provided addressees with ambiguous or incomplete experiences, inviting them to use their imagination and generate their own subjective interpretations. This resulted in a change in the relation between artefact and addressees. Inspired by installation art, scenography emerged as an approach to space and performance design that is more autonomous in relation to the dramatic text – seeking to expand and strengthen the visual dimension of the performance and the experience of spectatorship beyond textual reference.

Installations and sculptural works of Light Art have also enriched our understanding of the ability of light to act autonomously upon the spectator's perception. This chapter focuses on the development of Light Art, especially since the early 1960s, by introducing several representative works of art and keystone notions. The works discussed were selected to exemplify the possible poetic uses of artificial lighting, variations of which will also be found in the contemporary theatre performances analysed in Chapters 5 to 9.

Around the end of the 19th century the search for alternative forms of artistic expression and interaction with addressees was common to both the visual arts and the theatre. In *Theatre, Performance and Technology: The Development of Scenography in the Twentieth Century*, Christopher Baugh notes that the great theatre-makers of the 20th century were to "propose an art that is independent of dramatic literature and that will generate artistic self-sufficiency within itself" (Baugh 2005, 10). This was related to the rapid advance in technology and the increasing proximity between art and philosophy since Modernism. We witnessed a remarkable technological development in the medium of

light throughout the 20th century; enriching both the diversity of formal characteristics (aesthetics) that light is capable of generating, and the means of poetic expression
available to artists creating with light. This technological development had a major
influence within the theatre and Light Art alike. Offering new forms of stimuli and
eventually leaving its 'fingerprints' in the image, technology exerts a major influence
on the reception of contemporary work. State-of-the-art philosophical debates on *the
representation of the sublime* and the new function of the image within modern, postmodern and contemporary visual art had later inspired theatre-makers in their work. This
chapter provides a brief overview of Light Art and the route of the medium of light
towards autonomous expression, touching upon several central philosophical notions as
embodied in artworks of light with relevance to the art of light in the theatre.

Light in the visual arts

For centuries, light has been one of the greatest sources of inspiration for artists, fulfill-
ing different functions in the aesthetics and poetics of the traditions and conventions
of different periods. Medieval art, for example, showcases extensive use of shiny metals
and precious stones to represent the divine light of God. The more reflection of physical
light was linked with the portrayal of angelic or Christian icons, the higher the degree
of holiness, and vice versa. The occasional absence of shadows on the represented body
followed the same Christian convention. In the Renaissance, light was liberated from its
religious context and used in secular feasts, spectacles and light festivals to celebrate the
gaiety of life overcoming darkness. "In the fine arts", as Anne Wagner writes, "light had
served mostly as a formal and emotive vehicle, vivifying sculptural surfaces and providing the templates for many of the most dramatic of painting's depicted effects. Light,
and its antonym, darkness, created the art object's atmosphere, in every sense of the
word" (Wagner 2013, 31). Wagner also notes that light's central role was to assist in
creating an illusion of depth and the sense of passing time. Later, Baroque artists generated the dramatic effect of light and shade through the *chiaroscuro* technique and intensified the theatrical impression of movement in sculptures by contrasting illuminated
and shadowed parts. In his essay *The Development of Light Art*, Peter Weibel refers to the
appearance of painted light sources (such as fires or candles) and rainbows in various
paintings from the 18th century by Joseph Wright of Derby (Weibel 2006, 90–5). In
these works, light appears not only as a means to reveal details in the gloomy surrounding but also to link the painted light and the paintings' subjects: scientific exploration
or industrial activity that metaphorically refer to the Enlightenment. According to
Weibel, the end of the 19th century saw a line drawn between earlier art and modern
art movements. The former imitated light by depicting images of daily life (as a 'vehicle'), and the latter used the material of paint to create images about light and visual
perception itself and, later, added actual physical light. Among these movements, to
mention but a few, were Impressionism, Pointillism, Divisionism and Monochromatic
panel painting. The advent of photography had provided yet another reason for painters
to reconsider the aesthetics of art through the medium of painting. Realism in painting declined. The medium sought anew its distinction from photography with regard
to representation of reality and light. We find artificial lighting sources adapted by the
visual arts most significantly since the early 1920s, as a response to scientific discoveries
in the fields of physics and neurology.

In their essay *Light as a Medium of Art* Peter Weibel and Gregor Jansen note that since the end of the 19th century the phenomenon of 'synaesthesia' – experiences that cross various sensing modalities[1] – gained increasing scientific and artistic attention (Weibel and Jansen 2006, 27). Likewise, artistic experimentation seeking for harmony between colour and music further expanded especially since the 19th century, following, for instance, earlier artistic experiments that included Louis-Bertrand Castel's *Colour-Music* system (1725) and the introduction of the *clavecin oculaire* (colour-organ; 1730), and the later electrified colour-organ of Alexander Wallace Rimington (1895). In the tradition of painting, colours were the principal means to portray light. Around the 1870s, the Impressionists were greatly inspired by the research of light in physics and publications of colour theories that followed, one of which was the influential colour theory *De la Loi du Contraste Simultané des Couleurs* by Michel Eugène Chevreul (Paris, 1839). The reference to light as energy, as dynamic electromagnetic waves of light – of which only a limited range in the optical spectrum is visible to the human eye – encouraged later the use of genuine light in the visual arts.

The cinema, a new art-form in which image and music work simultaneously, was considered by some visual artists as an appropriate substitute for static painting: it allowed them to explore new possibilities for a synaesthetic experience using materials and technologies previously unknown. This resulted in the first abstract films in and around 1921. But already as early as 1916, long before he could watch such films, the Swiss art critic Bernhard Diebold prophetically wrote in *Expressionismus und Kino*:

> The painted art film [. . .] plays with forms in a free and completely natural way. Like in music, male and female forms dance and struggle, appear and vanish. They appear to change shape continually, in dissonances and variations, according to the rules of the most exact of all arts, and then to return to their original form. In the meantime storms, flames, winds, and waves, painted or sketched in lines, wander around, meet, follow and overlap with each other in rhythmic arrangements, fight, become entangled, cancel each other out and, finally, dissolve or culminate in a dominant configuration in red against the vanquished, hostile blue.
>
> (quoted in Selwood 2006, 416)

It is highly significant that Diebold associates the movement and metamorphosis of lines and shapes – images of light on a two-dimensional flat screen – with characters, gender and signs of human communication. Envisaging such moving forms as active performers with 'behaviour' analogous to that of human beings or forces of nature is the result of imaginative representations which the addressees construct with – and in – the artwork. Diebold's groundbreaking formalistic approach influenced all the manifestos of abstract filmmakers who, in turn, noted dichotomies between female and male forms, natural and geometric forms, unification and confrontation of forms in space, among others (Selwood 2006, 416). Among the artists who created the first 'Abstract Cinema' were Walter Ruttmann (*Lichtspiel Opus 1*, 1921), Hans Richter (*Rhythmus 21*, 1921), Viking Eggeling (*Symphonie Diagonal*, 1921), Fernand Léger (*le Ballet Mécanique*, 1923–4) and Marcel Duchamp (*Anemic Cinema*, 1926).

Ruttmann, the first artist to screen abstract films in public, considered this genre as 'painting in time' (Figures 2.1, 2.2 and 2.3). He was excited by the "infinite possible uses of light and darkness, of calm and movement, of straight lines and curves,

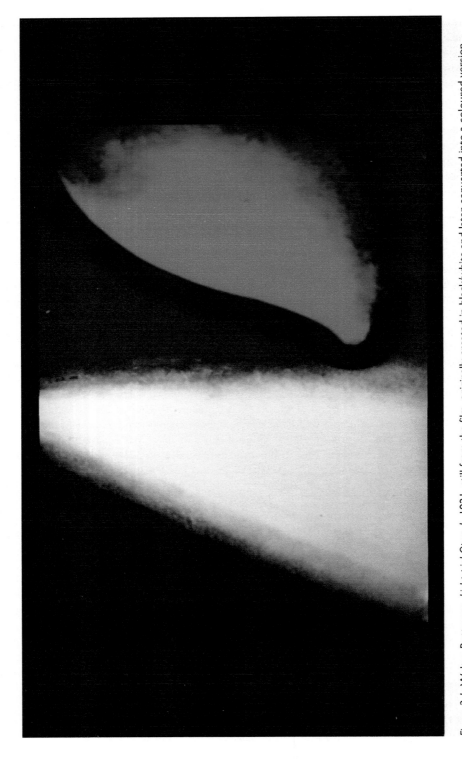

Figure 2.1 Walter Ruttmann, *Lichtspiel Opus I*, 1921, still from the film, originally created in black/white and later converted into a coloured version. Courtesy of Filmmuseum München

Figure 2.2 Walter Ruttmann, *Lichtspiel Opus I*, 1921, still from the film, originally created in black/white and later converted into a coloured version. Courtesy of Filmmuseum München

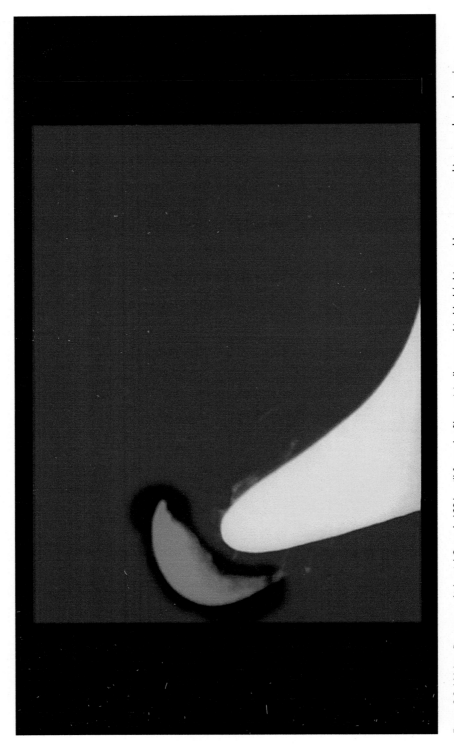

Figure 2.3 Walter Ruttmann, *Lichtspiel Opus 1*, 1921, still from the film, originally created in black/white and later converted into a coloured version. Courtesy of Filmmuseum München

of mass and fine structure and the innumerable stages in between, and accumulations" of what he considers "a raging mixture of light and dark elements, until somehow by victorious intensification harmony and balance are introduced" (Weibel 2006, 168). Both Ruttmann and Léger were fascinated by film as a cumulative experience that is reinforced in time and by the film's capacity to generate movement of forms with light of which painting was incapable. In 1918, about three years before screening his first abstract film, Ruttmann commented: "There's no sense in continuing to paint [. . .]. One has to set painting in motion" (Selwood 2006, 418–19). Likewise, Léopold Survage commented in 1914 that in painting "the groups of colors are fixed on a static surface [. . .] their relationships do not change", and therefore "I want to animate my painting and give the concrete action of the abstract picture rhythm and movement [. . .] The instrument will be the cinematographic film, the true symbol of concentrated movement" (quoted in Russett and Starr 1976, 39).

Abstract films were produced on the basis of different concepts, and with a variety of techniques: Ruttmann wanted to visualize the music and generate a *"dynamism of optic events"*, while Oskar Fischinger experimented with coloured liquids, stencils, moiré patterns, wax and sound, and developed silhouette animations and films using numerous projectors (Weibel 2006, 169). In 1921 Theo van Doesburg, known as one of the leaders of the De Stijl movement, writes: "It could be insightful to compare abstract film with visual music, because roughly in the same way as with music, here the entire composition arises visibly within the open field of light" (Weibel 2006, 168). In *The Future of Painting* (1923), Willard Huntington Wright announced that a "new art of color" would replace painting on canvas with pigment-based colour, because, for the latter, "there is no future". (. . .) "The medium of this new art will be light, namely, color in its purest, most intense form".[2]

Another type of work that used light prominently was the Lumia (Figure 2.4), invented by the Danish artist Thomas Wilfred in 1921 and first shown to the public in 1922. The Lumia was a kinetic system that, by pressing a keyboard, produced ever-changing metamorphoses of light, colour and forms. Wilfred passionately claimed the Lumia to be a new, eighth art-form and stressed its nature as a visual art, but one that was silent in contrast to the colour-organs. In the late 1920s he began building smaller and more compact Lumias, suitable for home use. In 1930, soon after introducing this technology, Lumia projections had their debut on Broadway, in the theatre performance of Ibsen's *The Vikings*.

In 1922, the Bauhaus artists Ludwig Hirschfeld-Mack, Josef Hartwig and Kurt Schwerdtfeger began to develop Colour Music performances, inspired by the work of Wassily Kandinsky and Paul Klee. They did so, however, using actual objects and lights that move in space and change over time. Hirschfeld-Mack notes that his goal was:

> . . . to intensify colored shapes, which in a painted picture only simulate movement through their relations, into a real, continuous movement. Take a work by Kandinsky or Klee: here all the elements for real movement are present – tensions between surfaces and space, rhythm, and musical relations, all in non-time based picture.

> (cited in Selwood 2006, 413)

In search of the unique features of the medium and its future, the abstract colour fields of Kasimir Malevich, Yves Klein, Barnett Newman or Mark Rothko all showcase a tendency

Figure 2.4 Thomas Wilfred, *Thomas Wilfred with Lumia*, 1960. Thomas Wilfred Papers (MS 1375). Manuscripts and Archives, Yale University Library

toward a 'truer' expression of ideas and emotions by dismissing the perceptual features of visual reality and excluding the recognisable forms of daily life. "Pure painting perhaps means pure light", writes Apollinaire.[3] Such is also the case with movement: as the visual arts imitated light using paint and later replaced it in favour of a genuine physical light, imitated movement (in Cubism and Futurism) was replaced by real physical movement in the work of Constructivism and Kinetic Art. With the emergence of new art movements, one of which was Light Art, material paint lost its former precedence. *Light in its genuine physical form* became of greater interest to artists than the imitation of light in painting (Weibel 2006, 95). László Moholy-Nagy, one of the pioneer artists working with light, notes that "a direct beam of light could create a very much more intense effect if it could be controlled to the same degree as painting with pigment. And that is indeed the future problem for the visual arts: the creative use of direct light" (Baugh 2005, 124). In his kinetic sculpture *Licht-Raum-Modulator* (1922/1930) – a truly important landmark in the history of Light Art – Moholy-Nagy used light to alter the characteristics of the exhibition space in the spectators' perception.[4] Artificial light modulated and deconstructed the space in perception by illuminating through moving sculptural elements according to a 'scored' sequence, changing the look of the object and casting shadows, including those of the spectators, on the surrounding walls (Zyman 2006, 467–70). The experience was one of constant metamorphosis and renewal (Figure 2.5). Light, space and sculpture together immersed the spectators in a highly theatrical situation.

The title of the artefact is also interesting and highlights some of its poetic aspects. Beyond itemizing components of the piece, the title *Licht-Raum-Modulator* indicates the

Figure 2.5 László Moholy-Nagy, *Licht-Raum-Modulator,* (1922–1930) Replica 1970 c/o Pictoright Amsterdam 2015. Collection Van Abbemuseum, Eindhoven. Photo: Peter Cox, Eindhoven

function of the sculpture as the modulator of both light and a space. Nevertheless, the title could also be read as modulator of a 'light-room', that is, *a room that is essentially made of light*. The latter interpretation suggestively indicates a room made of special qualities, the existence of which is not embodied in material but depends upon visual perception and, therefore, determined by the distribution of light and the kinesis of the modulator. Interestingly, the original title at the Paris exhibition in 1930 was *Light Prop for Electric Stage* (*Lichtrequisit einer elektrischen Bühne*) and the new title came only later, with the 1970 replica (Wagner 2013, 33–4). The change of titles reflects the different roles that Moholy-Nagy intended for the piece to play: at first, it was a supportive stage element ('prop') but, since 1970, it has become a modulator of visual perception, or the modulator of a room made of light.

In 1934, four years after having presented this piece of art, Moholy-Nagy notes: "I dream of light machines with which one can hurl handmade or automatic-mechanical light visions into the air, into large spaces and on to screens of unusual character, onto mist, gas and clouds" (David 1991, 9). In another place, he states: "I want a bare room with twelve projectors so that the white void can be activated by the criss-crossing of beams of colored light" (David 1991, 9). *Licht-Raum-Modulator,* and the new thinking about light expressed by Moholy-Nagy's statements paved the way to what Cliff Lauson calls "the widespread broadening of the category of sculpture around the 1960s – 'the transition from "objecthood" to environment' – that saw artists fully maximizing light's potential both as a sculptural medium and for altering the viewer's perception of space" (Lauson 2013, 17).

No development worth mentioning took place from the late 1930s until the early 1960s. But from the 1960s on, artificial light increasingly appeared in the visual arts – in the form of light graphics, light boxes with reflective materials, light columns and even whole spaces that contained moving light sources. This trend was borne by the growing interest of artists in studies on *light as energy* and *light as a medium in art*, both in the United States and in Europe. Popper mentions the ZERO group, whose artistic goal was "to reduce all things figurative and [to pursue] a purist concentration on the clarity of pure color and dynamic vibration of light in space" (Popper 2006, 436). The 1960s also saw the emergence of Installation Art, a new form of visual work in which artists explore spatial possibilities and interaction with the spectators. Some spaces invited the spectators to walk 'inside the piece' and become more or less interactive participants. The completion of the work depended upon the presence and activities of the address-ees, and so, instead of seeking 'meaning' in the artefact, the addressees focus on their own subjective experiences. (Lauson 2013, 22). Light Art installations significantly contributed to the discourse on artistic experience in the 1960s. The truly unique type of 'light installation' incorporates some of the most fundamental ideas regarding (the instable nature of) visual perception and reception of art, materiality of the medium and the increasingly complex relation with the piece as negotiated by the addressee. Let us ponder these notions for a moment through a discussion of a few selected artworks.

Dan Flavin, one of Minimalism's key figures, is among the pioneering, most influen-tial artists in light since the 1960s. His body of work greatly contributed to the acknowl-edgment of artificial light as an artistic medium. For three decades he developed all of his artworks using a restricted palette of commercial fluorescent tubes, limited to ten hues and a few tube lengths. He has celebrated the formal features of lighting technology itself and treats the tubes and fittings as his 'brush strokes'. Although he is a minimalist concerned merely with the use of fluorescent tubes, Flavin's quite constructivist structures as opposed to the diffused light, occasionally in subtle mid-tones, create a rich diversity of relations between the visitors, the surrounding space and the light-sculptures.

The piece *Untitled (to the "innovator" of Wheeling Peachblow)* from 1966 consists of a frame made of four fluorescent tubes and their white metal fittings. Two horizontal white tubes face forward and two vertical yellow tubes face the gallery walls. Occupying a room corner in the gallery, and highlighting an area that is conventionally deprived of any art, this piece is placed on the floor. The formation of these four fluorescents creates a soft gradation scale of peach and rose hues. With reference to the tradition of framed painting, the 'canvas' in this case is the architecture of the gallery space itself. Devoid of any figurative element, the visual stimuli were derived from the vibrant tubes, i.e. the lighting source and the diffused light these distributed on the walls. In the theatre, the proscenium arch 'frames' imitated reality on the stage, opening onto the world of illusion and clearly separating our 'real' world (auditorium) from the place of artistic representation (performance). In *Untitled (to the "innovator" of Wheeling Peachblow)* Flavin problematizes the presupposed separation between the artefact and its environment, between the 'heightened' aestheticized dimension of artistic experience and the 'ready-made' off-the-shelf fluorescents that simultaneously illuminate not only inward, into the corner, but also outward, onto the spectators.

If Flavin's work celebrates the use of artificial light as a medium by exposing its emitting source and technology, James Turrell, in contrast, conceals the apparatuses and concentrates on visual perception itself, influencing it by using natural and artificial light. With light and architecture, he creates environments that challenge the visual and spatial perception of the spectator and bring about an even more complex spatial exploration than witnessed in most of Flavin's work. Turrell's installations are highly immersive, transient and unstable while the qualities of light as perceived in them shift between opaqueness and transparency, solidity and immateriality, between the tangible and the subliminal. Since the late 1960s, Turrell has explored light as 'the medium of perception'. His work occasionally consists of two separate chambers: an *observation space*, from which one draws one's experience, and a *perception* or *'sensing space'*, toward which one directs one's gaze. He often problematizes what we know about a given space and what we see in it, contrasting the visual with the epistemological. The (physical) position and the motions of the spectator inside the 'observation space' influence the spatial and emotional experience of the 'sensing space'. The duration of the visitor's attending, likewise, plays a role in the experience. "The 'image' changes as a function of the viewer's movement, demanding a constant revision of what you see" (Kirschner 2009, 74). And so, what we 'know' of the space becomes relative and subject to constant change. For example, in *Afrum-Proto* (1966) the light on the wall alters during perception, depending on the distance of the viewer from the corner: to the viewer standing near, the light appears as a flat geometric form. From afar, however, the shape seems to become a solid, three-dimensional cube, floating out of the corner (Figure 2.6). At first, the shape is perceived as a cube, but knowledge that the intersecting walls are flat and the shape is projected light overrules the first observation.

The various phenomena Turrell explores in his work direct our attention to ourselves, becoming aware of the 'work' we do as spectators and the visual and emotional effect the bewitching light has on us as time passes. We become gradually aware of the relative, fragile, even capricious, corporeal experience we gain by visual perception. About his work, Turrell states: "First of all, I am not dealing with an object. The object is perception itself. Secondly, I am not dealing with an image, because I want to avoid any

Figure 2.6 James Turrell, *Afrum-Proto*, 1966. Photo: Florian Holzherr

associative symbolic thought. Thirdly, I'm not dealing with a special purpose or focal point either . . . You are looking at yourself looking" (Kirschner 2009, 71). Turrell's occasional use of a single saturated colour in a space continuously causes the addressees to subconsciously calibrate their colour perception in search of a white balance. Since monochromatic space is 'unnatural', the human brain seeks to reassess whether seeing a singular colour is in order or demands colour correction, as if searching for 'white-balance'. Turrell states: "In a lucid dream, you have a sharper sense of color and lucidity than with your eyes open. I am interested in the point where imaginative seeing and outside seeing meet, where it becomes difficult to differentiate between seeing from the inside and seeing from the outside".[5] A prolonged exposure to single coloured light brings about a shift toward the complementary colour in the brain of the observer, and "makes light seems atmospheric and colour almost tangible. The latter effect is an optical form of 'the Ganzfeld', a state of disorientation caused by a confusion of the senses in response to continuous, uniform simulation" (Lauson 2013, 23).

In her essay On "Making-Room" or How Seeing Takes Place in a Light Space, Daniela Zyman refers to such sub- and conscious experiences taking place in the works of Light Art. She proposes two perspectives from which the works can be discussed (Zyman 2006, 467). The first focuses on the properties of the piece, requiring them to be described objectively. These are properties or formal characteristics that we consider as deriving from the material quality of the artefact. The second perspective focuses on the process and subjective nature of the aesthetic experience inherent in the reception of the work. However, in the case of light and space, a separate analysis of the two perspectives poses a problem. Unlike architecture, light is an 'immaterial' medium and is, indeed, essential for visual perception to become possible at all. Since without light there is 'no space', at least not in perception, most of us are accustomed to perceive space and light together. Yet for the sake of analysis a separate approach to light and space is recommended. This distinction is important, in particular, for works of Light Art in which light manipulates our perception in non-conventional spaces, calibrated under carefully organized shifts, disorientations and resolutions (Zyman 2006, 466–7 and 474). James Turrell's later installations could be characterized as highly calibrated light-spaces, where light becomes the prominent means to challenge visual perception. In 1987, Turrell stated:

> When I work with light it is important to me that I create an experience of wordless thought, shaping the quality and sensation of light as something real, something tangible. The quality of the substance of light cannot be touched, but it can be rendered physically visible. [. . .] My work deals with light to the extent that that light is present in it: my work is not a treatise on light or even a kind of documentation. It is light itself. [. . .] I form light to the extent that this material allows me to do so — and in a manner that allows you not only visually but also physically to experience the substance of the light that fills a room. [. . .] By absorbing a room in your perception you can watch yourself seeing. That act of seeing, that conscious perception, fulfils the room with awareness.
>
> (Weibel 2006, 222)[6]

The Wolfsburg Project, Turrell's largest indoor installation to date, consists of a seemingly dimensionless space, where light and architecture blend into one another in the perception of the viewer (Figures 2.7 and 2.8). There are two chambers: one for

Figure 2.7 James Turrell, *The Wolfsburg Project (Bridget's Bardo)*, installation, Kunstmuseum Wolfsburg, Germany, 2009. Photo: Florian Holzherr

Figure 2.8 James Turrell, *The Wolfsburg Project (Bridget's Bardo)*, installation, Kunstmuseum Wolfsburg, Germany, 2009. Photo: Florian Holzherr

viewing and another for sensing. A long diagonal bridge descends from the entrance of the installation towards the 'perception ('sensing') space'. The sensational light completely immerses the spectators, ironically disturbing them from successfully calibrating the dimensions of the space. Hartmut Böhme, in *Das Licht als Medium der Kunst, Über Erfahrungsarmut und ästhetisches Gegenlicht in der technischen Zivilisation*, writes about works of light-space as *space in the process of becoming*, first in perception and later as representation (Böhme 1996). He notes:

> Light artists such as Turrell, Nordman, and Verjux are aiming at a space which is in the first instance brought forth by light. Light is, after all, a sculptor of space, the space sculptor par excellence. Further, light is a medium, a medium of perception (even before it becomes a medium of representation). It is right that the expression 'light-space' exists. It means that space only begins to dawn in light. Space is first of all clarification. In light-spaces we are present at processes of becoming space. The dawning of space is in it a dawning that takes place in viewers themselves. Clarification is a perceptual process in which, as Goethe said, one can learn to notice, observe, sense the feats accomplished by light: that is, grasp something of the link between light, space and perception, a link which is usually inconspicuous or forgotten in everyday living. In this respect all light artists and their works are exercises in perception.[7]

The rounding and smoothening of all intersections of the walls with the floor and ceiling, and the exclusion of any architectonic detail that could assist in orienting oneself result in an unsettling experience (Figure 2.8). Every inch of the space is painted with highly reflective paint, which increases light intensity and saturation, and helps to eliminate the visitors' shadows. The 'sensing space' near the low end of the bridge surprisingly eludes spatial perception and reveals an empty 'hole' in the field of vision, which results in an immersive Ganzfeld effect (Figure 2.7). In this case, the 'sensing space' shifts (in perception) between an infinite horizon and a near-flat surface. The coloured light slowly shifts between hues of red and magenta, deeper purple and blue. Intense and monochromatic, the light upsets the eyes of the viewer and may lead to an increased feeling of excitement, exhaustion, unbalance, disorientation and impaired time perception.

Aspects of the Ganzfeld effect can also be found in a light installation called *Your black horizon* by the artist Olafur Eliasson, in collaboration with architect David Adjaye, created for the 51st Venice Biennale in 2005 (Figures 2.9 and 2.10). The piece consists of two sub-spaces: a preparatory corridor and the main space. Before entering the main space, one walks along a rather dark passage, where one's pupils dilate gradually and adjust to the poor light conditions in the following space. After a short walk, one enters an empty dark space, the dimensions of which are difficult to determine, due to the sharp contrast between the brightness outdoors and the darkness indoors. One horizontal slit of light, shining within and along the black walls, unfolds at eye level; the slit seems to float out of the black void enveloping the visitors (Figure 2.10). During a sequence of 15 minutes, this single source of light continuously changes its colour, featuring all the colours present in the visible spectrum of daylight, as Eliasson had measured it in Venice. The minimalist design of the walls contributes to the Ganzfeld effect and although the horizon helps in orientation, our visual perception is deluded by the difficulty to calibrate the dimensions of the space.

Figure 2.9 Olafur Eliasson, *Your black horizon*, 2005. Installation view: Thyssen-Bornemisza Art Pavilion, Lopud/Croatia, 2007. Courtesy of Studio Olafur Eliasson. Photo: Michael Strasser/TBA 21, 2007

Figure 2.10 Olafur Eliasson, *Your black horizon*, 2005. Installation view: Thyssen-Bornemisza Art Pavilion, Lopud/Croatia, 2007. Courtesy of Studio Olafur Eliasson. Photo: Michael Strasser/TBA 21, 2007

The movement of the spectators inside the installation is a fundamental factor in their experience of the piece. When one stands near the walls, the light seems to penetrate from outside, but as one takes one's distance the walls almost disappear and the line seems to emerge from the surrounding black void. It is what Gunnar Kvaran describes as "presentation and representation of ephemeral phenomena, events limited in space and time" (Kvaran 2007, 73). In his work, Eliasson explores contemporary cultivated views on nature – increasingly mediated by technology – and their influence on the social dimension through the relationship between the human individual and (new immersive) environments.

With the piece *Your black horizon* we experience the disability to calibrate the dimensions of the space we are in while becoming aware of our visual perception at work and its shortcomings. It proves to be less trustworthy than we consider it to be in daily life. Eliasson distorts our perception of space and time, and evokes a sense of dissolution of our corporality. The only object we can hold on to is the horizontal slit of light, so fragile, and yet so troubling. He states:

> *Your black horizon* is about orientation in inner and outer space. The movement of your own body is what makes it possible to map the space and determine the special parameters. In fact, it's not only about getting to know your surroundings, it is just as much about getting to know yourself. All kind of strange optical effects are triggered: after-images, subtle perceptual delays, syncopations. All those things that happen behind your eyes, as Panza would have said.[8]

The Weather Project in the Turbine Hall of Tate Modern in London (2003) has become one of Eliasson's most famous artworks, attracting more than 2.3 million visitors between October and March 2003–4 (Figures 2.11 and 2.12). Located at the far end of an immense space, a huge bright yellow circle was suspended below a mirror ceiling – its lower half a real illuminating surface and its upper half a mirror reflection. The lower part, a semi-opaque body equipped with Low Pressure Sodium lighting fixtures from behind, distributed highly saturated yellow light. In addition, thin mist steadily filled the space and a thicker haze occasionally drifted in the air, blurring the spectator's perception of the space. The soft diffused Sodium light 'coloured' the architecture through the haze and imposed a monochromatic view of the entire surrounding. Mirrors on the ceiling of the huge Turbine Hall reflected the half yellow circle, the visitors, and the hall, as if doubling its height.

Most probably, one first associates the big yellow circle with the sun, or with cinematic images of a sunset at the beach. Another artificial element, the haze, enhances the atmospheric, almost fantastic impression of the image and is reminiscent of water droplets near the seashore or natural mist. Upon entering the space, one's senses are confused – while the eyes recognize light, intensity and colour cognitively embodied in visual memories we associate with physical warmth, the body experiences no heat whatsoever (Sodium-based lighting is cold). The contrasting signals from eye and body produce a contradictory cognitive outcome. Yet many visitors were sitting or lying down on the floor facing what the mind interprets as 'sun', staring at it and at the mirror ceiling and *seeing themselves seeing – seeing themselves sensing.*

The surprising behaviour of the majority of visitors attending *The Weather Project* seems to derive from Eliasson's success in using light to evoke their primal instincts and a feeling of relaxation, as well as subjective memories, even emotional reactions

Figure 2.11 Olafur Eliasson, *The Weather Project*, 2003. Photo: Studio Olafur Eliasson

Figure 2.12 Olafur Eliasson, *The Weather Project*, 2003. Photo: Studio Olafur Eliasson

that challenge social codes and cultivated behaviour usually associated with visits at prestigious art institutions such as Tate Modern. It seems that for those who visited the gallery during the cold London winter and found joy in sitting or laying on the floor, this artificial sun was a visual substitute for the 'real thing', should I say, a variation of Nordic 'light therapy'. For others, it may have been a pleasant nostalgic image of the sunset as embedded and familiarized in our image culture. The spectator is invited to become a participant in the situation, to change the piece as the piece changes her or him, to be present and engage with it.

However, Eliasson's reference to *the contemporary representation of nature* is sophisticated and ambivalent in that the piece lets us fall into such a representation of nature, while it simultaneously exposes the artificiality of the situation in many ways. "Nature is never presented 'as is', but always as a reconstruction under control of the artist" (Kvaran 2007, 76–7). Eliasson brings the 'sun' indoors and makes no effort to conceal the architecture of the building, nor the apparatuses involved in the making of our experience – the smoke machines are visible and the Low Pressure Sodium fixtures could be seen from below. He once noted that by knowing what constitutes the piece, from both representational and technical perspectives, we can *deconstruct the piece and then replay it*, while taking a more critical position. In this respect, the mirror ceiling complicates the situation even more: you see yourself watching, you see 'your' space from a new perspective (the bird's-eye view) and from the floor you see the whole doubled depth of the real and the reflected space. At least three perspectives, therefore, are at work simultaneously. In a text for The Museum of Modern Art, New York (2001), Eliasson notes that artists not only stage the artefacts but also, and even more importantly, the ways in which the artefacts can be perceived by the addressees. "It is crucial not only to acknowledge that the experience is part of the process, but more importantly, that experience itself is presented undisguised to the spectator" (Eliasson 2001). This notion is elaborated in a conversation with Daniel Birnbaum, where he remarks:

> . . . to evaluate the experience that we have by being able to step out of ourselves and see the whole set-up with the artefact and the subject and the object – that particular quality is also the quality that gives us the ability to criticize ourselves . . . it's about giving the subject a critical position, or the ability to criticize one's own position in this perspective.
>
> (Eliasson 2007, 37)

Light works by Anthony McCall, on the other hand, call to mind Appia's notion of *active light*, embodying light as a sole performer in a dark space filled with mist. McCall's work drifts among the media of sculpture, film and drawing. It is a sculpture insofar as the light seems to be tangible and solid when illuminating the haze in the air, constituting a three-dimensional body that can be viewed from 360 degrees. It is a film because the source of light is a projector that screens animated linear images, slowly changing over time. One watches a light-image in the dark space, but as opposed to most films, the image does not refer to some illusory space and time, and one is free to choose and change position and perspective at will. It is, finally, a drawing because its aesthetics consists of straight and circular lines, appearing on the wall opposite the projector.

In his innovative piece *Line Describing a Cone* (1973), McCall employed a 16mm film projector and concerned himself with the metamorphosis of the light beam itself rather than the image it projects. When first presented, the piece was regarded as a work of "cinematic deconstruction" (Luckett and Manchester 2013, 121). This 30-minute-long film opened with a single white dot that steadily and slowly extended into a line, eventually drawing a complete circle (or closing a light tunnel when looking towards the projector). McCall realised that by slowing down animation speed, not only could the spectators follow the movement of the lines and the beam more attentively, but they could also walk through the light and discover spaces internal to the beam at any moment. The more recent piece *You and I, Horizontal* (2005) is a valid example of McCall's horizontal light works (Figure 2.13). In a lecture given at the Braunschweig University of Art in Germany, McCall remarks that when movement is quick, the spectators freeze and behold. On the other hand, when a slow animation is projected, they increasingly engage with the light work, move around and explore it, so that ideally "the spectator has to be the fastest object in the room".[9] Both in London and in Berlin, I had the opportunity to see how intriguing and playful these works were for the visitors. People who occupied the beam while I watched it entered the image/sculpture and by casting their shadows upon the animation became part of my experience of the piece. With the mist in the space, the work of solid light also incorporates solid shadows of visitors, stretching out and moving in the air.

In the 1970s, the 16mm projector technology still limited McCall's light works to horizontal layouts. The later invention of digital beamers allowed lighting from the ceiling, facing downward, and has enabled him, since 2004, to develop vertical works as well. Luckett and Manchester note that his work has recently undergone a shift in emphasis, as McCall himself stated (in 2009): "Over the past few years I've thought of my solid-light works as referring to the body, or as suggesting the idea of reciprocity between bodies".[10] The verticality brought about the suggestive presence of a standing figure, breathing like a lung. The reference to the corporeal is even enhanced when two cones are positioned next to each other, as demonstrated by the piece *Between You and I* (Figure 2.14). In this vertical work, two light cones stand and perform in slow motion, almost in a freeze, evoking a Japanese Butoh dance. The stream of information is also slowed down, enabling the addressees to become more attentive to detail. When standing near the cones, your imagination tells you there is a 'thing' over there, solid and tactile, even if touching the beam or walking through it breaks the illusion. The forms drawn by the light consist of widening and narrowing ellipses, moving sinus-waves and floating lines that unite altogether and emerge like a mysterious alien sign language. The logic underlying the metamorphosis of the light-cone is perhaps subliminal but strongly sensed. A unique behaviour for each cone of solid light is the result of changing relations and intersecting forms (ellipse, sinus and line), each change affecting the appearance of the beam.

Conclusion

In this chapter on Light Art works, I discussed various types of light-spaces and lighting technologies that artists have used to explore phenomena relating to visual perception and eventually, the reception of the addressees. As early as the 1930s, Moholy-Nagy foresaw the potential of artificial light as an artistic medium: "This will constitute the new ACTION OF LIGHT, which by means of modern technology will use the most intensified contrasts to guarantee itself a position of importance equal to that of all other theatre media" (Baugh 2005, 124). Light Art became highly inspirational for contemporary

Figure 2.13 Anthony McCall, *You and I, Horizontal*, 2005. Installation view at Institut d'Art Contemporain, Villeurbanne, France, 2006. Photo by Blaise Adilon

Figure 2.14 Anthony McCall, *Between You and I,* 2006. Installation view at Peer/The Round Chapel, London, 2006. Photo by Hugo Glendinning

theatre, as it contributed to light's becoming autonomous as an artistic medium in the performance. That said, the new position of light in the theatre was certainly not related solely to the rise of the Light Art movement; it was also enabled by changes intrinsic to contemporary theatre, on its way to become a more conceptually elaborate and complex art-form. The greater degree of 'openness' of the contemporary theatre piece is directly related to the important part the addressees play in interpreting and complementing the theatrical performance. Artists in contemporary theatre, compared to the theatre of Realism, have gained an increasing awareness of the visual dimension of the performance and are much less occupied with a verisimilar simulation of reality. A similar process of abandoning the exact representation of reality based on verisimilitude occurred in the visual arts, in favour of a more *experiential engagement* between the spectator and the work. In addition, the new range of lighting technologies available for light design today brought about a wealth of opportunities for such an *engagement*. The unique qualities that light is now capable of generating, the sensation of light and its poetic expression, and the liberation from the traditional hierarchy of media altogether, give rise to this experiential engagement with light. The capacity to evoke more intensive sensorial (subconscious) experience, and emotional and conceptual (conscious) experiences using light in the theatre, therefore, increases *the autonomy of light*. In its capacity to orchestrate its own painterly and sculptural 'voice', light becomes a narrator in its own right.

Notes

1 An additional reference to synaesthesia can be found in the following chapter.
2 W. Huntington Wright, *The Future of Painting,* New York: Huebsch, 1923, p. 38 and p. 47, quoted in S. Selwood, "Color Music and Abstract Film", in *Light Art from Artificial Light, Light as a Medium in the 20th and 21st Century Art,* edited by Peter Weibel and Gregor Jansen, Ostfildern: Hatje Cantz, 2006, p. 408.
3 Quoted by Robert Delaunay in *Zur Malerei der reinen Farbe,* München: Verlag Silke Schreiber, 1983.
4 A short film that shows the (reconstructed) sculpture in action can be seen on the Internet by typing the following link; http://www.youtube.com/watch?v=nVnF9A3azSA&feature=related.
5 http://www.artfund.org/turrell/james_turrell.html (last accessed 7 September 2012).
6 *Kartographie des Raumes, Ein Topologische Übersicht des Werkes von James Turrell*, exhibition Catalogue. Kunsthalle Basel, 1987, p. 33f, in P. Weibel, "The Development of Light Art", in *Light Art from Artificial Light, Light as a Medium in the 20th and 21st Century Art,* edited by Peter Weibel and Gregor Jansen, Ostfildern, Germany: Hatje Cantz, 2006, p. 222.
7 H. Böhme, *Das Licht als Medium der Kunst, Über Erfahrungsarmut und ästhetisches Gegenlicht in der technischen Zivilisation*, inaugural lecture: 2 November 1994, Humboldt-Universität, Berlin, Philosophische Fakultät III, Institut fur Kulturwissenschaften, no. 66, Berlin, 1996, http://edoc.hu-berlin.de/documents/ovl/boehme-hartmut/PDF/Boehme.pdf, quoted in D. Zyman, "On 'Making-Room' or How Seeing Takes Place in a Light Space", in *Light Art from Artificial Light, Light as a Medium in the 20th and 21st Century Art*, edited by Peter Weibel and Gregor Jansen, Ostfildern, Germany: Hatje Cantz, 2006, p. 466.
8 D. Birnbaum, *Olafur Eliasson, David Adjaye, Isola di San Lazzaro*, in *Dumos*, no. 883, July/August 2005, p. 20, in D. Zyman, "On 'Making-Room' or How Seeing Takes Place in a Light Space", in *Light Art from Artificial Light, Light as a Medium in the 20th and 21st Century Art*, edited by Peter Weibel and Gregor Jansen, Ostfildern: Hatje Cantz, 2006, pp. 478–9.
9 *Anthony McCall: Recent Work and Current Projects*, online lecture at 30:40", https://www.youtube.com/watch?v=HvuqdpsmS-s (last accessed 6 August 2014).
10 C. Beaufort and B. Rouge, interview with Anthony McCall (published in French) La Lumiere dans l'Art depuis 1950 (Figures de l'Art No. 17), 2009, quoted in H. Luckett and E. Manchester, "Artists Text", in *Light Show*, London: Hayward Publishing, 2013, p. 126.

References

Baugh, C., *Theatre, Performance and Technology: The Development of Scenography in the Twentieth Century*, general editors: Graham Ley and Jane Milling, Basingstoke, UK and New York: Palgrave Macmillan, 2005.

Böhme, H., *Das Licht als Medium der Kunst, Über Erfahrungsarmut und ästhetisches Gegenlicht in der technischen Zivilisation*, "inaugural lecture: 2 November 1994, Humboldt-Universität, Berlin, Philosophische Fakultät III, Institut fur Kulturwissenschaften, no. 66, Berlin, 1996, http://edoc.hu-berlin.de/documents/ovl/boehme-hartmut/PDF/Boehme.pdf.

David, C., *Vision, Motion, Emotion: Moholy-Nagy experimenteller Einsatz*, in László Moholy-Nagy, exhibition catalog Museum Fridericianum Kassel, Cologne, 1991.

Diebold, B., *Expressionismus und Kino*, in *Neue Züricher Zeitung*, no. 1453, 27 July 1916.

Eliasson, O., *Projects 73*, leaflet edited by the Museum of Modern Art, New York, 2001.

Eliasson, O., "Statements", in *Olafur Eliasson, Colour Memory and Other Informal Shadows*, Milano: Postmedia books, 2007.

Howard, P., *What is Scenography?*, London and New York: Routledge, 2002.

Huntington Wright, W., *The Future of Painting*, New York: Huebsch, 1923.

Kirschner, E. B., "From Space to Surface to Space: On the Works in the Exhibition", in *James Turrell: The Wolfsburg Project*, Kunstmuseum Wolfsburg and Hatje Cantz Verlag, 2009.

Kvaran, G. B., "Technological Humanism", in *Olafur Eliasson, Colour Memory and Other Informal Shadows*, Milano: Postmedia books, 2007.

Lauson, C., "Light Art: An Immaterial Material", in *Light Show*, London: Hayward Publishing, 2013.

Luckett, H. and Manchester, E., "Artists Text", in *Light Show*, London: Hayward Publishing, 2013.

Popper, F., "Light Kinetics", in *Light Art from Artificial Light, Light as a Medium in the 20th and 21st Century Art*, edited by Peter Weibel and Gregor Jansen, Ostfildern, Germany: Hatje Cantz, 2006.

Schlemmer, T. (ed.), *The Letters and Diaries of Oskar Schlemmer*, translated by Krishna Winston, Evanston, IL: Northwestern University Press, 1990.

Selwood, S., "Color Music and Abstract Film", in *Light Art from Artificial Light, Light as a Medium in the 20th and 21st Century Art*, edited by Peter Weibel and Gregor Jansen, Ostfildern, Germany: Hatje Cantz, 2006.

Survage, L., *Le Rhythme coloré*, in Les Soirées de Paris, no. 26–7; July–August 1914, cited in Russett, R. and Starr, C., *Experimental Animation, An Illustrated Anthology*, London and New York: van Nostrand Reinhold, 1976.

Wagner, A., "Vision Made Visible", in *Light Show*, London: Hayward Publishing, 2013.

Weibel, P., "The Development of Light Art", in *Light Art from Artificial Light, Light as a Medium in the 20th and 21st Century Art*, edited by Peter Weibel and Gregor Jansen, Ostfildern, Germany: Hatje Cantz, 2006.

Weibel, P. and Jansen, G., "Light as a Medium of Art", in *Light Art from Artificial Light, Light as a Medium in the 20th and 21st Century Art*, edited by Peter Weibel and Gregor Jansen, Ostfildern, Germany: Hatje Cantz, 2006.

Zyman, D., "On 'Making-Room' or How Seeing Takes Place in a Light Space", in *Light Art from Artificial Light, Light as a Medium in the 20th and 21st Century Art*, edited by Peter Weibel and Gregor Jansen, Ostfildern, Germony: Hatje Cantz, 2006.

Chapter 3

Theoretical framework

So far this study has focused on the artistic function of light, presented through the historical discourse of theatre lighting, and the adaptation of artificial light as a medium in the visual arts, followed by the emergence of the movement of Light Art. Throughout the 20th century, attempts to adapt various theoretical approaches to theatre studies sought to assist us in understanding the processes of making meaning in the theatre and the sensorial systems that shape our experience while watching a performance. Numerous studies initially concentrated on the language/dramatic play as the driving force of the performance, later shifting attention to the performer and her/his body in space, followed by more recent studies of scenography, seeking to define its function, boundaries and relationship with other media in the theatre. Theatre scholars have often neglected light for too long, perhaps due to its highly technical orientation, transparency and fleeting qualities. Another possible reason could be that lighting design has only been recognised as an artistic practice within the theatre since the mid-20th century, along with dedicated study programs in universities and art academies, and international conventions that focus on light, even though artificial light has long been used in the theatre, one way or another.

In order to explore the new aesthetic and poetic tendencies of light within contemporary theatre, and to be able to examine how we experience and interpret the artistic function of light within a performance, an appropriate theoretical framework is required. Since no previous publication has suggested any conceptual framework exclusively fit for the analysis of light, my goal here is to lay the theoretical foundations for a new conceptual framework for the interpretation and analysis of light in contemporary theatre. The hermeneutic discourse, and the dynamic relation between the artefact and the addressee against the background of meaning-making and complementing the artwork, both underwent tremendous change throughout the 20th century. This chapter introduces key notions from existing theories of semiotics, phenomenology, media studies (mediology), and recent studies on the experience of art from the perspectives of cognitive sciences and neurosciences. I will introduce my theoretical basis and discuss the work of selected theatre scholars who adapted the various theories to theatre studies, referring then to the consequences these theories have on the interpretive process. This chapter will constitute the theoretical 'infrastructure' of the new analytical framework for light presented in the next chapter.

Semiotics

The study of semiotics explores the processes involved in *signification* and *communication* — the generation and exchange of signs in human culture. Semiotic studies examine the relation between the signifying object ('sign') and the signified ('meaning') in sign-systems used by society, at first closely related to the study of linguistics and its methodologies. The making of meaning using signs has been extensively approached through three fundamental perspectives: the *semantic* dimension (meaning based on the arbitrary cultural convention of the sign and its signified object); the *syntactic* dimension ('grammar' – structural rules by which the configuration of various signs generates meaning); and the *pragmatic* dimension (meaning generated by the way the user makes use of the sign, beyond, and even in contrast to, the semantic relation). From early on, the study of semiology/semiotics has known two traditions based on the work of dominant thinkers: that of Ferdinand de Saussure (1857–1913) and Charles Sanders Peirce (1839–1914). For Saussure, 'semiology' was a science that studies the role of signs as part of social life, while for Peirce 'semiotics' was the formal doctrine of signs that was closely related to logic.[1] Saussurean semiology emphasizes a two-sided relationship between signifier (*sign-vehicle*) and signified (*meaning*), and considers the semiotic process as one of *signification* whereby two human beings take part and intentionally communicate with one another. As Saussure's semiology refers to a process occurring between humans, the mental effort of interpretation is already embodied in the process, both by the emitting party, who intentionally executes a sign, and the receiving party, who possibly identifies it and makes meaning of it. On this, Umberto Eco comments in *A Theory of Semiotics*:

> Saussure did not define the signified any too clearly, leaving it half way between a mental image, a concept and a psychological reality; but he did clearly stress the fact that the signified is something which has to do with the mental activity of anybody receiving a signifier . . . Thus the sign is implicitly regarded as a communicative device taking place between two human beings intentionally aiming to communicate or to express something.
>
> (Eco 1976, 14–15)

American logician and philosopher Charles Sanders Peirce explores the processes and functions of signification and elaborates a theory of logical relations. Peirce's definition of semiosis involves an irreducible triadic relationship between three semiotic entities, not necessarily human subjects, featuring: the *sign* (the 'representamen'), its *object* (namely, the sign's subject matter) and the *interpretant* (in short, the sign's meaning or the ramification/effect of the encounter between a sign and its receiver). These three roles in the signification process are fixed, although the ideas and subject matter used to transmit them are interchangeable; for example, an interpretant can possibly become a new sign for another interpretant in a continuous chain, ad infinitum (Eco 1976, 15).

Another characteristic distinction between the perspectives of Peirce and Saussure regards 'intentionality' in the production of the sign. While Saussure considers something to be a sign only when its emitter intends to signify and its receiver identifies the stimulus as a sign, Peirce holds only the receiver responsible for taking a subject matter to be a sign. According to Peirce, a sign is "something that stands to somebody for something in some respect or capacity" (Peirce 1931–2, 228). In this sense, Peirce broadens the scope of semiosis even to the signification of ideas by a non-human emitter of signs (for example, a mathematical formula representing a logical idea for a reader) while the other is a human interpreter.

Some of Peirce's notions were widely accepted and adapted for the semiotic analysis of theatre, in particular his categorization of signs and his ideas concerning the semiotic drift of the interpreter. Peirce defines three major categories of signs: *icons, indices* and *symbols*. The different categories of signs are interlinked and several categories can relate simultaneously to the same sign. *Iconic signs* are based on (perceptual) similarities between the sign and its object. A high degree of similarity is found in an iconic sign between the sign's sensory appearance and its subject matter. Peirce himself suggests the figurative painting and the photograph as examples of iconic signs. Philip Butterworth notes that iconic signs are highly important in the theatre; perhaps more so than any other type of sign, due to their dominant visual dimension and the great diversity within this category of signification. *Indices* are signs that refer to their objects through a relationship of cause and effect, or indicate a logical connection between sign and object. Keir Elam lists the following examples: "The rolling gait of the sailor, indicating his profession, a knock on the door which points to the presence of someone outside it, and the verbal deixis (personal and demonstrative pronouns such as 'I', 'you', 'this', 'that', and adverbs such as 'here' and 'now', etc.)" (Elam 1980, 22). *Symbol* is a sign for which the relation to the object (subject matter) is arbitrary and its signification is agreed upon in a certain culture. "A symbol is a sign which refers to the object that it denotes by virtue of a law, usually an association of general ideas", notes Peirce (Peirce 1931–2, 249). Both addresser and addressee require the use of an a priori previous cultural knowledge about the meaning of symbols, in particular when using linguistic signs.

Within the category of the 'iconic', Peirce specifies three kinds of signs in accordance with the degree of perceived similarity between the sign and what it represents. The three subcategories are: *image, diagram* and *metaphor*. An image is an iconic sign whose appearance resembles that of the object to which it relates. Similar formal characteristics are to be found in both the signifier and that for which it stands. A diagram is a sign for which the formal characteristics are close to the object, or to an idea visually represented "through rational relation rather than appearance" (McKinney and Butterworth 2010, 159). Metaphoric signs signify less by verisimilitude with the intended object and more by asserting or evoking further associations and ideas regarding their objects. Metaphor, as a type of iconic sign, involves an identification of a general structural similitude between the sign and the object. Metaphor encourages the addressee to work with the sign and generate subjective imaginative information about it – a highly important feature for contemporary theatre in light of the increasing autonomous signification of various media in the theatrical event.

Another fundamental notion of Peirce's semiotic theory is 'the semiotic drift' – a state in which the addressee is engaged with signs in the ongoing process of interpretation, using her or his associations, imagination, memories and knowledge. New interpretations are continuously generated, leading to new considerations of the sign's meaning and, consequently, to a wider scope of subjective interpretations of the sign.

Umberto Eco further develops the notion of 'the semiotic drift' in his semiotic theory, in which he uses the term 'unlimited semiosis'. Although published as early as 1962 (initially in Italian), Eco's influential book *The Open Work* (*Opera aperta*) was – and still is – considered an innovative study in the field of *reader response criticism* and ahead of its time. The relevance of *The Open Work* to the philosophical discourse on contemporary theatre is so immense that it is hard to read Eco's reflections from 1962 and not think about the experimental characteristics of contemporary theatre labelled as *postdramatic theatre* by Lehmann almost four decades later. Surprisingly, many of Eco's early notions have retained their potency with reference to the hermeneutic discourse in the context of state-of-the-art contemporary theatre.

Open works, according to Eco, are complex artefacts characterized by suggestivity, ambiguity and uncertainty within a rhizome of possible traces of meanings that addressees can choose to explore and complement with subjective interpretation. Metaphorically, an open work resembles an *'encyclopaedia'* that explains key terms by means of interweaving threads of knowledge. It invites readers to migrate from one context to another, and to use their imagination in understanding relationships among various fields of interest through more complex processes A *'dictionary'*, on the other hand, reflects an arbitrary and narrower signification of codes (words) indicating synonyms, and does not offer the broad range of movement of thought between different codes that the encyclopaedia does. The idea of *'dictionary'*, therefore, refers to a limited movement of thought between meanings. For example, a dramatic piece with a linear coherent plot, arranged according to causal development, could be related to 'dictionary-like' qualities, due to a narrower scope of associative movement within the piece compared with a fragmental 'open work'. Eco describes an open work as a *'field of possibilities'*, in which the addressee is able to make interpretive choices, as long as she or he interprets it in a way that respects the line of thought that the artist initially included in the artefact.[2]

Since the early 1960s, with the extensive philosophical discourse on the *crisis of representation (of the sublime)* and the decline of Modernism and, later, Postmodernism, in the arts, artists and post-structuralist philosophers became increasingly aware of the complexity inherent in the negotiation of (uncertain) meaning. The mutually dependent symbiotic relation between the artists who create artefacts with their own set of meanings, and the addressees who use the works to reconstruct meanings, puts the autonomy of the piece at risk and the authorship of the piece in question. 'A work in movement', is a distinctive category of open work in which the relations between artist/artefact/addressee become highly unstable. This situation emerges when artists insert intentionally ambiguous and incomplete elements and structures into their work, in order to facilitate access to the work via diverse approaches and through various perspectives, conferring upon the piece kaleidoscopic qualities. The addressee confronts a *'controlled disorder'* when engaging with this kind of work, trying to make sense of the stimuli the piece provides. The vaguer the connection between the parts of a message, the more difficult it is to comprehend its meaning – the *more information* is produced and *all the more cognitive activity* occurs. The added value for some addressees in experiencing this kind of works or, alternatively, the exhausting and possibly disengaging situation for others, lies in the ambiguity and incompleteness that await us, the addressees. The public thus shares with the artist the responsibility for the 'success' of the artistic experience. In this spirit, almost 30 years after the publication of *The Open Work*, Paul Ricoeur notes: "The reader is invited to do the work that the artist delights in undoing" (Ricoeur 1991, 150).

Another fundamental notion in Eco's semiotics, first introduced in *The Open Work* and then elaborated in his later book on *The Limits of Interpretation* is the *'unlimited semiosis'* (Eco, 1990, 41–2). The term refers to a potentially infinite model of interpretation processes, somewhat resembling Peirce's 'semiotic drift'. Here, however, Eco relates to the 'encyclopaedic' character of the process, in the ongoing motion of thought. In applying Peirce's semiotics to theatre studies, writes Elam, signs from different systems (e.g., actors, dramatic text, light, sound, mise-en-scène) are able to interchange using analogous relations – keeping in mind that the Peircean theory does not deal with the unique materiality of the signs as if they were all equivalent, but concentrates on logical schemas and functions. 'Unlimited semiosis' reflects the fluid ability of the interpreta-tion process to enrich, deepen and extend its scope through the associative relations between signs and meanings. The drift from one meaning to another in the cognition of the addressee is based on the shifting of sign-into-meaning-into-sign-into-meaning, repeatedly, in an associative process. Consequently, as long as the addressee is engaged in the interpretive process, the poetic dimension of the piece is also constantly under construction. This continuous and gradual evolution in the fluid relationship of the sign/meaning according to Eco's *'unlimited semiosis',* recalls, to a certain extent, Derrida's notion of *'free play'* – an infinite interpretive process involving the signs and the signi-fied objects in reality.

On the adaptation of semiotics to the framework of theatre studies

I turn now to the application of semiotic studies in the context of theatre performance analysis. The first attempt to appropriate the study of semiotics to theatre studies is attributed to the Prague School, with the publication of two radical studies (1931): *Aesthetics of the Art of Drama* by Otakar Zich and *An Attempted Structural Analysis of the Phenomenon of the Actor* by Jan Mukařovský (Elam 1980, 5–6). During the 1930s and 1940s, the adaptation of semiotic perspective resulted in considering the theat-rical event as a complex of various 'sign-systems', aiming at distinguishing one sys-tem from the other and examining them separately, to a certain extent (McKinney and Butterworth 2010, 152 and Elam 1980, 7). Semiotics analysed a literary work as a single sign-system with internal meanings encoded by its author, awaiting the reader to decode or unfold the meaning of its signs. Theatre performances, consisting of many different sign-systems in addition to written and spoken language, have a far more complex structure and signification processes that cross different sign-systems. A new innovative approach to the analysis of performance, as a collective of sign-systems, emerged following the recognition of each medium as possessing unique functions and significance, separate from the text.

Given that theatre performance is a complex of sign-systems, many of which consist of iconic signs with some degree of visual similarity to their objects, this allows the transformation of signs from one sign system into another, replacing, for instance, a ver-bal text by a body gesture. According to Elam, transformability among sign systems can also take place by changing the way we use the same sign to poetically signify a different thing (Elam 1980, 12). In this case, the addressee indentifies the relation of *visual, acous-tic or functional analogy* between signs from different systems of signs. Moreover, when the user of the sign uses it in a way that differs from cultural convention, transform-ability is ultimately reached by the new 'interpretant' – *the ideas that the sign stands for.* "The same stage item stands for different signifieds depending on the context in which it appears; 'each object sees its signs transformed in the most rapid and varied fashion' (Bogatyrev 1938a, p. 519)", writes Elam (Elam 1980, 12). Transformability (poetically) reconfigures the signs in the performance, and influences their distance from mundane signification. The theatre of Realism is stricter with regard to the transformability of signs, for its illusion of reality is based on a basic similarity with the ways in which signs are used in daily reality. The Elizabethan theatre, however, in which the actual stage space was devoid of any scenery supporting the creation of illusion, would portray the fictive environment of all scenes by means of spoken language (Elam 1980, 24–5). Consequently, through linguistic signs (symbolic) and gestural signs (indices and icons), the addressees were to envisage for themselves the absent visual dimension – words and body movement helped the audience to complement the dull image of an empty stage and so, the same stage in *Macbeth*, for example, became an iconic sign (metaphor) for Duncan's palace or the battlefield. From a semiotic perspective, the transformability of signs, therefore, relies on the flexibility and fluid connection between the sign and its object (subject matter) and the idea the sign calls for (the interpretant), through analogies in the mind of the addressee. Furthermore, a sign that bears less perceptual similarity to its object (like a symbol, diagram, or metaphor) functions with the aid of cultural conventions. Knowing these cultural conventions is a necessary precondition for the users of the signs in order to identify and interpret exchange between signs-systems.

In *The Semiotics of Theater,* Erika Fischer-Lichte writes that what spectators hear and see in the theatre are *signs of signs.* The multidisciplinary art of theatre adapts sign-systems from daily reality and reconfigures them in imaginative ways. This implies that the sign-systems used in the theatre emanate from the already-existing cultural systems of signs (Fischer-Lichte 1992, 7–10). Conjoining these systems under syntactic rules constitutes the aesthetics of the piece and lends the signs a new poetic dimension. Provided that the addressee recognizes this 'theatrical code' and locates the performance within a certain familiar genre, the reading of its signs is conditioned by cultural convention. According to Fischer-Lichte, a theatre performance creates its internal theatrical code, which addressees possibly consider culturally-dependent theatrical signs and associate with performative genre. The configuration of signs from various sign-systems constitutes the theatrical code – "the code regulates which material creations are to apply as vehicles of meaning" and "in what way and under what conditions these signs can be combined selectively with one another" (Fischer-Lichte 1992, 10). The diversity of theatrical codes, emerging from the distinctive syntax and use of signs in performances, is what constitutes and characterizes different genres of performing arts. Therefore, the addressee must first identify the theatrical code before attempting to decode the meaning of any sign in the performance (Fischer-Lichte 1992, 11).

For example, musical signs in opera play a more dominant role and interact differently with the narrative compared to the working of music in a theatre performance of realistic drama. Likewise, movement signs in pantomime and in contemporary dance-theatre each feature a different degree of illustration or abstraction of reality, as well as different physicality and use of movement in space. A 'no smoking' icon on a 'realistic' theatre stage will probably be interpreted as it is in everyday life. However, taken as an iconic sign within the scenography, the icon is now seen in the context of a fictive space. In this example, the 'poetic dimension' of the iconic sign is not that rich, since the sign signifies in the performance the same object that it does in daily reality. Whether the adaptation of existing cultural systems of signs into aesthetic and poetic context creates a rich poetic dimension or, instead, almost replicates daily reality – the process of signification constitutes a subjective reflection upon culture. Each genre creates its own theatrical code, a semiotic configuration through which the addressees can decode the signs and interpret their meaning, depending on their identification of that theatrical code.

The generic distinction between performances has become less applicable for both spectators and theatre studies since the onset of modernism, as the spirit of experimentalism that followed the theatre of Realism continues in contemporary theatre to dissolve the boundaries of familiar genres and reject uniformity. In this respect, Hans Belting writes, in *Art History after Modernism*, artists have become increasingly emancipated from the idea that their creation belongs to, or continues a historical linear development into the future. Art history is no longer an obligatory tradition but is, rather, used as 'material' for art that engages with the question of *what art is*. Belting agrees with Danto that because artists are now able to create with more freedom than ever, the emergence of a unified *contemporary style* has become impossible (Belting 2003, 115–17). Likewise, theatrical codes multiply and diversify through artists' search for new forms of expression.

In her attempt to apply structuralist semiotics to the analysis of theatre performance, Fischer-Lichte defends the idea that exchange between different sign-systems can take place in the theatre, in order to signify the same meaning. She writes:

> Here, a human body can indeed be replaced by another body or even by an object, and an object can be replaced by another random object or a human body, because, in their capacity as theatrical signs, they can signify one another. For their material existence is of interest for theatre with regard neither to its uniqueness nor to its specific functionality, but alone in terms of its ability to be used as a sign of sign. What is crucial is not existence as such but rather the meanings to be created using existence as a sign.
>
> (Fischer-Lichte 1992, 140)

Fischer-Lichte considers all the stimuli and phenomena one perceives in a theatrical event to be deliberately generated signs of signs, by which the artist wishes to signify a certain meaning – a point that Patrice Pavis strictly rejects. However, in *The Semiotics of Theatre*, Fischer-Lichte does not seem to consider the possibility that by substituting signs from one sign-system to another, the material and projection of the sign changes, the perception is modified and, consequently, the experience of the addressee and the process of interpretation are influenced (Fischer-Lichte 1992, 133–41). Not all meanings are fixed or culturally agreed upon and, therefore, the vehicle of the sign (signifier object) remains crucial in the experience of the addressee and in the process of interpretation. The exchange between systems of signs will lead to new contexts and unavoidably also to other interpretations. Studies in the fields of phenomenology, mediology and neuroscience have dealt with these aspects in depth, where the material plays a more significant role than in semiotics.

Before proceeding to the critique of structuralist semiotics in general, and then to its shortcomings with regard to theatre studies in particular, I would like to address Willmar Sauter's notes on the importance of semiotics for the development of theatre studies. In *The Theatrical Event: Dynamics of Performance and Perception*, Sauter notes three ways in which semiotics has influenced theatre studies: first, it increased scholarly recognition of the importance of an encompassing theory, as "semiotics shifted the debate within the discipline from methodological and research strategies to a level of profound theoretical thinking" (Sauter 2000, 24). The second accomplishment of semiotics was in moving theatre scholars further away from the tradition of historical studies of past theatre performances through the reproduction and restoration of visual and written documentation, and in urging them to deal with "the nature of the object which they were so desperate to reconstruct". Finally, the third and perhaps most influential aspect was to locate the performance itself within the analytical discourse. Therefore, the application of structuralist semiotics for theatre studies has brought about valuable advantages, despite rapidly revealing its shortcomings – resulting from new theoretical influences in philosophy and the acknowledging of semiotics' insufficiency for analyzing the complexity of the theatrical event, in which the addressee is a fundamental entity.

In his essay in *Semiotica* (168/2008), Fernando de Toro describes the gradual decline of the structuralist approach. He observes that while striving for a scientific status, the theoretical effort of semiotic studies prevailed over the development of a practical analytical method closely familiar with the artistic practice (de Toro 2008, 112–13). Nevertheless, de Toro defends the validity of structuralist perspective, which contributed greatly to the study of signification and shaped the way we approach theatre:

> And this 'thinking' has remained and made enduring contribution to the study of culture in general. What was rejected, I believe, was what Elam himself points out; that is, the type of 'tools' that were used and how they were used . . . I believe that we are still very much working with 'semiotic thinking' albeit in a quite different manner; one that relates to issues in culture, literature and theatre, one that attempts to connect with the whole of society and its realities, and one that indeed had and will continue to have an enduring legacy.
>
> (de Toro 2008, 123–4)

A critique of structuralist semiotics for theatre analysis

Structuralist semiotics and the attempts to adapt it for theatre analysis began to decline with the critique of philosophers like Michel Foucault, Jacques Derrida and Roland Barthes, whose work relates to post-structuralist philosophy, simultaneously with the renaissance in the field of phenomenology with Hans-Georg Gadamer's hermeneutics in the mid-20th century. Structuralism as a philosophy sought to explain cultural elements in relation to a meta-structure by which people perceive, think, feel and act, and – in the case of semiotics – by which signification and human communication could be theorized and explained. The main concern, therefore, was with structures and systems of codes, rooted in logical models of human thinking, which can potentially encode meaning as written/spoken language does. Derrida states that:

> The concept of centered structure is in fact the concept of freeplay based on a fundamental ground, a freeplay which is constituted upon a fundamental immobility and reassuring certitude, which is itself beyond the reach of freeplay . . . it became necessary to think the law which governed, as it were, the desire for the center in the constitution of structure and the process of signification prescribing its displacements and its substitutions for this law of the central presence - but a central presence which was never itself, which has always already been transported outside itself in its surrogate.
>
> (Derrida 1989, 960–1)

Michel Foucault also criticizes structuralism's claim to certainty and stability:

Structuralism, or at least that which is grouped under this slightly too general name, between elements that could have been connected on a temporal axis, an ensemble of relations that makes them appear, as juxtaposed, set off against one another, implicated by each other – that makes them appear, in short, as a sort of configuration.

(Foucault 1984, 22)

Structuralist semiotics assumed the existence of systems of signs with a stable arbitrary meaning – an idea that post-structuralist philosophers, among them Derrida, strictly rejected. While structuralist semiotics sought the structure in the text, post-structuralism observed with more suspicion the unstable changing relations and vectors of conflicting movements and ideologies (conventions) that constitute cultural reality. And so it focused on a *free play* within the structure of signs in search of fleeting meaning, leading to an infinite interpretation process. The flexibility, the instability of the (Saussureian) *signified* in relation to *the signifier* became pivotal in the hermeneutic process and in discussions about *the primacy of the signifier*. The interpretation process of the individual reader gained prominence over the assumed intention of the author. The variety of interpretations deriving from the background of the readers' cultural differences, gender, class and racial identity – which structuralist semiotics had previously neglected – were now called for reconsideration. Post-structuralist criticism, therefore, based its analysis on multiple, even sometimes contradicting perspectives, and withdrew from seeking complete validity for a single possible interpretation.

The critique of structuralist semiotics did not refrain from noting the failings of semiotics in applying to theatre performance analysis. The inadequacy of semiotic studies for theatre performance analysis was also due to the fact that many of the leading semioticians were not theatre scholars, and so, devoid of insight regarding theatrical phenomena, their elaborate theories attempted to impose themselves on the structure of performance (Sauter 2000, 24). As an example, Sauter refers to Tadeusz Kowzan's essay *Le signe au théâtre* (1968) in which Kowzan presents thirteen categories of signs, divided into visual and auditory signs and subdivided on the basis of their degree of relation to the performer: "His focus is solely the spectacle on stage and the way in which meaning is produced. The spectator and the process of reception are completely ignored, as was the case in many books on theatre semiotics" (Sauter 2000, 25). A sort of theoretical distance between theory and object remained unsolved. Even those semioticians who did specialize in theatre did not always succeed in constructing a semiotic theory that also addressed other theatres than the rather traditional theatre of Realism and its significant conventions.

In *Analyzing Performance: Theatre, Dance and Film*, Patrice Pavis stresses that since theatre performance is a complex, multi-sensorial event, consisting in more than just a system of linguistic signs, we cannot reduce our experience in the theatre and refer to it as a stable systems of signs with only arbitrary meanings. Performance consists partly in signs perceived by the senses and partly in ephemeral 'vectors of energy' that affect our overall experience. In addition, performances consist of signs, artificially generated by the artists, as well as things that are real, authentic, without any intention to signify. A situation of uncertainty concerning what is a (made) sign and what is real calls the use of semiology into question, as Pavis argues:

Not everything in the performance is reducible to a sign; there remain authentic moments, unforeseeable and unrepeatable events. How can one know whether the whiskey drunk by an actor is actually a whiskey after all, or whether the plaster cast covers a leg that is really broken? Therefore, if everything can be a sign, and if nothing is absolutely certain, is it still useful to secure the services of semiology?

(Pavis 2003, 311)

From a different perspective, also in the context of the fleeting meaning of the image, Barthes discusses the unstable relation the viewer has with an image, while acknowledging three categories of meaning within the visual domain: the *informational*, the *symbolic*, and a *'third' meaning* that is less comprehensible, but possibly enables one to find a more penetrating and 'poetic' meaning than the other two kinds. An image is a much weaker, and more unstable object to interpret than language – in terms of codes related to meanings – since visual signs 'tolerate' more the drift of 'unlimited semiosis' and are more fluid than words. Barthes notes that for images "there are potentially as many meanings as there are viewers" (McKinney and Butterworth 2010, 194).

Among other scholars, Bert O. States even argues that it is impossible to dismantle a theatrical event into separate sign-systems since we experience the performance as a whole:

The problem with semiotics is that in addressing theatre as a system of codes it necessarily dissects the perceptual impression that theater makes on the spectator. And, as Merleau-Ponty has said, "It is impossible . . . to decompose perception, to make it into a collection of sensations, because in it the whole is prior to the parts".

(States 1985, 7)

The focusing on *the production* rather than on *the addressee*, and discussing the *meaning on stage* (through the use of *sign-systems*), rather than the *meaning generated in the imagination* of the addressee through processes of *reception*, eventually became crucial failings in the appropriation of semiotics to theatre studies, writes Sauter (Sauter 2000, 24). The semiotic search for the *grammar of the production* instead of the experience of the theatrical event as a communicative encounter, downplayed the sensorial and emotional experiences directly affecting the reception on a primal level. Through the prism of a linguistic approach these corporeal experiences turn into something else: namely, a word, a mediated concept. For example, on the loss of sensorial experience in the 'translation' process of visual signs into linguistic signs, Pavis notes: "Nothing obliges (nor allows, for that matter) spectators to translate into words the experience of contemplating a light, gestures, or music in order for that experience then to be integrated into the global meaning of the stage" (Pavis 2003, 14). This aspect of semiotics has also been re-approached by Régis Debray in his book *Media Manifestos*, in which he proposes a revised semiotic model that aims to expand semiotics, and includes a phenomenological perspective concerning the materiality of the signs, as well as other aspects previously neglected by structuralist semiotics.

Phenomenology

Phenomenology deals with the understanding of human existence as felt through the bodily experience of sensations around us, describing the structure of that experience in phenomenal terms. Edmund Husserl, one of the founding fathers of the field, considers the body the locus of conscious existence. Phenomenological studies examine the conscious experience of subjective reality that human beings live through, using their senses, perception, imagination, memory, thoughts, desires and emotions. It is also the study of the *appearance of things* ('phenomena') or how things appear to be in our experience, in contrast with *the way they are* in reality. The written or spoken description of such an experience is based on an empirical perspective that is clearly subjective and individual.

Phenomenology evolved into two directions: one branch is *language-based hermeneutics*, the science of interpretation, with which the work of Martin Heidegger, Hans-Georg Gadamer, and Paul Ricoeur is associated. Hermeneutic phenomenology is epistemologically driven, as it seeks to broaden the scope of its analysis and asks: what is the object we would like to understand and what is the process of understanding? (Sauter 2000, 29). The other branch of phenomenology focuses on interpreting the perception and the embodiment of the human experience. The phenomenology of embodiment is based on the interpretation of conscious human experience and its immediate corporeal dimension, "before intellectual analysis begins to sort, edit and render it as an artificial 'reconstruction'", McKinney and Butterworth note, after Maurice Merleau-Ponty (2010, 167). Both branches respond to a different relationship between the addressee and the artefact, in which attention shifts from the piece[3] to the addressee in the interpretive process – strikingly different from the structuralist semiotic approach presented earlier.

Let us discuss several representative ideas from the innovative writings of Ricoeur in the early 1980s on hermeneutic phenomenology.[4] Not only was Ricoeur a pioneer in redefining the role of the addressee as a truly crucial participant in the hermeneutic process, insofar as the responsibility for the making of meaning is shared between the addressee and the author of the work of art, but he also proposed a theoretical model integrating semiotic and phenomenological perspectives. Ricoeur's theory on the process of interpretation includes a number of ideas inspired by Gadamer's hermeneutics. The theory was conceived in the same period when the responsibility for meaning-making was considered to be shifting gradually from the artist (who encodes signs in the piece) toward the piece (being a complex of signs awaiting the receiver to decode its meaning), and then to the addressee (who generates a subjective, yet studied, interpretation). The duality in Ricoeur's approach spans structuralist semiotics and hermeneutics, and reflects the decline in the position of structuralist semiotics around the late 1980s, while, nevertheless, aiming to synthesize the hermeneutic approach with structuralist semiotics, in an attempt to achieve scientific validity for the act of interpretation.

On the one hand, Ricoeur bases his interpretive method on a thorough semiotic analysis of the text and on 'decoding' information from the infrastructures that structuralist semiotics aims at locating in the piece, in order to interpret the written text according to its inner 'subtext'. On the other hand, in this framework, the engagement with the addressee receives a new dimension that thinkers prior to Ricoeur had considered external to the piece and, therefore, irrelevant for its interpretation. In this respect, Ricoeur's significance lies in reconsidering the addressee's position and responsibility to exchange and negotiate meaning in the hermeneutic process, and to legitimize interpretations based on information external to the piece, while still in accordance with the author's direction of intent.

In his essay *Mimesis and Representation*, Ricoeur proposes an analytical method for the reading of a literary work, consisting of three consecutive levels of interpretation.

On each level, a different approach to the text is taken, without hierarchy but rather in a continuously expanding manner. For the sake of clarity: Ricoeur uses the term 'mimesis' to refer to an imitation of human action and not to a representation that imitates the features of reality. We all practice mimesis in everyday life, and so do artists who use it slightly differently in artistic productions. In everyday reality, mimesis is any operation involving the imitation of human action; while within the arts, mimesis is the imagined imitation of human action using an imaginative reconfiguration, and the renewal of already-known artistic traditions of the imitation of human actions. The origin of the word 'mimesis' lies in the context of artistic production, and particularly with reference to the Greek epic – tragedy and comedy. In these works, Ricoeur notes, "*mimesis* is the *mimesis* of an action, and what makes such imitating a *poiesis*, i.e., a productive activity, is the activity of arranging incidents into a plot" (Ricoeur 1991, 138, italics in the original). "For Aristotle", writes Ricoeur, "mimesis takes place only within the area of human action, or production, or poiesis. It is an operation". Later in this chapter, I will readdress the contemporary use of the term 'mimesis' from the perspective of cognitive sciences on the study of the arts, as a human practice of imitation, potentially used by artists for cultural self-reflection. Ricoeur, however, identifies three levels of mimesis in his analytical framework:

Mimesis₁

In his *Poetics* (part XIV), Aristotle elaborates upon the imitation of reality in tragedy through *human actions*. Actions, as interwoven in a plot, are highly likely to happen according to the fictive circumstances in view of cause and effect – it is not merely an imitation of human beings acting. The essence is in the actions, moral code, ethics and intentions that cause the characters to act. When portraying an action in the form of a written text, the poet stimulates the addressees to imagine the narrative, and to consider what this description actually means. Readers engage with a fictive situation suggested by the text by actually reviving it through their imagination and 'reliving' it using their memories. Ricoeur writes: "To follow a story is to actualize it by reading it" or, in another place, "the written work is a sketch for the reader" (Ricoeur 1991, 151–2). The readers' initial understanding of a fictive action originates from the meaning of that same action, if it would have been carried out in their everyday reality. The first stage of the analysis concentrates, thus, on the semantic dimension of signs and their relation to everyday reality. Mimesis₁, therefore, is:

> . . . This pre-understanding of what human action is, of its semantics, its symbolism, its temporality. From this pre-understanding, which is common to poets and their readers, arises fiction, and with fiction comes the second form of *mimesis* which is textual and literary.
>
> (Ricoeur 1991, 142, italic in the original)

Mimesis₂

On this level, mimesis is referred to as the creation of a "quasi-world of actions that are arranged by certain rules of emplotment", a configuration of signs. This 'quasi-world' is not a mere replication of human actions but, rather, a complex of signs organized in a comprehensible structure (called 'schema' by Ricoeur) and referring to reality as we know it (Ricoeur 1991, 149). Below the 'surface level' of the written text, lies a secondary 'infra-text' that the semiotic logic exposes – a reductive schema. Separate linguistic units, arranged according to the laws of syntax, structure this text. The focusing on the signs, on their arbitrary 'signifieds' and on the syntax, narrows the scope of reference to the internal world of the written text, without yet linking it to the cultural experience of the reading subject.

Schemas are products of traditions and are subject to cultural change, both by artists who adapt and appropriate the schemas and by members of the culture who consume the artistic work and position themselves in relation to the tradition. Artists create and exchange within the framework of traditions. However, once in a while, art movements suggest new thoughts concerning traditions, reflecting upon or opposing them. The notions of structuralism concerning the a-temporality of logical structures and the syntactic principles of language are of no assistance in unfolding the poetic richness that emerges in the breaking from traditions. Ricoeur attempts to resolve and complement the shortcomings of the semiotic analysis in mimesis$_2$ by the subjective interpretation of the addressee in mimesis$_3$. As already noted, mimesis$_2$ is, therefore, the configuration in signs of human actions and their organization by means of narrative schemas according to syntactic structures.

Mimesis$_3$

At this stage, the reader is endowed with her or his own appropriation of meaning, following the initial understanding of the text, by contextualizing the fiction and relating to the structure and the narrative schemas (including the relation to traditions, as manifested by the piece). In this respect, the similarities between Ricoeur's *'appropriation of meaning'* and Gadamer's idea of *'application'* have to be elucidated. For Gadamer, the reader is invited to discover new *'horizons'* within the written text, and the fusion of several horizons culminates in a deeper understanding of the text (Gadamer 1986, 272–3). Nevertheless, Gadamer's interpretive theory is distinct from that of Ricoeur in regard to the authorship of meaning. Whereas Gadamer presupposes that *meaning already exists in the text* and is inevitably revealed differently by different readers, Ricoeur begins to discover the meaning as a result of negotiation between the text and the addressees. Ricoeur, thus, considers the reader as an active participant in the hermeneutical arc and the creative process of interpretation, i.e. the meaning partly exists in the text (internal) and partly depends on the addressee (external). Ricoeur reminds us that Aristotle had already regarded the addressee as an active component in the mimetic process, and so he concludes: "It is in the audience or the reader that the process [parcours] of mimesis ends" (Ricoeur 1991, 148).

Mimesis$_3$ is the stage at which personally appropriated meanings might confront culturally conditioned meanings that the addressee interpreted regarding the piece in earlier stages of the analysis. At this stage, the appropriation of meaning by a well-informed reader remains linked to the text, while potentially endless variations of related (subjective) interpretations enrich the reader's imagination. Ricoeur writes: "If, therefore, we accept, as I think we must, the problematic of the reception of a work as an integral part of the constitution of its meaning, the question arises how we are to understand this final stage of mimesis and how to link it to the second one" (Ricoeur 1991, 150). After the semiotic analytical level of the interpretation, in which the reader focuses on signs and their arbitrary meanings in culture, s/he can inquire into the validity of her or his interpretation based upon personal associations and imaginative work with reference to the text. Jacques Derrida is in agreement with Ricoeur concerning the infiniteness of the hermeneutical process and its ability to recreate traces to ideas or contexts that originate in the text but then evolve beyond it, depending on the hermeneutic process. This is especially the case with the new postmodernist and contemporary aesthetics, in which tendencies to openness, fragmentation and intended incompleteness provide 'black holes' for the addressee/reader to fill in. The higher the potential for a diversity of interpretations (and uncertainty), the more the concept of an absolute truth in regard to the interpretation of signs is at stake. Therefore, instead, Ricoeur suggests using the (softer) term of *'rightness'*, but does not offer any criteria by which to asses the rightness or validity of an interpretation.

Moreover, by taking into account the appropriation of meaning, Ricoeur seeks to give hermeneutics a method by which to overcome the distance between the culturally conditioned signs and the reality of the addressee, a distance which results from the isolation of the signification sphere from day-to-day reality. The appropriation of meaning reflects the effort by the addressees to minimize the distance between the culturally agreed upon meaning of signs and their interpretation with reference to one's own life experience and imagination – a reference that was previously considered external and irrelevant to the text. The reader, then, 'complements' the text with a dimension of informed and subjective, yet related, meaning, and does not merely make sense of it. "By virtue of its sense", Ricoeur writes, "the text had only a semiological dimension; now it has, by virtue of its meaning, a semantic dimension" (Ricoeur 1981, 159). Following this line of thought, interpretation of text may culminate in the reader's re-interpretation of herself or himself, after positioning themselves differently in light of the work. The focus on structures, signs and signification processes, distance from the reality of the addressee, and the work taken as the core of the semiotic exploration – all were to change with the growing interest in phenomenology. Consequently, attention shifted from the interpretation of structures and signs towards the embodied experience of reality through the senses, and the engagement with the work was examined through the corporeal perspective.

On the phenomenology of embodiment

Since the mid-20th century, the branch of phenomenology of embodiment, in which the body plays a fundamental role in shaping the process of understanding through the human experiencing of the world, is highly associated with the work of Merleau-Ponty. In his *Phenomenology of Perception*, first published in French in 1945 and translated into English only in 1962, Merleau-Ponty elaborates upon the significance of the body in relation to the self, to the world and to others. He regards perception as a synaesthetic process, allowing the various senses to mutually communicate all the sensorial impressions acquired by a first person in her/his environment. We are our bodies and it is through the body that 'I' perceive the environment; therefore, as Merleau-Ponty argues in opposition to Cartesian thought, the dualism of separate body and mind is inapplicable and likewise, the perceiving body is not separate from its surroundings. Merleau-Ponty rejects the idea that the mind alone is the entity responsible for higher mental activities while the body is the (unreliable) system of sensory perception – a rejection that was later supported by many cognitive and neuro-scientists. Merleau-Ponty notes:

> In so far as, when I reflect on the essence of subjectivity, I find it bound up with that of the body and that of the world, this is because my existence as subjectivity is merely one with my existence as a body and with the existence of the world, and because the subject that I am, when taken concretely, is inseparable from this body and this world . . . The belief in an absolute mind, or in a world in itself detached from us is no more than a rationalization of this primordial faith.
>
> (Merleau-Ponty 1962, 408–9)

Nevertheless, Merleau-Ponty does not ignore the nature of human activities that can be referred to as 'mental' in favour of a purely stimuli-based/materialistic approach (which some cognitive scientists would defend); instead, he advocates finding within corporeal existence mind-related aspects as well. For this, he introduces the term *'body-subject'* and seeks to complement the concept of the body with a dimension of thinking subjectivity. The body-subject does not merely collect stimuli but is engaged in a process of 'creative receptivity', of shared responsibility in selectively constructing the *'body-image'* of reality. The duality in which a body experiences its environment – being in and part of it but, simultaneously, perceiving and distinguishing itself from its environment – reflects the unity in which the body-subject and its world exist. Both are caught in a temporal experience and constitute one *experiential whole* with one's own body in its environment. This experience affects our corporeal functionality on a meta-sensorial level, by organic psychological responses of the body involving muscular rather than audio-visual sensations, for example. In his later essay *Eye and Mind*, dated 1964 and dealing with the painter and his body, Merleau-Ponty elaborates upon the meta-sensorial experience of the body, while experiencing itself:

> The enigma is that my body simultaneously sees and is seen. That which looks at all things can also look at itself and recognize, in what it sees, the "other side" of its power of looking. It sees itself seeing; it touches itself touching; it is visible and sensitive for itself. It is not a self through transparence, like thought, which only thinks its object by assimilating it, by constituting it, by transforming it into thought. It is a self through confusion, narcissism, through inherence of the one who sees in that which he sees, and through inherence of sensing the sensed – a self, therefore, that is caught up in things, that has a front and a back, a past and a future . . .
>
> (Merleau-Ponty 1964, 162–3)

Being in a space and looking at an object implies that we evaluate the distance between that object and ourselves, and understand the perceptual features from different points of view. Looking at an object can evoke in us memories of bodily experience or imagination concerning how it feels to become engaged with the object. "For Merleau-Ponty, phenomenology is concerned with attempts to capture experience, in direct and 'primitive' essence and at a stage before intellectual analysis begins to sort, edit and render it as an artificial 'reconstruction'", note McKinney and Butterworth (2010, 167).

On the adaptation of phenomenology to the framework of theatre studies

It is perhaps not surprising that the increasing interest in phenomenology and the decline of structuralist semiotics occurred simultaneously around the early 1960s, with the emergence of new experimental performative forms, such as the Happenings, the Theatre of the Absurd, new forms of music drama, and the later 'post-dramatic' theatre – for the analysis of which semiotics proved to be unsuitable. Structuralist, and later post-structuralist semiotics lost their leading position as analytical frameworks for performance analysis toward the end of the 1980s (Sauter 2000, 29). The works of contemporary theatre differed greatly from the theatre of Realism and problematized its analyzing from a semiotic perspective, making it necessary to create a new analytical framework. Theatre scholars, several of whom were theatre-makers or closely related to the creative process of performances, sought to adapt phenomenology to theatre studies – among them Bert O. States (playwright and critic), Herbert Blau (theatre director), Maaike Bleeker (dramaturge), Patrice Pavis and Susan Bennett, to mention but a few.

With forms of experimental theatre like Performance Art and Happenings emerging and making the boundaries between art and daily life more fluid and less clear, the certainty concerning the intentionality of the signs that semiotics was so associated with was also questioned. The structuralist idea of an overall structure was abandoned in favour of what the addressees could ascertain: namely, their own conscious corporeal experience, directly influenced by their selective reception – the threshold which regulates what in the conscious experiences becomes subjectively significant. In his book *The Audience*, Blau refers to the different states of spectatorship while watching live theatre performance and film. Regarding the theatre, he argues that the presence of a live performer potentially allows not only an emotional but also a physical engagement. Theatre (and especially Greek tragedy) allows us to look at a spectacle while keeping a certain 'protective' physical distance from it, as we imagine the intimidating unknown that might appear from afar.

> "There is nothing that man fears", writes Canetti at the opening of *Crowds and Power*, "more than the touch of the unknown. He wants to *see* what is reaching towards him to be able to recognize it or at least to classify it". . . . In the dark, the fear of an unexpected touch can mount to panic . . . But as Canetti observes, all the distances that we create and keep around us are dictated by the fear of some unknown thing at the distance.
>
> (Blau 1990, 86–7, italic in the original)

The art of theatre deals constantly with this (physical and poetic) distance. Different periods in the history of theatre have revealed how theatre-makers increased or reduced the distance between the body, with its sensory organs for seeing and hearing, and the spectacle. Two of the productions analysed in the following chapters (*On the Concept of the Face, Regarding the Son of God* and *Rechnitz*) present highly interesting ways by which the performance overcomes that distance by means of immersion, and generates a certain degree of fear or uneasiness among the addressees. The relationship between the presenting body, viewed on the stage, and the body of the viewer, who becomes engaged with the viewed and aware of the state of spectatorship, has been theorized extensively. In this relationship, the spectator undergoes a transformation while watching a performance, not only with regard to the making of meaning, from a philosophical point of view, but also in terms of cognitive and neuronal activities, dealt with later in this chapter. In *Visuality in the Theatre: The Locus of Looking*, Bleeker writes:

> What seems to be just 'there to be seen' is, in fact, rerouted through memory and fantasy, caught up in threads of the unconscious and entangled with the passions. Vision, far from being the 'noblest of the senses' (Descartes, 1977), appears to be irrational, inconsistent and undependable. More than that, seeing appears to alter the thing seen and to transform the one seeing, showing them to be profoundly intertwined in the event that is visuality.
>
> (Bleeker 2008, 2)

On the 'unstable' characteristics of seeing in the theatre, Bleeker writes in her earlier essay *Disorders that Consciousness Can Produce*: "Seeing appears to be irrational, inconsistent, and undependable. It is caught up in the threads of the unconscious and entangled with the passions. Ways of seeing are historically determined and culturally mediated" (Bleeker 2002, 132). The complexity of the act of seeing in the theatre is also examined by additional research in other disciplines. Recent studies in the neurosciences, and studies on cognition and the arts mentioned later in this chapter, have to a certain extent broadened the scope of our knowledge of the conscious experience of watching theatre, and assisted in revealing the mechanisms of mimesis and neural-cognitive principles involved in creating and engaging with art. Contemporary art, and particularly a multidisciplinary art-form such as theatre, engages more complex cognitive networks than art did in earlier periods: technically – because of the diversity of available media used in the arts today; and conceptually – due to the 'open' character of contemporary art concerning the 'meaning' of artworks and the responsibility of the addressee to negotiate a meaningful experience. Alluringly, contemporary art calls into question the functions of art in culture, the relation between art and technology – how art should be constructed aesthetically and poetically, and art's relationship with its addressees. Some media studies, among them 'Mediology' by Régis Debray, seek to combine a semiotic approach with emphasis on the medium used to signify and the materiality of the signs. Let us follow some of the main ideas in Debray's study that will be relevant for the later discussion on the analysis of light's aesthetics in contemporary theatre.

Mediology

Debray's 'Mediology' is the study of the higher social functions of signification, in relation to the material and technical aspects involved in the transmission of meaning; a study that seeks to integrate between semiotics (in the broadest sense) and the phenomenological approach concerning the reception of signs.[5] From early on, Debray argues, semiotics has neglected the reception of signs on the sensorial level and, consequently, the systematic conceptual de-coding (influenced by linguistics) handicapped the development of the study (Debray 1996, 65). Debray criticizes structuralist semiotics for concentrating on the signification sphere and establishing the arbitrary relation between linguistic signs and their fixed meanings, while failing to incorporate in the interpretation process important contexts of the signs linking them to everyday reality. Mere signification using codes creates a *cultural distance from reality*, i.e. semiotics does not integrate the essence of the signifying objects and their pragmatic relation to reality; namely, their *materiality*, their *medium*, and the ways one uses the objects in daily reality as opposed to artistic work. In that spirit, Claude Lévi-Strauss notes in his book *Structural Anthropology*:

> In positing the symbolic nature of its object, social anthropology does not intend to cut itself from realia. How could it, when art, in which all is a sign, utilizes material media? One cannot study gods while ignoring their images; rites without analyzing the objects and substances manufactured and manipulated by the officiant; or social rules independently of the things that correspond to them. Social anthropology . . . does not separate material culture and spiritual culture.
>
> (Lévi-Strauss 1976, 11)

With 'medio' incorporated in the name of his theory, Debray relates to the *mediation of ideas by media*, emphasizing the dynamics of change and instability of signification within the media. While the structuralist semiotic model concentrated on the ways in which signs generate meanings, the model of mediology focuses on analyzing *how meanings are materially transmitted*. 'Transmitting' refers to the power of materially embodied ideas to carry, or 'to mediate', information between two parties by technological means. By nature, the mechanical apparatus involved in the transmission of any sign influences its aesthetic character, maintaining a technological 'fingerprint' or integrating into the sign external contexts that are not self-evident. Mediology, thus, does not dismiss or ignore the semiotic practice but, rather, revises and increases the scope of the semiotic theory and practice to include other significant influences that assist in exploring and unfolding the sign's form and matter. It includes an analysis of the pre-semiotics stimulus (the 'signal' in Debray's terminology), its production method, the system of transmission and the reception of the stimulus as a sign by an addressee, from technological, social (daily reality) and cultural (aesthetic/poetic) perspectives. When adapting any object to use as sign in the service of art, its 'elevated' semiotic function is examined, as opposed to its function in everyday reality and in a non-aesthetic framework.

By considering how the same signifying object is used not only in the poetic context but also in daily reality, the semiotic analysis benefits from new tools with which to address the formal features of the sign and to examine the unique materiality of the sign. The process by which the object was produced juxtaposes social and cultural contexts that constitute fundamental facets when the object is used as a sign. The potential information we gain and examine about the sign consequently increases. Mediology thus gives primacy to the (complementary) material perspective of the signification process, and to the associations that signs give rise to beyond their arbitrary meanings, as mentioned above.

Another notable method of mediology – inspired, perhaps, by Peirce's notion of the 'semiotic drift' – helps to interpret the sign more openly than the structuralist semiotics. Debray describes a process of zooming in on the signifying object and zooming out at continuous intervals – looking at the object from the broader technological, social and cultural perspectives, and then examining the object in its semiotic configuration and artistic context. The more we examine the origin of the sign and its use in non-aesthetic contexts, the more valuable the information that we disclose about the sign. Therefore, notes Debray, "the pragmatics of usages determines the semiotics of the code" (Debray 1996, 67).

Notwithstanding the reconsideration of the material aspects of signs, the study of mediology does not reach as far as phenomenology in considering the sensorial experience of the addressee in the hermeneutical process. However, it does aim at a closer examination of conditions by which an addressee acknowledges a sign and how interpretation occurs. The instability in the act of interpretation begins with one's personal threshold and cognitive capacities, even prior to the acquired cultural background. While people partly distinguish some objects or stimuli as symbols, a great deal of other information might fade away as an unobserved 'noise'. These aspects will be further elaborated in the context of studies on art and the neuro-cognitive sciences.

On art and the neuro-cognitive sciences

During the last decades of the 20th century, new discoveries in neuroscience and cognitive science have enhanced the attention given to the central role of the body, and particularly of the brain, in the subjective and personal experience *Homo sapiens* has of its environment, and the experience of art as a particular category of environmental experience. Phenomenology and the neurosciences share a common interest in "intentionality, memory, the gestalt nature of perception and the human ability to bracket off some phenomena to better understand others" (McConachie and Hart 2006, 6). Various scientific insights illuminate how the body and brain function, what 'mind' is from a corporeal perspective, as opposed to its philosophical definitions, and help us to understand some of the essential processes we conduct, consciously and unconsciously, when approaching art. We also know now that the human genome we are born with carries certain universal aesthetic preferences (for beauty) that we apply in daily life and likewise, while judging art, just as we acquire different abilities to assume the intentions of other members in our society in order to maximize our chances for survival. In the final section of this chapter, I will briefly introduce various aspects of perception modes and embodied experiences, such as empathy caused by the expression of human emotions, sensitivity to light and colour, mimetic skills and the origin of the arts. A better understanding of the cognitive processes we perform while interpreting our situation, or while engaging with a work of art, will enable us to become more conscious of the complexity of the theatrical event, especially at a time when theatre is increasingly evolving its 'performativity' rather than the 'staging' of the text, and the rise of the visual and other dimensions challenges the tradition of the playwright's theatre.

In *The Psychology of Art and the Evolution of the Conscious Brain*, Robert L. Solso focuses on the essential role that our conscious brain plays in perceiving and experiencing art, referring to the perceiving individual and the environment she or he perceives through the body, as elements that together constitute a momentary experience of unity and wholeness. His neuropsychological perspective concerning the engagement with art seems to support the earlier phenomenological studies of Husserl and Merleau-Ponty, in which art is regarded as belonging to the environmental stimuli:

Both mind and art are part of a single physical universe. Separate analyses of art and of mind lead to misunderstanding of each. Heroic attempts to show the relationship between art, as an "out there" physical stimulus, and what it does to us as an "in here" psychological reaction lead to a strained connection between the two. Art and mind are of a single reality – they are constructed from the same base. We now have a much better understanding of how perceived objects (such as art objects) are processed by physiochemical reactions that take place first in the eye and subsequently in the brain. In addition, we have specific knowledge of the overall workings of the brain as reflected by neurological principles.

(Solso 2003, 21)

Solso distinguishes between two kinds of perception that humans constantly integrate in daily life, as well as in the experience of art. The first kind is *nativistic perception* ('bottom-up'): the translation of environmental physical stimuli into chemical and neurological signals, activating chain reactions that can move along the 52 networked regions within the brain; regions that are specialized for different functions. *Directed perception*, the second kind, is based on the subject's personal knowledge and history of experiences as registered in the memory, initially triggered by the external stimuli that the nativistic perception distinguished. The distinction between the two kinds of perception helps to explain and identify the source of the stimulus and the direction in which the neurons move, whether it is a trigger from the sensorial organs into the brain, internal triggering in the brain (by 'reviving' a memory, for example), or a chemical reaction that the brain sets in motion in the rest of the body (producing adrenalin in the case of fear, for example). In fact, the two perceptions are interwoven and work simultaneously at all times.

It should be noted that various sensory networks linked to these types of perception are initially designated to fulfil primal functions and to enable better chances of survival in the world; only at a later stage of evolution are humans believed to have started using these capacities for the appreciation of art. Moreover, nativistic perception, which is specialized in apprehending the physical structure of the world, is not complemented only by a culturally conditioned knowledge of the world, but, as Steven Pinker argues, is also subconsciously influenced by instinctive and universal emotions and aesthetic pleasures (Pinker 2002, 412). He notes, for example, that small children prefer calendar-like images of landscapes over deserts and forests, while three-month-old babies look at beautiful faces longer than at plain ones; likewise, they prefer consonant musical intervals over dissonant ones. In view of the above, Derrida's notion of 'free play' within the process of interpretation proves to be cognitively invalid, since interpretation is an embodied process. The virtually unlimited potential for interpretation is narrowed and grounded in each individual (and subjective) visceral system, unconsciousness and conscious experience of reality. Bruce McConachie and Elizabeth Hart write:

Cognitive science undercuts the major assumptions upon which Derrida built deconstruction. Ironically, though, most cognitive scientists would agree with conclusions deriving from modifications of Derrida's insights. While attribution of meaning to a text or performance is not cognitively free, the enormous flexibility of the mind/brain does make it impossible for even a single reader or spectator to pin down any fixed or final meaning.

(McConachie and Hart 2006, 4)

The state of consciousness includes the recall of knowledge of three different kinds: *self-knowledge* about our own situation; *world knowledge* of things we have learnt and recall from our memory; and recall of *collective knowledge* (Solso 2003, 31–3). Our mind complements the sensory experience of external stimuli in various ways, including psychological and emotional reactions and the exchange of modalities. For example, while seeing an image, one might have in mind the sensation of hearing, tasting or smelling (without external stimuli), based on recall of knowledge and personal memories. Signals crossing various regions in the brain, responsible for different sensing modalities, embody the experience of synaesthesia. The activity of the nervous system in the brain creates networks between different designated brain regions. However, as Antonio Damasio explains, the subjective body experiences its environment also through a subliminal level of perception called *somatosensory*, beyond the already known sensory modalities of sight, hearing, smell and taste. About the somatosensory perception McKinney and Butterworth note:

> This last term refers to sensory systems inherent in the body and includes the sensing of changes in 'the chemical environment' of cells through the operation of the nervous system and the visceral dimension of our internal organs. These are influenced by flows of blood which might be registered as feelings of calm or agitation, flushing skin or sweating palms.
>
> (McKinney and Butterworth 2010, 178)

The component of collective knowledge is linked to the shared capacity of any individual human living in a group (and the limited capacity of several species of other mammals) to experience empathy for one another, so that "one is conscious of another's consciousness as well as his actions. And an important part of this personal insight is that it opens the door for human empathy as well as seeing oneself in another's actions" (Solso 2003, 32). Since the human being is a social organism, it is important to have the ability to effectively communicate emotions and intentions among the members of the group. According to McConachie and Hart in *Performance and Cognition: Theatre Studies and the Cognitive Turn*:

> Cognitive science suggests that empathy and emotional response are more crucial to a spectator's experience than the kind of decoding that most semioticians imagine . . . TOM [Theory of Mind] advocates now understand simulation, the basic psychological mechanism that deploys empathy, as the major means of interpreting and predicting human behaviour and as more important than rational approaches to understanding others.
>
> (McConachie and Hart 2006, 5)

This embodied social feature is also connected to the discovery of *mirror neurons* in the experiments by Giacomo Rizzolatti and his team in the early 1990s – experiments whose results indicated that both the performer and the viewer of a goal-directed motorized action share some similar patterns of neurological activity. Similar patterns of neurons were registered in Macaque monkeys that carried out a goal-directed motor act (such as holding, grasping and manipulating), and in monkeys that watched another monkey, or just heard and knew that another individual was conducting this action (Rizzolatti and

Sinigaglia 2008, x–xi). The same neurons were fired when the monkey itself grasped food, for example, and when it watched the experimenter grasping food; nonetheless, mirror neurons did not fire when watching the food or any other object alone, but only when a goal-directed motor action was performed with the object (Rizzolatti and Sinigaglia 2008, 79–80). Mirror neurons depend on the viewing of specific motor acts (picking up, grasping) while a body organ (hand, mouth) interacts with an object (food, tool) – simply miming such actions without an actual object does not result in the discharging of mirror neurons. It is interesting to note that while different distances did not affect the production of neurons, different neuronal performances were registered according to whether the experimenter used his right or left hand.

The firing of mirror neurons seems to occur with reference to motor actions with clear goals, when the act is related to a practical purpose that we assume we know, based on our past experience. Rizzolatti and Sinigaglia disagree with Marc Jeannerod's theory concerning the function of these neurons, according to which the role of mirror-neurons is "to generate an 'internal motor representation' of the observed motor act, on which the possibility of learning by imitation relies", although they do not reject the possibility that such learning indeed happens.[6] Rizzolatti and Sinigaglia argue that the primary role of mirror-neurons is involved in "the understanding of the meaning of 'motor-events', i.e. of the actions performed by others" (Rizzolatti and Sinigaglia 2008, 96–7). In a lecture given at the *Forum on Art and the New Biology of Mind* (24 March 2006), Vittorio Gallese discussed an experiment regarding mirror-neurons and the performing arts, conducted with professional classical ballet and Capoeira dancers. The results showed that more neurons were fired among the dancers while watching the genre at which they were highly skilled, and vice versa, "so the more you get acquainted with something, the more your brain resonates along with what you are looking at".[7] Among the conclusions of that experiment was that: "the 'mirror system' integrates observed actions of others with an individual's personal motor repertoire, and suggests that the human brain understands actions by motor simulation".[8] The understanding of a goal-oriented action involves numerous cognitive processes and modalities in which mirror-neurons constitute merely a part. However, this part generates an embodied empathy in the viewer toward the acting individual, as Rizzolatti and Sinigaglia write:

> Emotions, like actions, are immediately shared; the perception of pain or grief, or of disgust experienced by others, activates the same areas of cerebral cortex that are involved when we experience these emotions ourselves. This shows how strong and deeply rooted is the bond that ties us to others, or in other words, how bizarre it would be to conceive of an *I* without an *us*. As Peter Brook reminds us, the players on the stage overcome all linguistic and cultural barriers to encompass the spectators in a shared experience of actions and emotions.
>
> (Rizzolatti and Sinigaglia 2008, xii–xiii)

Almost half a century before the discovery of mirror neurons, Ernst Cassirer wrote in *An Essay on Man: An Introduction to a Philosophy of Human Culture*, about the notion of '*emotional language*', of the impulses and instincts on which animal communication is based. Although some species have developed limited cognitive capacities considered to be rational, for each species – according to its extent of evolution – animal communication consists of an immediate and instinctive transition of signals. Animal communication does not mediate ideas using signs configured in structures – a key-domain of cultural development. The primary communication in nature is, therefore, one of emotions and senses. The exclusive and most important capacity of humankind is symbolic thinking and symbolic behaviour, a capacity even more important than rationality, writes Cassirer (1944). This capacity is progressive and additional to the primary emotional understanding between individuals.

Symbolic thinking is essential for the creation and the experience of art, both of which involve the cognitive ability to reflect upon human culture itself. Being a product of human culture, art is self-reflective. Since Modernism, in particular, art has reflected upon the cognitive processes of the artist and the addressees that are involved in the creation and engagement with art – thereby making art meta-cognitive. In *Art and Cognitive Evolution*, Merlin Donald writes that, since prehistoric times, art has arisen within the context of cultural and cognitive evolution, and it has been linked to the constant development of human mimetic skills (Donald 2006, 14). Donald mentions four central mimetic abilities that humans are particularly good at: *mime, imitation, gesture* and *the rehearsal of skill* – all of which are connected to action. Developing imitation skills in a reflective way was a fundamental and exclusive feature in the evolution of the primate brain and the later emergence of art. Donald writes:

> Mimesis seems to have evolved as a cognitive elaboration of embodiment in patterns of action. Its origins lie in a redistribution of frontal-cortical influence during early stages of the evolution of species *Homo*, when the prefrontal and parts of the premotor cortex expanded enormously in relative to size and connectivity . . . This also gave them some ability to reflect on the cognitive process itself, and the option of deliberately reflecting on, and shaping, their own actions.
>
> (Donald 2006, 15–16, italic in the original)

As Denis Dutton recognizes in *The Art Instinct: Beauty, Pleasure and Human Evolution*, there are seven universal features in human culture, related to the creation and appreciation of art at any evolutionary stage with its respective adaptations:

1   *Providing direct pleasure* – Humans enjoy the experience of art for art's sake, without it providing them with any material benefits.
2   *Style* – Artefacts are produced according to recognizable formal features and conventions that belong to a style. Style is also expressed emotionally through the artist's individual creative and novel 'signature', beyond the canonized characteristics.
3   *Criticism* – Works of art tend to be surrounded by social recognition and reflective activity. Likewise, art's stimulation of many regions in the brain also reflects the intellectual challenge that its experience provides for the addressee.
4   *Imitation* – People take pleasure in artworks that are based on verisimilitude to experiences from reality.
5   *Skill and virtuosity* – The demonstration of learnt skills with outstanding quality delights people and leads to admiration for those artists who show themselves to be capable of such skills.
6   *Special focus on artefact* – Special attention, heightened by daily reality, is given to the creation and appreciation of art.
7   *Imaginative experience* – Humans find pleasure in the representation of fictive situations and the play of make-believe in the 'theatre' of their mind.

The evolution of the human culture, according to Donald, consisted of three major phases: first was the *mimetic phase*, in which action-metaphor was central for establishing communication in the forms of gesture, pantomime, dance, visual analogy and ritual. Subsequently, the later *mythic phase* consisted of the emergence of spoken language, especially through the storytelling of myths, which helped establish notions concerning authority, gender and morality. The current *theoretic phase* in the cognitive evolution of human culture is marked by the development of written language and scientific progress – more intensively since the Enlightenment at the end of the 17th century and throughout the past several centuries. "Theoretic culture", Donald notes, "is symbol-based, logical, bureaucratic, and heavily dependent on external memory devices, such as writing, codices, mathematical notations, scientific instruments, books, records, and computers" (Donald 2006, 8).

Likewise, Solso emphasizes the parallel progression of the evolution of the cerebral brain with its cognitive capacities, and the degree of complexity with which artefacts are constructed. Artefacts should be seen in a symbiotic relationship with the developments in cognition that have influenced the creation of cultures and artefacts alike – and not merely for their historical and archaeological values (Solso 2003, 41). This remark is highly interesting with regard to the increasing development of conceptual art at an astonishingly rapid pace since the rise of modernism at the beginning of the 20th century and up to the present day, with the increasing influence of theory on art reception. Tom Wolfe notes in *The Painted Word* (1975) with reference to modern art: "Not 'seeing is believing', you ninny, but 'believing is seeing', for *Modern Art has become completely literary: the painting and other works exist only to illustrate the text*" (Wolfe 1975, 5, italics in original).

And yet, one of the achievements of art lies in its potentially evoking a meaningful experience, i.e. a cognitive outcome, by proposing a new imaginative perspective on reality and a new way of knowing the world. This is always dependent on accomplishing a certain control over the attention and state of mind of the addressee. Donald writes: "Art should be regarded as a specific kind of cognitive engineering . . . control of attention, which carries with it a propensity to deliberately engineer the experiences of others . . . " (Donald 2006, 4). Artists launch the cognitive processes that the addressees then carry out in their minds; in a sense, the artists initiate a multisensorial event, a cognitive complex for addressees to perceive, engage with and generate creative interpretations, using their memories and imagination. In *The Blank Slate*, Pinker notes that experiments on the visual tastes of people revealed repeated preferences for elements that cause them aesthetic pleasure; and in *The Art Instinct*, Dutton writes about the all-human meta-cultural ideals of beauty and preferred aesthetics of art. Both mention the universal and intuitive tendency of people to like panoramic views of landscapes with blue sky, a savannah with blossoming, fruit-laden trees and animals, a flowing stream and a path in the midst of open terrain, offering suitable habitat in which to dwell, signifying safety and fertility. The interesting fact is that people living in countries featuring very different landscapes and weather conditions also showed preference for these features, despite not being accustomed to them. Pinker notes: "the study of evolutionary aesthetics is also documenting the features that make a face of body beautiful. The prized lineaments are those that signal health, vigor, and fertility" (Pinker 2002, 405). By being more familiar with how our mind works, artists in light can more consciously 'engineer' cognition, the ways we perceive, feel and think about what we see, in the theatrical event. As some of the later examples of Light Art works and contemporary theatre performances will show, light has the ability to draw our attention to the processes of our visual perception, to the emotional impact of light, and to the conflict between what we know by seeing and what we think we see.

Light, colour response and neuroscience

In *How the Mind Works*, Pinker relates to pre-semiotic cognitive activity, referring to human survival instincts manifested in the visual experience: "We pay attention to features of the visual world that signal safe, unsafe, or changing habitats, such as distant views, greenery, gathering clouds, and sunsets" (Pinker 1997, 537). Light, one of nature's most powerful major forces, and visually most dominant medium in the theatre, makes us alert and *instinctively emotional* with every change of light in the habitat.

In *The Lighting Art: The Aesthetics of Stage Lighting Design*, Richard H. Palmer elaborates upon the influence of colour on the attention and emotions of the spectators. According to Faber Birren in *Light, Color and Environment,* spectators are more attentive to colours in the centre of the visible spectrum of the light than at its ends (white, yellow and green more than red and blue), although white light attracts little interest due to its lack of chromaticity (Birren 1969, 47). Saturated colours (red followed by green, yellow, white then blue) call for more attention than subtle colours. Blue is perceived as more distant than red, because blue light is of shorter wavelength. Palmer notes the highly effective subjective experience of colour, whose influence depends on the observer's cultural background, visual sophistication, gender and age – among other factors (Palmer 1998, 99). Brightness or size of coloured areas, as well as changing colours or the movement of coloured light, are factors influencing our attention; however, all these findings are based on quantitative studies that have provided differing and controversial results. For example, the probability distribution of the effects on individual spectators differs greatly and does not clearly indicate tendencies; likewise, studies have indicated that various coexisting factors on the stage could compete with each other, preventing a successful separation in order to study each effect separately.

Previous attempts to analyse the emotional effects of coloured light have provided more complex and contradictory results, caused by the differences in cultural background of the examinees, their visual education and individual personality, while physiological studies failed to conclude that a certain colour results in one given effect. Numerous researches of colour response presented spectators with a colour and asked them to choose words from a list of associations. These tests too, however, led to unclear findings, varying according to the character and temperament of the spectators, their cultural background, their visual training, their symbolic associations and aesthetic preferences. Palmer states that coloured light is clearly able to influence blood pressure and heart rate, breathing tempo, sweating, brain waves, blinking rate and muscular tension (Palmer 1998, 100). In *Color and Human Response*, Birren notes that blue has a relaxing effect on spectators while red increases the rate and level of the parameters mentioned above. Green results in neutral levels; the effects of yellow and orange are similar to these of red, but not to the same extent. The efficacy of purple and violet is similar to that of blue, but here too, on a smaller scale (Birren 1978, 24).

Measurements have shown that any effect of colour on the body of the spectator is usually temporary and that shortly after its sudden reaction to the stimulus, the body either restores its functions to their previous levels or alters them in the opposite direction. The repeated appearance of a colour will not be as effective as its initial use. Warm and cool coloured light have shown a differential influence on people's moods and also their attitude toward the illuminated environment or object. An appearance of a pleasurable colour after a less pleasurable one will also elicit an emotional effect, and vice versa. From a commercial perspective, the 'positive' effect of warm light is measurable in increasing sales of such lights.

Languages also adopt a 'colour symbology' of emotions associated with words, as Palmer explains, and these expressions, with which theatre-goers become familiar, are occasionally used by lighting designers as theatrical conventions: for example, 'green with envy', 'feeling blue' or representation of insanity with yellow, passion/death with red. The cultural knowledge of these associations among members of a specific culture becomes a shaping part of the emotional experience and the hermeneutic process that the addressees perform with reference to coloured light in a performance. However, with all the findings of coloured light affecting corporeal-physiological activity and the conceptual influence (of linguistic association) on the spectators, there is not as yet sufficient evidence to conclusively define the way by which each coloured light affects audiences in the theatre. Palmer writes:

> There is presently inadequate scientific evidence to support conclusively the effects of colored light, but we do know that light stimulates the pituitary and pineal glands and possibly other regions in the brain controlling the production of hormones that influence the way we feel; so there is a basis to justify further investigations of colored light, which in turn may lead to a better understanding of emotional responses to color.
>
> (Palmer 1998, 101–2)

Works of Light Art can occasionally be extreme and immersive, in terms of how these works invite us to explore the influence of light on the visual perception and cognition of the addressees, while placing the act of seeing at the core of the artistic sensation, both corporeally and philosophically. Most art is metacognitive, Donald argues, since it is a self-reflection of the process that created the work itself; namely, the mind of the artist and the culture from which this artist emerged. Artistic traditions and art movements are also metacognitive systems that reflect the changing views on the social and cultural functions of art, as these develop from one period to another. Technology has great influence on the cognitive networks that artists can create, through the aesthetic qualities that one technology or another instils in art objects, and brings to the cognitive process. Moreover, technology is occasionally a preconditioning factor in the conceptual and creative process of art- making, affecting the reception of the piece and potentially expanding cultural cognition by presenting new technologies. Donald writes:

> They [media] influence memory, shape public behaviour, set social norms, and modify the experience of life in their audiences. In these terms, the various techniques and media of art are a small but important part of the larger evolutionary trajectory of the human mind.
>
> (Donald 2006, 7)

The evolutionary trajectory of the human mind advances constantly by creating and disseminating cognitive networks in culture, involving a great number of participating brains in the exchange of knowledge. Art is an example of such a network, playing a unique role in the development of complex cognitive capacities and networks in the culture within and among its individual members. The memory storage capacities of the participants are interconnected into a cognitive network that exceeds the capacity of the individual brain, and so "perceptions can emerge and undergo major transformation anywhere in the network. Representations become a shared resource, and the sources of creative change can be found in many different locations at once" (Donald 2006, 12). In this respect, Solso notes: "One's past knowledge and interest direct one's attention. Each of us brings to the viewing of art an entire set of past experiences and expectations that largely influences what we perceive and how we interpret what we see" (Solso 2003, 3). Therefore, it is the collective and diverse experience of art that evolves the ways by which artists create, addressees experience and scholars theorize, contemporary art.

The precarious condition of multifaceted experiences and interpretations, to which both Donald and Solso refer, seems to have increased immensely in regard to contemporary theatre, where meaning is no longer considered to reside in the performance but is, rather, the cognitive outcome of the process of engagement and negotiation between the artefact and the addressees. The process relies on the individual's memory system, which is extremely complex in itself and, therefore, the artist cannot predict the cognitive outcome in the reception of the artefact. The human brain is able to reflect upon and interpret an artist's view of reality in endless ways, some of which may not have been envisaged by the artist. The artist, thus, can influence only part of the process and is limited in predicting the reception experience.

Addressees, in turn – when perceiving art – 'know the world' through the unique perspective of the artist on human culture if they reconstruct it 'correctly', inviting us to engage with and through the aesthetic prism of an artefact. "Art attacks the mind, not usually through its logical and analytic channels, but more commonly through its senses, passions and anxieties". As a cognitive scientist, Donald still reflects upon the author's meaning as being internal to a work of art, and argues that by engaging with the separate formal artistic elements, the addressees seek to grasp the artist's intent (Donald 2006, 13). The various scholarly perspectives introduced in this chapter reflect the changing position of the artist in regard to the piece, and present some central ideas in the theoretical discourse concerning the relevance of the author's meaning to the experience of the addressees. The author's intentions remain relevant indeed and significant for a large public of art-lovers, but this is not so for many other addressees of the more experimental contemporary art.

Conclusion

Light in the theatre is probably the most fleeting medium experienced by the public. Even more than music, light can be a 'transparent', immaterial and intangible medium and, thus, its analysis becomes a complex task. The tendency of contemporary art toward the realm of philosophy (Danto), differing so tremendously from the theatrical tradition up to the 20th century, makes the reference to light design an even more complex task. This chapter introduced several key notions, applied to theatre studies, from the fields of semiotics, mediology, phenomenology, and cognitive and neurosciences. In order to develop a coherent and rich theoretical – yet practical – perspective for the analysis of light in contemporary theatre, selected notions from the scholarly work I discussed earlier are woven complementarily. The following notions will be relevant, in particular, for the analysis of light: categories of signs and semiotic drift (Peirce), open work, encyclopedia and unlimited semiosis (Eco), the transformation of signs from one sign system into another (Elam, Fischer-Lichte), informational/symbolic/'third' meanings (Barthes), appropriation of meaning (Ricoeur), embodied experience and body-image of reality (Merleau-Ponty), influence of the materiality of a medium (Debray), evolutionary aesthetics and art (Pinker, Dutton), universal human ideals of beauty (Dutton) and art as cognitive engineering (Donald). A (new) analytical framework must be developed in order to approach the processes by which experience and meaning of light are created in contemporary theatre. In the following chapter I will propose a new conceptual framework for analysis of the experience and meaning of light in contemporary theatre, of light's aesthetics, semiotics and poetics, with reference to the performance as a multi-sensorial event in which the addressees become active participants in the total theatrical experience and in the making of meaning.

Notes

1 The choice of the name 'semiotics' rather than 'semiology' reflected the aim to validate and categorize the study of signs among the other disciplines of the exact sciences, with fewer connotations to the humanities. Umberto Eco's semiotics attempts to integrate the two in one systematic theory.

2 Eco's conditional notion concerning the artist's intent became slightly mitigated in his later publications. See also in: U. Eco, *The Limits of Interpretation*, Bloomington and Indianapolis, IN: Indiana University Press, 1990, p. 24.

3 When appropriating ideas from theories on the reception of text and appling them into the study of theatre, I use the term 'performance', or alternatively, 'piece'. Merleau-Ponty applies phenomenology to the context of visual arts and reversaly uses the term 'text' metaphorically.

4 I didn't find any reference to Ricoeur's ideas on mimesis and representation, nor on the interpretive process by theatre scholars. It is remarkable since his hermeneutics point back to Aristotle's *Poetics*, which is so relevant to theatre studies.

5 States defends the validity of semiotic analysis, when simultaneously employed with phenomenology, in order to unfold and contemplate a larger scope of information as relevant for the interpretation of the experience of reality, as that of art. For elaboration, see also B.O. States, *Great Reckonings in the Little Rooms: On the Phenomenology of Theatre*, Berkeley, CA and London: University of California Press, 1985, p. 8.

6 Later in this chapter, I elaborate on Merlin Donald's work concerning the importance of imitation as a human learning skill, and the imitation in the arts in particular, in the creation of *cognitive networks of knowledge*.

7 https://vimeo.com/39351287 (6:10").

8 https://vimeo.com/39351287 (6:23").

References

Aristotle, *Poetics*, part XIV, translation with an introduction and notes by M. Heath, London: Penguin, 1996.

Belting, H., *Art History after Modernism*, translated by Caroline Saltzwedel and Mitch Cohen with additional translation by Kenneth Northcott, Chicago: University of Chicago Press, 2003.

Birren, F., *Color and Human Response*, New York: Van Nostrand Reinhold Co., 1978.

Birren, F., *Light, Color and Environment*, New York: Van Nostrand Reinhold Co., 1969.

Blau, H., *The Audience*, Baltimore: John Hopkins University Press, 1990.

Bleeker, M., *Disorders that Consciousness Can Produce*, in *Bodycheck: Relocating the Body in Contemporary Performing Art*, Amsterdam and New York: Rodopi, 2002.

Bleeker, M., *Visuality in the Theatre: The Locus of Looking*, Basingstoke, UK: Palgrave Macmillan, 2008.

Cassirer, E., *An Essay on Man; An Introduction to a Philosophy of Human Culture*, New Haven, CT: Yale University Press, 1944.

Collins, J. and Nisbet, A., *Theatre and Performance Design: A Reader in Scenography*, edited by Jane Collins and Andrew Nisbet, Abingdon and New York: Routledge, 2010.

Debray, R., *Media Manifestos, on the Technological Transmission of Cultural Forms*, translated by Eric Rauth, London and New York: Verso, 1996.

Derrida, J., "Structure, Sign and Play in the Discourse of the Human Sciences", in *The Critical Tradition*, edited by Daniel Richter, New York: St Martin's Press, 1989.

Donald, M. "Art and Cognitive Evolution", in *The Artful Mind: Cognitive Science and the Riddle of Human Creativity*, edited by Mark Turner, New York and Oxford: Oxford University Press, 2006.

Dutton, D., *The Art Instinct: Beauty, Pleasure and Human Evolution*, Oxford: Oxford University Press, 2009.

Eco, U., *A Theory of Semiotics*, Bloomington, IN and London: Indiana University Press, 1976.

Eco, U., *The Limits of Interpretation*, Bloomington and Indianapolis, IN: Indiana University Press, 1990.

Eco, U., *The Open Work*, translated by Anna Cancogni, with an introduction by David Robey, London: Hutchinson Radius, 1989, translation of *Opera aperta*, 1962.

Elam, K. *The Semiotics of Theatre and Drama*, New York: Methuen & Co. Ltd, 1980.

Fischer-Lichte, E., *The Semiotics of Theater*, translated by Jeremy Gaines and Doris L. Jones, Bloomington and Indianapolis, IN: Indiana University Press, 1992.

Foucault, M., "On Other Spaces", first published in the French journal *Architecture-Movement-Continuite*, October, 1984, appears in *Theatre and Performance Design: A Reader in Scenography*, edited by Jane Collins and Andrew Nisbet, Abingdon and New York: Routledge, 2010.

Gadamer, H. G., *The Historicity of Understanding*, in: *The Hermeneutics Reader*, edited by K. Muller-Vollmer, Oxford: Basil Blackwell, 1986.

Lévi-Strauss, C., *Structural Anthropology*, vol. II, translated by Monique Layton, New York: Basic Books, 1976.

McConachie, B. and Hart, F. E., *Performance and Cognition: Theatre Studies and The Cognitive Turn*, edited by B. McConachie and F. E., Hart, London and New York: Routledge, 2006.

McKinney, J. and Butterworth, P., *The Cambridge Introduction to Scenography*, New York: Cambridge University Press, 2010 (1st printed 2009).

Merleau-Ponty, M., *Eye and Mind*, translated by C. Dallery, in *The Primacy of Perception: and Other Essays on Phenomenological Psychology, the Philosophy of Art, History and Politics*, edited by James M. Edie, Evanston, IL: Northwestern University Press, 1964.

Merleau-Ponty, M., *Phenomenology of Perception*, translated by Colin Smith, London and Henley: Routledge and Kegan Paul, New Jersey: The Humanities Press, first published in French in 1945, first English edition in 1962.

Palmer, R. H., *The Lighting Art: The Aesthetics of Stage Lighting Design*, 2nd edition, Upper Saddle River, NJ: Prentice-Hall, Inc, 1998.

Pavis, P., *Analyzing Performance: Theatre, Dance and Film*, translated by D. Williams, Ann Arbor, MI: University of Michigan Press, 2003.

Peirce, C. S., *Collected Papers*, vol. 2., Cambridge, MA: Harvard University Press, 1931–58.

Pinker, S., *The Blank Slate: The Modern Denial of Human Nature*, London: Penguin Books, 2002.

Pinker, S., *How the Mind Works*, London: Allen Lane, The Penguin Press, 1997.

Ricoeur, P., *Mimesis and Representation* in *A Ricoeur Reader*, edited by M. J. Valdes, Toronto: Toronto University Press, 1991.

Ricoeur, P., *What is a Text? Explanation and Understanding* in *Hermeneutics and Human Sciences*, Cambridge: Cambridge University Press, 1981.

Rizzolatti, G. and Sinigaglia, C., *Mirrors in the Brain, How Our Minds Share Actions and Emotions*, translated by Frances Anderson, Oxford: Oxford University Press, 1st English edition, 2008.

Sauter, W., *The Theatrical Event: Dynamics of Performance and Perception*, Iowa City: University of Iowa Press, 2000.

Solso, R. L., *The Psychology of Art and the Evolution of the Conscious Brain*, Cambridge, MA: The MIT Press, 2003.

States, B. O., *Great Reckonings in the Little Rooms: On the Phenomenology of Theatre*, Berkeley, CA and London: University of California Press, 1985.

de Toro, F., "The End of Theatre Semiotics? A Symptom of Epistemological Shift", *Semiotica* (168), edited. by Yana Meerzon, 2008.

Wolfe, T., *The Painted Word*, New York: Picador, 1975.

Chapter 4

A new conceptual framework for the analysis of light

Light is the most important part of theatre. It brings everything together, and everything depends on it . . . If you know how to light, you can make shit look like gold.

(Robert Wilson (quoted in Holmberg 1998, 121))

Everyone thinks they know what light is. I have spent my life trying to find out what light is, and I still do not know.

(Albert Einstein)

In the previous chapter, I introduced two different perspectives (the semiotic and the phenomenological) by which theatre studies have attempted to analyse the meaning and experience of the complex theatrical event. Neither of these frameworks has particularly addressed the exclusive features of light, which are relevant for a detailed analysis of its artistic role within the performance. The few semioticians who have briefly referred to light came short of a full study. Due to their unfamiliarity with the practice of light design and their limited understanding of this intangible medium, theoreticians have offered 'sterile' and impractical approaches that were based upon conventions of the theatre of Realism.[1] In the meantime, technological developments in theatre lighting have also enabled designers to use light in new and highly sophisticated ways, to create light-images with optical qualities and precision that could only have been dreamt of a few decades ago, and to evoke ever more complex embodied experiences in the body–mind–brain of the spectators. These experiences can be better understood by applying cognitive semiotics to the analysis of theatre lighting, as in the present study, which takes the first steps on this path.

At the same time, the increasing acknowledgment by institutes for the performing arts, universities, art academies and theatre practitioners of the artistic potential of light to offer new ways of designing and perceiving theatre today, raises the necessity, now more than ever, of an efficient analytical method that is grounded in practical experience of light design. In addition, the recent professional discourse on the scope of scenography, resulting in modifying the name of the international *Prague Quadrennial of Performance Design and Space* (PQ) almost every four years, shows that for too long, light, video and sound design have been considered subliminal elements under the wings of scenography. The reference to light was – at best – secondary to scenography. In both the *PQ* and the parallel international exhibition *World Stage Design*, light design has recently gained its well-deserved recognition as a substantial artistic creation and, consequently, a separate prize in the category of light design is now awarded for excellence in light design. That said, the necessity to provide a method by which to analyse the unique expression of light, its complex bodily effect and its 'meaningful' experience (in the broadest, most open sense), becomes self-evident and requisite.

Critical studies such as the present research call for the formulation of a conceptual framework, and the demonstration of its usefulness by means of test cases. Five contemporary theatre performances will thus be analysed with the new conceptual framework – functioning as test cases. In attempting to outline my framework for the analysis of the experiential dimension and the poetics of light in contemporary theatre (using cognitive semiotics), several difficulties arise.[2] First, I am not aware of any existing coherent conceptual (not technical!) methodology in the field of light design for theatre, since Appia's writings from the end of the 19th century; especially not one that incorporates semiotic and phenomenological-cognitive approaches. Through the approach that I take here, I hope to establish such a (new) conceptual framework, based on existing theories of semiotics, poetics, phenomenology, media theories and cognitive science. For this reason, the methodology in the following chapter derives from – and stands as a direct inseparable outcome of – the reflections in the previous, theoretical chapter. In view of the complexity of the phenomenon at hand, and the limited scope of the theoretical approaches discussed, I will integrate concepts and terminology from different fields in a 'rhizomatic' way. For example, while recalling the Peircean categories of signs, I do not ignore the corporeal experience. A partial reading of the two chapters might lead to errors in identifying the breadth of my intentions, or end up overlooking the application of *cognitive* semiotics to the study of light. Moreover, I will focus, in the analysis, on the meaning and experience of light from the perspective of the addressee, and I will not attempt to decode the author's intentions and compare them to the spectators' interpretations.

An additional challenge is how to write appropriately about such an intangible visual stimulus as light. Beyond the generally similar action of the eye, the physiology and the neurology and the neurological effect of light on the body, such as: heartbeat, perspiration, after-image, embodied aesthetic pleasure (Palmer 1998, 62–83), it is mostly a matter of subjective psychology. The suggestive, fleeting and somehow spiritual experience that light brings to the theatre can only be described, to a certain extent, by means of critical writing. With the photos included in my later performance analyses, I aim to assist the readers (who did not attend the performances in the theatre) in visualizing and engaging with the analysis of my own watching experience and consequent interpretation of selected images of light. It is also my aim, however, to encourage them to realize an experience of their own. From a theoretical point of departure, I set out to present a new, scholarly and practical approach that is intended to expand our awareness of, and enrich the discussion among theatre-makers, critics, scholars, students and theatre spectators on the manifold dimensions of light in contemporary theatre.

A few notes on practicality

In any theatre performance, one or multiple images of light are organized in a sequence of 'lighting states'. Each state is composed of either a single or several light source(s) and consists of various intensities, colours, shadows, shaped illuminated areas, different optical qualities and, possibly, physical movements of light beams. A lighting console stores all the light-images of the show and sequentially calls up each image with its pre-programmed transition. Accordingly, the metamorphoses of the light during a performance are 'scored' as cues and tied to both the timeline and the spatial manifestation (the sculpturing of space) – light exists as an actual object, but light and space are interdependent. We cannot perceive space in the absence of light, and vice versa. The experience of both is embodied and is a continuously accumulating *process*.

For methodological reasons, we will distinguish between two ways of looking at light; in each we will concentrate on different aspects of the phenomenon. In fact, these two perspectives are fused and simultaneously take part in the cognitive processes that occur with light; one enables us to *experience light on a corporeal level* (its aesthetic, embodied, emotional and pre-semiotic experience), while the other level is that of *significance* (this being the realm of cognitive semiotics, including the phenomenal function) and *representation* (poetics). (By no means, do I limit my use of the term 'representation' to an object standing for something else on the basis of verisimilitude. I use the term in line with the cognitive sciences that refer to the *imaginative* representation, initially triggered by the artefact and further processed by the addressee's imagination in the most open manner. It is not, therefore, the representation in the sense of theatre of Realism that is intended here.) Although methodologically required, the distinction between the two dimensions of light is made for the sake of clarity, as they constantly intermingle and affect one another when a performance is viewed. By distinguishing between these two dimensions of looking, I hope to draw attention to the broader spectrum of the different qualities of light in contemporary theatre, and to generate more information concerning light through the analytical process.

1   *Aesthetic analysis* – we will first process the perceptual characteristics of the light-image. Using this as a basis of the analysis, we can obtain a *descriptive observation* of the light, and describe what we actually see on a pre-semiotic level, borrowing from the technical jargon of lighting, as used by theatre practitioners. The focus is first on light alone, namely, what light – and no other medium – is doing. However, since all media in the theatre interact and create a complex web of interrelations, it is impossible to analyse one medium in a 'vacuum', that is, apart from the collective of media used. As mentioned above, light, for example, cannot be analysed without referring to the physical space accommodating it.[3] The analysis of light must first concentrate on light itself as much as possible, dwelling on the aesthetic level, and then spread out to address the relations between light and other media in the theatre. In the course of this analysis, we will determine what constitutes a light-image and how light interacts with other media, in terms of perceptual characteristics. The various components distinguished in the light-image will provide us with a basis upon which to construct the next stage.

2   *Semiotic and poetic analysis* – At this level, we consider which lighting elements are used as light-signs, what these signs are about and how these signs are used in a poetic way, per light-image. (As already stated, my framework focuses on the spectator's interpretation of the watching experience, and not on the activity (or supposed 'encodement') that the artist envisages while creating light-images. The perception and reception of light is at stake, while the intention of the absent

author remains, in fact, external.) Aesthetic features of light can become significant when light follows a cultural convention and matches a set of expectations on the part of the addressees (their schemata and scripts, in terms of cognitive psychology). Aesthetic features of light can also become significant when deviating from cultural conventions, as when, by illuminating the auditorium suddenly during the performance, the watching experience is interrupted. In addition, considering the formal characteristics of light with relation to the activity of another medium can make light meaningful as, for example, a concrete 'light-space' that acquires a poetic dimension by the activity of the performers within this space. Likewise, a certain coloured light aside an opera libretto reinforces the poetic dimension by way of mutual reflection. Another way by which we identify light-signs is when we become aware of the subliminal emotive effect that light has on our being and our conscious experience while watching a performance. In all these cases, as already noted in the previous chapter, light involves two kinds of perception that Solso calls 'nativistic' ('bottom-up') and 'directed' (the personal knowledge of the world as registered in one's memory).[4] The evoking of memories through association in the process of interpretation can make signs of light representational, in the sense of the Peircean 'semiotic drift' or the cognitive 'conceptual blending'.[5] This second level allows us, while combining semiotic and phenomenological perspectives, to analyse in greater depth the poetic strength of single light-images in invoking subconscious emotions into consciousness (feelings) and recalling personal memories or acquired ideas. The embodied experience and imaginative representation of light in the contemporary theatre will, thus, be analysed per light-image, with reference to *six grounds of representation*, which I will elaborate upon in due course.

Consequently, this analysis will pave the way for a broader, yet detailed view on the poetics of light and, later, to an expanded discussion of *the dramaturgy of light* in the performance under analysis.[6] This process is continuous and cumulative, but, for methodological reasons, we will first analyse separate light-images before retrospectively fusing them into a coherent *dramaturgy of light*. The dramaturgy of light comprises all the light-images that appear throughout the entire performance and, therefore, one can speak of it only after having watched the whole performance. By the term 'dramaturgy of light', I refer to *the overall development of light's poetics as progressing in time.* Light dramaturgy functions like a musical score, organizing the visual concepts during the whole performance according to a set of artistic decisions. It results in a structure with a poetic dimension that may be either clear or ambiguous but is, nevertheless, sensed to be carefully composed as a 'phantom' performer and a subliminal behaviour that cannot be based upon arbitrary decisions. When a light artist works with strong visual concepts of light, each individual light-image exists with a sense of purpose within the tapestry of the media, and is aimed at a certain effect on the addressees.

What should we seek out through the aesthetic analysis?

In contemporary theatre one can find an extensive palette of lighting technologies, more than theatre has ever known before. Likewise, the visual stimuli light is now capable of providing (and indeed does provide) call for a more adequate attention to the aesthetics of light. This conceptual framework proposes to examine first the perceptual characteristics of a single light-image. In the initial stage of the analysis, a descriptive approach is chosen to tackle the materiality involved in the making of the image. Here, we will study the composition of the light-image through the various technical components and the qualities of light and shadow, intensity, colour and shape, optics, kinetics distribution of light[7] or visible lighting objects in the space. One may then ask, regarding the light:

- *Which lighting elements generate what I see?*
- *What are the formal relations between various lighting elements (one supports the other, mutual-intensification or contrast)?*
- *How is the composition organized?*
- *If the lighting sources are visible – what are these 'objects', what do they look like and how can they be used?*
- *If the distribution of light originates from an object external to theatre lighting – from which initial context does the object originate?*

The last few decades have also shown an increasing interest on the part of light designers (and artists of Light-Art) to adopt and use objects with illumination capacities other than 'traditional' theatre lighting as legitimate instruments, even when the object was invented for different, non-artistic use in daily life. For example: fluorescent lamps for working spaces, low-pressure gaslight from industrial environments, HMI gaslight originally invented for the film sector and LED light that was first employed by optical-fibre telecommunications and used for little indicators on various devices. It is important to track the original context of non-traditional lighting sources, as this background information is valuable for the next stage of analysis.

For all lighting sources, the technical jargon of stage-lighting handbooks is used to describe various formal features of light and shadow, and to name lighting angles and optical qualities of different lenses. In addition, the internationally numbered coloured filters and gobos[8] are described using the standard technical terminology of the medium.

Having concentrated first on the perceptual or aesthetic features of light itself, we can then describe, one light-image at a time, the interrelations between the medium of light and the other media. For example, the way a light-image organizes a visual composition to draw more attention to specific areas in the space, using aesthetic features of light (such as intensity, shadow, colour, shape, optical qualities or kinetics) or the deconstruction of scenography by creating *'a (light-) space within a space'*. However, the interaction between lighting elements, space (scenography), performer, costume, video, music or text is examined and analysed, at this stage, without generating interpretations, since we concentrate on the perceptual, pre-semiotic configuration of the elements.

What should we seek out through the semiotic and poetic analysis?

On the basis of the observations of the aesthetics of light, we can proceed to the second stage of the analysis. At this stage, we examine single light-images through (cognitive-) semiotic and phenomenological perspectives and we first analyse the representational dimension of light alone, before proceeding to the analysis of the interrelations between light and other media. Regarding each light-image, we will ask:

- *How are the aesthetic features of the light corporeally experienced, and/or used as signs?*
- *What are the signs of light about? What ideas does the imaginative representation involve?*
- *What part does technology have in the embodied experience or representation?*
- *How are the signs used in a poetic or artistic way?*

Recalling Peirce's notions of *ground* and *quality* (Peirce 1868, 287–98), in which the ground is a pure abstraction of a quality or, alternatively, a quality (with its aesthetics) is something embodying a ground, I adopt and appropriate these concepts for my analytical framework. In the context of our discussion, the quality (the aesthetics) is carried by a light-image, while the ground of an imaginative representation points back to an abstraction, namely, the poetic dimension of light. We will therefore examine each light-image in relation to its functions and the processes it generates. As our point of departure, the questions given above will help us in articulating and defining the grounds of the function of light.

Six grounds of representation

I would like to introduce six fundamental grounds of representation that can be considered in relation to any light-image in contemporary theatre. These grounds are based upon my integration of the theoretical and historical studies of the medium of light with about twenty years of experience as a professional light designer, and are validated through the test-case performance analyses following this chapter. In no way do I want, through the conceptual framework I present, either to impose a strictly limiting categorization or to oversimplify the thinking about the embodied experience and representational potential of the medium of light. Rather, the six grounds that I am about to introduce are 'keys' for paving a path toward a thorough conceptual discussion of light-images, and light design as an artistic process. The future will reveal whether other scholars, light designers or theatre-makers will detect any additional grounds worthy to consider. Such observations will surely enrich the theoretical discourse on the medium of light in the theatre and hopefully also inspire artistic development and creativity. The final goal is not to pinpoint whether a certain light-image is drawn from one ground or another. Rather, the goal of the process is to analyse the representational ground embodied by the visual content of light and to produce more information (sensorial, emotive, semiotic) regarding that light-image. A second goal is to enhance the discussion on the poetic strength of the medium of light and to encourage the growth of its poetic potential for expression. This approach, which begins with an analytical observation of light's aesthetics and then continues towards the poetics of light using (cognitive-) semiotic and phenomenological perspectives, will increase the awareness of devoted theatre-goers and scholars, critics and theatre-makers regarding new possibilities of reference to the role light plays in the theatre.

I believe that the categorical presentation of light's *grounds of representation* in a schema (see the table below) will help in clarifying some of the subject's complexity, rather than oversimplifying it. Obviously, there are no clear or absolute boundaries between the various grounds. Light-images can combine a number of grounds of representation.

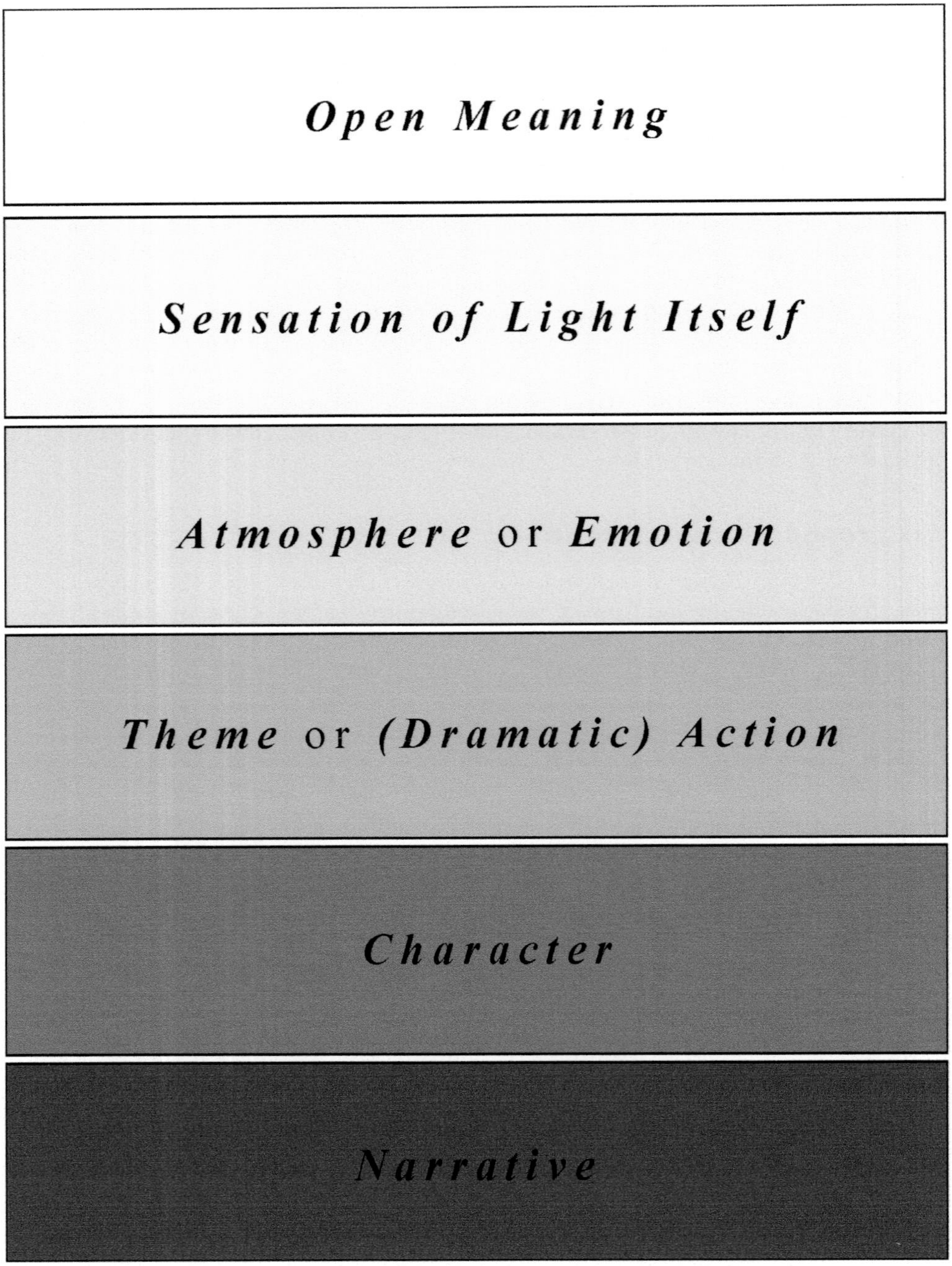

Figure 4.1 The Grounds of Representations of Light by Yaron Abulafia

The rationale underlying the order in which the grounds appear in the schema below derives from the increasing degree of autonomy and independence from the written/verbal text. This autonomy, or liberation from a mere illustration of the text, develops as we move away from the ground of 'narrative' – a characteristic aspect of contemporary theatre that I have elaborated upon in the introduction to this study.

I. Narrative – When the corporeal experience and the semiotic function of a light-image are grounded in the ***narrative***, light's aesthetic features are mainly designed to strengthen the illusion of fictive time and space, as these originate in the written or verbal text. The light then bears illustrative qualities, portraying aspects of the text on the basis of similarities. Light-images of this category visually complement the text's descriptive information while remaining loyal to the perceptual features pre-given by the text. Thus, there is a sort of doubling of signification through the two media and the stimuli reinforce each other.

The signs of light we detect in relation to *narrative* as ground can be:

1   *Iconic signs – image*: a high degree of similarity between the sign and its object; for example, when artificial lighting simulates daylight in angle, direction, and the colour of light according to the time of day.
2   *Iconic signs – diagram*: when the formal features of the sign (of light) represent an object by referring to structural similitude and establishing a logical relation between the two; for example, a white circle of light standing for the moon.
3   *Symbols*: in this case, the arbitrary relation of sign to object is subject to cultural conditioning, without any visual similarity between the two entities. In regard to theatre lighting, each genre develops its own conventions of representation. For example, a symbol of night-time in the theatre of Realism is often a deep blue illumination, although darkness has no particular colour.

The light-image embodying *narrative* as ground is linked to two kinds of text:

1   *Playwright's instructions* – written by the playwright and informing the artistic team, or other readers of the play, concerning the fictive conditions of light in the situation, space and time in any scene, entrances and exits of characters, their appearances and costumes, and some of the characters' activities. We learn about the physical environment in which the characters act, and so the readers can imagine the light as the text depicts. For example, the canonical *Macbeth* by William Shakespeare, Act I Scene I, starts with the instruction *"A desert Heath. Thunder and lightning. Enter three Witches"*.[9] When staging the play, it is up to the artistic team to choose whether or not to remain loyal to the descriptive representations that the playwright left in the body of the play.
2   *Spoken text in the performance* – this includes all the text with explicit or implicit reference to the light conditions of the scene, spoken by performers, in playback or in projected films. Nevertheless, there are performances, one of which is analysed later, that use no verbal text but point to metanarratives that are deeply rooted in our cultural identity, such as The Old and New Testaments. In fact, a light-image embodying the ground 'narrative' may also refer to a narrative when this narrative is 'silenced' and manifested in visual form.

The meaning of a light-image grounded in the narrative strengthens the (more or less evident) sense of fictive space and time as rendered by the text. Whether in a dramatic play, or in a contemporary text that tends to break with dramatic conventions, a light-image of this kind consists of aesthetic features that are already suggested *by the verbal text*. The light plays an illustrative role in relation to the written/spoken text and, indeed, the two media double each other's signs.

II. Character – When the corporeal experience and the semiotic function of a light-image are grounded in **character**, light's aesthetic features are designed to reflect upon the 'inner world' of a fictive character, its mental condition, or the interrelation between different characters, as informed by the written/verbal text. From a professional perspective, I would say that when creating a light-image of this kind, the designer relies on a higher degree of analysis and subjective interpretation of the text, focusing on the emotional and rational processes in which characters are involved in the course of the performance. The (imaginative) representation of the character's condition in light lets us see what we cannot hear. Nevertheless, due to our tendency to reason causally, the text still sets the tone as it diverts the interpretation of a visual experience in favour of a conceptual understanding – especially with such an intangible medium as light. Let me elucidate this ground using two examples: in one case, the light-image will refer to the dramatic escalation simultaneously with the actual happenings in the narrative; and, in the other case, the light will be 'looking ahead' of the progression of the narrative.

In the first case, imagine a sequence of light-images in which the first ones display a clear visibility with soft bright colours, gradually becoming more expressive and full of contrast, with harsh light against shadows; a development that represents the decline of a character as the narrative progresses.

In the second case, when looking ahead into the character's future fictive condition, light-images foreshadow the *peripeteia* (the sudden change of circumstances) and build up to a denouement throughout the performance. Some visual elements stand out as leitmotifs and evolve within earlier light-images until the moment of the *peripeteia*. The 'introductory' images prior to the *peripeteia* give rise to the aesthetic features that will later constitute the key image for the turning point of the character. Spectators can recall and retrospectively interpret the light-motif they watched earlier, by correlating the key image to the same stimuli that were introduced in the 'preparatory' images.

Development of visibility, in both cases, will be in accord with the development of the narrative; however, light will be adding an expressive dimension that does not explicitly originate from the text. Therefore, through reference to a fictive character, a light-image grounded in a character brings to the narrative expressive qualities that are unique to the medium of light and are created by the light designer. Light-images embodying this ground are interpretations of, and complementary to the verbal text, creating an expressive dimension that proceeds beyond that of the text.

The signs of light we detect in relation to *character* as ground can be:

1   *Iconic signs – diagram*: when the formal features of the sign (of light) represent an object linked to the fictive condition of the character on the basis of structural similarity, thus, establishing a logical relation between the two. For example: the gradual darkening and increasing expressiveness in visibility mentioned above.

2   *Iconic signs – metaphor*: the sign goes beyond the mere identification of the object on the basis of formal characteristics; for example, the case of light 'looking ahead', as noted above.

3   *Symbols*: in this case, again, the arbitrary relation of sign to object is subject to cultural conditioning, without any visual similarities relating the two entities. Regarding theatre lighting, each genre develops its own conventions of representation. For example, a symbol of affection in the theatre of Realism is often the illumination in warm skin tints, on a rose to red scale.

III. Theme or (dramatic) action – When the representation through a light-image is grounded in the ***theme*** or ***(dramatic) action***, light's aesthetics is used to reflect on the theme of the play, or on its central (dramatic) action, as distinguished from mere activity.[10] Light is now based upon a deeper analysis of the text, involving the narrative and the themes and (dramatic) actions that underlie the narrative plot. The play, then, is abstracted from its linguistic substance, and is regarded as the 'vehicle' or the 'agent' of the themes and dramatic actions.

Any reading of a dramatic or post-dramatic text for the stage will eventually lead to unique and differently formulated themes and (dramatic) actions for each production. The process is one of subjective interpretation of the text through the negotiation of its meaning by the reader (and by the light designer too!). Likewise, light-images that relate to this the (third) ground theme or (dramatic) action actually *mediate the dramaturgy of the written/verbal text into the medium of light*, following the interpretation of the text for a particular production according to the artistic team. Representation (of light) is thus still bound to the verbal text, albeit in a looser way. Rather than focusing on the literal text or the qualities of the acting within a scene, light embodies central ideas pertaining to the dramaturgy of the performance. Light-images of this sort are *metaphors* (Peirce) that encourage the addressee to explore the formal characteristics of light in order to contemplate their significance. A light-image embodying this ground can also be an *index*, when the perceptual characteristics of light lead to a theme or (dramatic) action through a relation of cause and effect.

That said, in performances that do not use any texts, as in the case of Romeo Castellucci's production which will be analysed hereafter, theme and action can still be embodied in light, subject to the stimuli from other media that we detect as signs. Since Performance Art and Happenings diverted the focal point from the Aristotelian dramatic action to physical activity occurring in space and time, contemporary (post-dramatic) theatre performances occasionally feature non-dramatic actions as fundamental performative elements. The qualities of the light-image can refer to this activity and can thus be based on ***non-dramatic action*** as ground. The light, in this case, can refer to culturally rooted narratives the performance points to without actually staging and narrating them. Well-known themes or non-dramatic actions, enriched by the signs of light, in a sense 'dissolve' into the performance, enriching its poetic dimension.

The signs of light we detect in relation to *theme or (dramatic) action* as ground can be:

1   *Iconic sign – metaphor*: the sign goes beyond the mere identification of the object by associating its formal characteristics in relation to its object, namely, the theme or the (dramatic) action that arise from the written play and/or the performance.

2   *Index* and *Iconic sign – diagram*: a sign that holds a relation of cause and effect with its object, or a logical relation; for example, by highlighting a key element in the space so as to reflect on the theme or the action.

3   *Symbol*: the arbitrary darkening of the auditorium during the performance is a cultural convention, and any deviation from it – namely, illuminating the auditorium, becomes a symbol.

IV. Atmosphere or emotion – The fourth possible ground of representation is that of *atmosphere* or *emotion*. The quality of light related to this ground is among the most acclaimed properties of theatre lighting, and theatre professionals and the audience at large often refer to it. Nevertheless, the broad scope of this quality requires elaboration. When the semiotic function of a light-image is grounded in an *atmosphere* or *emotion*, the influence of the verbal text and the narrative plot is even looser than was the case with the previous three grounds. A light-image embodying this ground (as well as the following two) gives on to the imagination of the spectator through the visual dimension more than through the verbal text. The aesthetics of light is now used to evoke *a transcendental realm of emotions and atmospheres*, raising levels of physiological and/or neural activity and aiming at an emotive experience. Bruce McConachie and Elizabeth Hart, in *Performance and Cognition: Theatre Studies and The Cognitive Turn*, refer to the role of emotional reactions in influencing the degree of attentiveness and the highlighting of selective moments in the course of the performance. They write:

> Because the mind/brain is part of the body – and because emotions and feelings (which are emotions brought into consciousness) produce physio-chemical responses – affective responses become an ongoing part of the feedback loop of spectating. In effect, the body's pro-active bio-chemistry shapes each percept and "tells" the mind/brain what is important, enabling the spectator to "pay more attention" to moments in the performance.
>
> (McConachie and Hart 2006, 6)

As a designer, I would say that this type of light-image not only intensifies the atmosphere of the text or represent the emotion of a character, but also casts its impact upon us – the addressees – directly, and becomes a first-rate source of atmosphere and emotional effect.

Light-images whose representational function is grounded in an atmosphere or emotion are often found in classical ballet and contemporary dance, dance theatre (inspired by *Ausdruckstanz*), Performance Art, movement theatre, and music theatre, where the text is no longer the first medium in the hierarchy. Because most of the genres mentioned above frequently do without (any) coherent and rounded off dramatic narrative, light designers have more freedom to contribute their own visual world of atmospheres and emotions with a broad palette of light and shade, of colours and patterns, affecting the perception and mood of the spectators. Consequently, the expressive dominance of light increases, though in tune, if proportionally and sensitively done, with the other media in the performance. Experiencing the light-images in this category truly becomes what Merlin Donald calls 'cognitive engineering', when he refers to the artist's deliberate effort to control attention and engineer the experiences of others.[11] Because light can be such an ephemeral and intangible medium, the effect on the conscious addressee can be perceived as 'transparent', resembling the film score or soundscapes that affect our emotions and create atmospheres without calling for explicit attention. Artificial light, because of the pre-semiotic, survival skills that link to light in nature, manipulates one of our primal sensory modalities and has a powerful impact on our sense of being, our mood, on our feeling safe or endangered (Pinker 1997, 537). No wonder that a sudden change in light conditions in the theatre can make us feel alert and vulnerable.

Therefore, in view of their stimulus–response properties and corporeal and emotional effects, the signs of light we detect in relation to *atmosphere or emotion* as ground belong to the category of the *index*. This has to do with the relation of cause and effect between the (indexical) sign and its object. Thus certain feelings can be provoked by means of specific forms of coloured light.

In contemporary theatre, when the ground of the corporeal experience and representational function of a light-image is *atmosphere* or *emotion*, light gains a more autonomous position. Light evolves to greater 'autonomy' by viscerally affecting our senses and arousing our deepest emotions, on the primal level on which humans experience light in both nature and culture. Light-images of this sort are distinctive in their highly sensed expressive potency and can be used very ambiguously by designers – first as direct stimuli and, if evoking rational thinking – as signs. Therefore, in performances that include no verbal text at all, light-images will mostly embody this, as well as the next two grounds of representation.

V. Sensation of light itself – When the semiotic function of a light-image is grounded in the ***sensation of light itself***, light's aesthetics generates the following one or two qualities:

Spectacularity, based upon a direct aesthetic pleasure derived from light, and the appreciation we owe to the precision and craftsmanship involved in the making of the light-image. In the previous chapter, I referred to seven universal aesthetic features distinguished by Denis Dutton, features that relate to the creation and appreciation of art in culture. Dutton's reference to human admiration for the performance of 'skill and virtuosity' in the arts is, perhaps, the feature that is most equivalent pertaining to the quality of light referred to here as 'spectacularity'.

Hypermediacy, as coined by Jay David Bolter and Richard Grusin in their book *Remediation: Understanding New Media*, refers to the (postmodern) emphasis on the explicit presence of media technology in the artefact (1999, 31–44).[12] Hypermediacy, in the context of this study, means that light's aesthetics underlines the presence of the medium of light, its materiality and actual application in the performance. In this circumstance the light-image does not influence our cognition using 'transparent' qualities, disappearing behind the scenes – so to speak. Rather, it exposes its constituent components and the *active presence* of technology is highly sensed.

Through both the qualities of spectacularity and hypermediacy, "complex technologies in performance may also serve as symbols of power and authority, at the simplest where the stage knows or 'owns' something that the spectator does not", as Christopher Baugh writes (Baugh 2005, 1). While Baugh in his historical study refers to the authority and power of the ruler, as manifested in his theatre, I have in mind the authority of the contemporary theatre-maker. "Technologies may have meanings in and of themselves, and are not simple servants to the mechanistic needs of scenic representation. They are an expression of a relationship with the world and reflect complex human values and beliefs" (Baugh 2005, 8). Furthermore, light-images may explore the idea of *lumière pour lumière*, or light's self-reference, not only as the tangible and material dimension of a representation, but also as an imaginative and meaningful dimension, contributing to the cognitive work of the addressees. As a means of arousing corporeal experiences and imaginative representations, light is a vibrant force.

Light Art shares with light design in the theatre the two qualities mentioned above. In Chapter 2, I discussed the emergence of Light Art as an influential movement in recent art history and examined several of its founding ideas and their relevance to new ways of thinking on theatre lighting. With both visual artists and spectators having realized that light is a medium in its own right, and that it is possible to take light to the fore as *the* object of artistic expression and experience, the impact on theatre lighting is groundbreaking – and I predict that these tendencies will develop even further in the near future.[13] Light evolved in the visual arts with brand new aesthetic and poetic qualities of expression, raising questions concerning visual perception and epistemology, engagement with the addressee, the relation between art and brain – to mention but a few that continue to inspire light designers, directors and choreographers in the contemporary theatre.[14]

The signs of light we detect in relation to *sensation of light itself* as ground can be:

1   *Iconic sign – diagram*: the formal features of the diagram (sign of light) can represent 'behaviour' or 'authority', as technology manifests through structural similitude and the establishing of logical relations between sign and object.
2   *Iconic sign – metaphor:* the sign of light abandons verisimilitude in favour of an analogous relation to its object, encouraging 'drift' in the associations concerning the meaning of the sign.
3   *Index:* when the sign points to its object in a relationship of cause and effect (for example, when we experience an aesthetic pleasure out of an active pattern of light and, likewise, of the ability to predict its 'behaviour').

To conclude: spectacularity and hypermediacy in a light-image can be genuinely independent of a linguistic substrate. The interrelationship of this kind of self-referential light-image and any other medium (including text) induces us to negotiate the meaning of the sensation of light in the context of the performance. This kind of light-image is highly remarkable in terms of liberating the medium of light from the traditional hierarchy whereby the written/verbal text is primary, and pointing to what light, and only light (!) can do best.

VI. Open meaning – The sixth and last ground of representation that constitutes this conceptual framework for the analysis of light is **open meaning**. Light-images that embody the ground of *open meaning* are highly complex and the signs of light are intriguing and challenging. Peirce writes that "A sign is something by knowing which we know something more" (Pierce, CP 8.332), and Eco elaborates: "The sign is an instruction for interpretation, a mechanism which starts from an initial stimulus and leads to all its illative consequences" (Eco 1984, 26). A light-image that embodies *open meaning* is an extraordinary instance of semiosis or interpretation, in which the addressee *'knows something more'* only after carefully investigating the signs and negotiating meaning. The process initially begins with identifying stimuli of light as light-signs, while their meaning remains obscure and cannot easily be decided upon. In a process of 'drift' (Peirce) or 'unlimited semiosis' (Eco), light-images that are based on *open mean-ing* as ground give rise to the mobilization of ideas in a 'rhizomatic', associative and adventurous way. In cognitive science this is known as 'blending' – an interpretation process involving relations of "change, identity, space, time, cause-effect, part-whole, representation, role, analogy, dis-analogy, property, similarity category, intentionality, and uniqueness" (McConachie and Hart 2006, 20). The hermeneutic effort involved in negotiating open meaning relies upon an extensive use of *directed perception* (Solso) – memory-based experiences and personal knowledge are stimulated as a reaction to exter-nal triggers that Nativistic perception identifies. Directed perception is simultaneously processed in cognition through *image-schemes* (Johnson) – mental patterns that provide a structured comprehension of various experiences. There is no single or direct relation between the stimuli and possible meanings; in that sense, the meaning is 'open'. No code is available.

Could it be that the artist in light leaves the spectators to complement the elements that he intentionally keeps uncertain? "The reader", writes Ricoeur, "is invited to do the work that the artist delights in undoing" (Ricoeur 1991, 150). A situation of this kind might be pleasant for some spectators while irritating others; challenging the engage-ment with the addressees can become a source of restlessness caused by a Sisyphean quest for a settling meaning. The 'openness' of a representation is not an arbitrary qual-ity but a constructed mechanism left by the maker. It plays a central role in the experi-ence of the addressees and the interpretation process they perform. One could say that *open meaning shifts the ground to the cognitive processes of the spectators*, to their feelings (the outcome of subconscious emotions turning into embodied quality we are conscious of), memories and imagination, and by so doing the cognitive process concerning any rep-resentation (or any light-image) extends in scope.

That said, the light-image still intrigues and incites us to produce meaning, since the visual information that light creates remains ambiguous and undefined, despite being captivating for the spectators. In his essay *Postmodern Design*, Arnold Aronson writes that: "Postmodern design is a dissonant reminder that no single point of view is possible, even within a single image. We are confronted with what Charles Russell calls "an art of shifting perspective, of double self-consciousness, of local and extended meaning" (cited in Aronson 2008, 14). The idea of open meaning also calls to mind Roland Barthes' notion of 'third meaning', a category of meaning that exceeds the more stable categories of informational and symbolic meanings. McKinney and Butterworth describe the encounter with Barthes's third meaning as follows:

> He identifies signifiers . . . but cannot say exactly what is being signified. This third kind of meaning is 'persistent and fleeing, smooth and elusive' and cannot be absorbed intellectually. It is 'obtuse' in the sense that it is difficult to explain, but this difficulty does not lessen its impact for the viewer.
>
> (McKinney and Butterworth 2010, 165)

I believe that when a light-image embodies *open meaning* as its ground, the signs of light are flexible to such an extent that their relevance to a category of signification (e.g. icon, index, symbol) depends solely on the cognition of the addressees. The ground is 'open' because the embodied process of interpretation effectively does not have to stop – it is engineered by the individual body-mind-brain of the addressee. The signs of light can be so distinctive and self-directed, almost narcissistically, that no meaningful relation is found by relating light to other media. A light-image grounded in *open meaning* represents the most autonomous performance of light in the theatre, and it functions similarly to works of Light Art, becoming, for the addressees, the locus for a visceral experience of light, space and time, visual perception and the negotiation of meaning.

An example of the engagement with light grounded in open meaning is taken from the production of *In the Solitude of Cotton Fields* by Bernard-Marie Koltès, directed by Yael Kramsky, with light and scenography designed by myself at the Herzliya Theatre, Israel, 2009. From the very beginning of the creative process, Kramsky and I chose to locate the performers on a bare black stage in which the light functions as a major force and affective entity that dictates the pace and enhances the visual dimension of the piece, by suddenly introducing atmospheres that reflect upon the emotions of the characters of the Dealer and the Client (as they are called in the play), and thus aim at affecting the emotions of the spectators.

One particular lighting element repeatedly haunted both the general public and theatre critics, being referred to as highly significant, mysterious and outstanding. This was a light-sculpture composed of long diagonal construction filled with bulbs in saturated orange, with the capacity for individual control (Figures 4.2 and 4.3). The light-sculpture performed pre-programmed intensity effects that created different patterns of movement within the line of the bulbs, simulating a stream, flickering, changing thickness etc. Consequently, the spectators' awareness of the medium of light increased profoundly, even more so because the presence of the sculpture did not directly emanate from (the text of) the play.

In the newspaper *Ha'aretz*, critic Michael Handelsaltz, the first critic I refer to, describes an empty, underlit stage with *a gallows along whose entire length some weak red lights flickered* (Handelsaltz 2010). Further on in this critique, Handelsaltz notes that near the end of the performance, the Client *'conquered' the oil lamp* of the Dealer and the Dealer was manoeuvred *under the gallows*. "Then we come to the question 'With which weapon' asked by the Client, and it is unclear whether the meaning is the goods, a duel or execution. *The red lights on the diagonal gallows increase and then turn off in a sequence, and we are left in the dark with many unsolved questions*" (Handelsaltz 2010; emphases added). Figure 4.4 presents these moments.

Shai Bar-Ya'akov, the theatre reviewer of *Yedioth Ahronoth* (Israel's most popular daily newspaper), notes:

> A large abstract sculpture that looks like a gallows, leans sideways or as *a static graph that drifts in the space and twinkles* with red points of light that switch on in different rhythms. Around this object, the lighting designer Yaron Abulafia created *an impressive weave of changing lights, the connection of which with the situation is not really clear*.
>
> (Bar-Ya'akov 2010; emphases added)

On the website *Habama* ('The stage' in Hebrew), Tzvi Goren writes that "in the centre of the stage stood, *as if it was about to fall*, an abstract apparatus with mounted red bulbs, which turn on occasionally, not necessarily in a clear order" (Goren 2010). "At the end", he adds, "when all the red bulbs burn together in the same apparatus, the feeling that it is a gallows is confirmed".

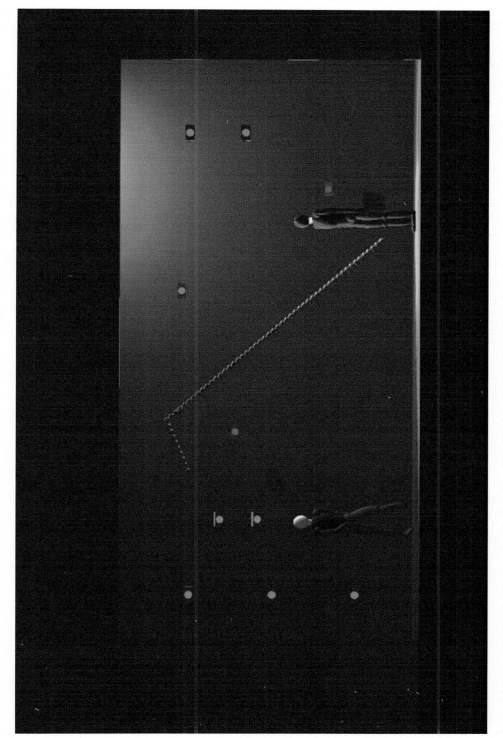

Figure 4.2 Yaron Abulafia: A computer rendering of the light for *In the Solitude of Cotton Fields*

Figure 4.3 Yael Kramsley, *In the Solitude of Cotton Fields* by Bernard-Marie Koltès Nimrod Bergman as the Client, light and scenography by Yaron Abulafia, Herzliya Theatre, Israel, 2009. Photo: Noam Wise

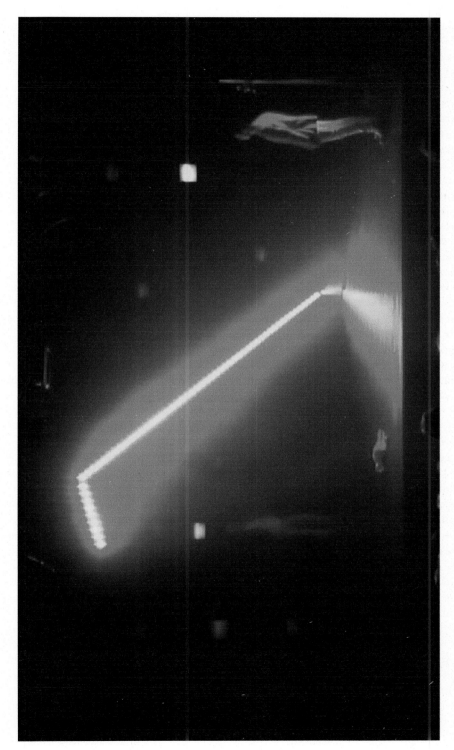

Figure 4.4 Yael Kramsley, *In the Solitude of Cotton Fields* by Bernard-Marie Koltès Doron Tavori and Nimrod Bergman in the final moments of the performance, just before the bulbs start turning off one by one, from up-left toward the floor. Light and scenography by Yaron Abulafia, Herzliya Theatre, Israel, 2009

Numerous spectators referred to the light in the performance, and the light-sculpture in particular, as if it was *a third actor*, sharing the space with the two human actors. It was an enigmatic lighting element for many in the audience, who wondered what this was, and commented that they had never seen such a 'thing' in the theatre. The absence of a clear meaning sparked increasing curiosity and speculation among the spectators. In the experience of many, the light-sculpture acquired a semi-human character through a process of personification of the light. One spectator noted that, for her, these lights "behaved as the pulse of the scene" – metaphorically suggesting a human context through an analogy between the activity of the light and the action in the scene; while at the same time, the reference used musical terms ('pulse'). Another spectator said that for him the sculpture was a phallic element, perhaps because the Dealer sat for a short while on the black platform with this array of lamps between his legs; or, perhaps he was sensitive to an erotic dimension developing, remaining yet unfulfilled, in the relationship of the Dealer and the Client.

Interestingly, critics and spectators not only gave different interpretations to their embodied experiences, but also complemented the object they looked at with emotions and associations of their personal knowledge in ways that affected what they saw (or what they believed they saw). For example, the drifting of the object that Bar-Yaakov writes about takes place in his imagination, since the sculpture was fixed, as if erupting from the stage. In his reference to the red bulbs, Goren associates the orange lamps with precious stones set in a piece of jewellery, as he uses the verb 'mounted' in his description. There is a measure of embellishment in the description of his embodied experience, indicating an aesthetic pleasure and a delightful experience derived from this lighting-element. Perhaps this pleasure relieved from the confusion and sense of effort involved in pinpointing a meaning for this stimulus.

What were these orange lamps for me? There is no visual reference to the sculpture as a gallows or any similar device, neither through the mise-en-scène of the actors nor in the written play. Among the many possible ideas we raised concerning the function of the light-sculpture, Kramsky and I did not think of or foresee the interpretation of a gallows. The image of the sculpture possibly resembled a collapsing 'street lamp' for some addressees, while on a more visceral and less illustrative level, the angle, position and dimensions of the object together could elicit anxiety and a sense of alertness concerning the performance space and proximity. The composition of this light-object freezes its movement downward and, at the same time, divides the stage image into two territories. It derived from a feeling I had regarding the play: that time is suspended, the space is vague, and the characters resemble agents that mouth philosophical notions rather than having any will of their own.

At the beginning of the play, the Dealer and the Client speak metaphorically about two points connected by a straight line, and draw conclusions concerning their encounter according to their rhetorical needs (the line is a 'bridge' between two sides, but is also the single existing path, with no alternative routes). Indeed, this versatile use of the orange lamps, with internal motion effects inside the sculpture caused by changes in dynamic intensity, constituted a visual 'pulse' different for each scene of the performance. In every scene, next to each monologue, different light-images and light effects characterized and defined the embodied experience of the addressees through variations of energy, motion and tempo, as an autonomous visual journey that one could take through the performance.

Therefore, when the semiotic and phenomenal function of light is grounded in *open meaning*, light becomes a phantom performer with its own 'behaviour', its own logic and reasoning – the 'drama' is within *light itself*, and *in between the medium of light and the addressees*. A light-image that embodies *open meaning* as ground, seeks its inspiration beyond the written drama and its conventions, and will shift the weight from the light-text interrelation to that of *light and addressee*. I would like to conclude with a quotation from Adolphe Appia that hauntingly reflects the ground of open meaning in light: "Where other arts say: 'That *means*', music says, 'That *is*' (Richard Wagner). Where form and colour try to express something, light says: 'I *am*'; forms and colours will only exist through me'" (Appia, *La Vie Musicale*, 1 April 1908 cited in Palmer 2013, 80).

Dramaturgy of light

Once we have watched a whole performance, we can retrospectively track the course of our embodied experiences derived from light, and reinterpret memorable scenes and selected light-images, also in relation to the use of other media. The last stage of the analysis, therefore, concentrates on the *dramaturgy of light*. This term stands for *the development of light's poetics in time*, the way(s) in which the light-images are structured and constitute the overall visual concept of light in the performance. As spectators, any sequence of light-images stimulates our unconscious emotions, conscious feelings, associations and ideas concerning the separate images, but also the relation between the images, how they interconnect, and what sense is to be made of them. In *Cognitive Science, Literature, and the Arts*, Hogan describes a process that occurs in cognition, as part of our watching experience (although there he refers to cinema): "Specifically, given an array of fragments, we construct agents, objects, actions, events, and causal sequences, hoping that we 'get the story straight'" (Hogan 2003, 116). Additionally, Hogan notes that this procedure is carried out using schemas familiar in a culture, patterns of thought that are familiar to the members of that particular culture: "As Branigan explains, 'a perceiver uses a schema to automatically fill in any data that is deemed to be missing' in the text'" (Hogan 2003, 117).

Thus, dramaturgy of light pertains to the organization of central ideas of the light designer and the creative team, using forms of light (aesthetics) to embody these ideas by a sequence of light-images. Dramaturgy of light reflects a suggestive interpretation of the piece by the light designer, including the constantly changing relations between the experience and signification of the light and the other media, for example: (1) a relation of *support and illustration*; (2) a relation of *mutual reflection*; and (3) a relation of *contrast or counterpointing*. Conforming to or deviating from known light-related conventions in a performance is a highly relevant characteristic in dramaturgy of light, for example: using the auditorium lights during the show, breaking away from the conventions of the performative genre. Moreover, the setting of tempo in a performance, as well as the experience that light can generate by calling attention to itself, to the medium of light at work, or by becoming transparent and 'disappear' in the background are integral in any dramaturgy of light. Altogether, the interpretation and reconstruction of the piece in light suggests new poetic ways through which to look at, and possibly to feel toward and think about a performance.

This retrospective 'close look' is the last stage in the conceptual framework for the analysis of the semiotics and poetics of light in contemporary theatre that I propose in this study. The framework is used in the analysis of five contemporary theatre performances in the following chapters in order to examine its usefulness.

Notes

1   *The Semiotics of Theater* by Erika Fischer-Lichte and André Helbo's essay "Light and Performance: A Few Methodological Remarks", *Semiotica* 136-1/4 (November 2001), pp. 403–8 exemplify the writing about semiotics of light with reference to the traditional conventions of the theatre of Realism such as 'camera work' (close-ups and blackouts as a sign for a new space and time), light supporting the fictive illusion of the performance and the supporting of other signs systems.

2   For the sake of clarity, the previous chapter focused on the advantages and shortcomings of each theoretical framework for the analysis of theatre performance, and led to the integrated use of various theories in the analytical effort; therefore, although I distinguish between the more general field of semiotics as the study of signs and signification processes in culture with its pragmatic, semantic and syntactic dimensions, and the field of poetics, which is the study of signs in an artistic context, I still refer to both dimensions in relation to the functioning of light.

3   Even visual artists such as James Turrell and Olafur Eliasson, who make a great effort, in their works, to unbalance and reestablish the relation of the viewers with the space they are watching, cannot escape the physical space while trying to concentrate on the perception of light.

4   See in Chapter 3 and R.L. Solso, *The Psychology of Art and the Evolution of the Conscious Brain*, Cambridge, MA: The MIT Press, 2003, p. 21.

5   For an elaboration on Peirce's, and later Eco's, notion of 'semiotic drift', and on conceptual blending, see Chapter 3.

6   A dramaturgical approach to light design is valid for any kind of contemporary theatre performance, whether the performance employs a dramatic or non-dramatic text, or even when text is absent. The contemporary approach to the construction of the theatrical event varies on that of the text-based theatre of Realism in many ways. More on this subject can be found in the introduction to this study.

7   Lighting technologies available and used in the theatre today are capable of projecting a still image, exactly like video can, or create effects of a kinetic image or texture like clouds, fire, water and smoke. Some visual and optical manipulations of an image can be done with lighting fixtures, as an alternative to video. On the other hand, video can project light to illuminate the space, or create atmosphere in a non-narrative manner. The latter lies within the scope of this study and is a phenomenon that I consider as a form of lighting. When it becomes a narrative element, I consider it as film.

8   Gobos are projection devices made of metal or heat-resistant glass that shape the field of light into selected forms or patterns.

9   *Macbeth*, Act I, Scene I, *The Complete Works of William Shakespeare*, London: Wordsworth Library Collection, 2007.

10   David Ball explains the structural aspect of dramatic action and compares it to the 'doings' of characters, like comparing fundamental strategy to limited tactics. Without dwelling on theory of drama here, a dramatic character often confronts other characters or powers (antagonists) that prevent him or her from reaching an overall aim; so dramatic conflict unavoidably comes to the fore. The conflict lasts as long as the character has its motivation to continue acting, until a stasis is reached. A stasis can be reached either when the main character accomplishes its goal or when realizing that the aim is unattainable. With the stasis the play ends. D. Ball, *Backwards and Forwards: A Technical Manual for Reading Plays*, edited by Curtis L. Clark, Carbondale and Edwardsville, IL: Southern Illinois University Press, 1983, pp. 19–31.

11   For elaboration see Chapter 3 on Donald or M. Donald, "Art and Cognitive Evolution", in Mark Turner (ed.), *The Artful Mind, Cognitive Science and the Riddle of Human Creativity*, New York: Oxford University Press, 2006, p. 4.

12   According to Bolter and Grusin, 'hypermedia' is a representational mode, the goal of which is to remind the spectator of the medium. Normally, this is done through the exposure of the techniques involved in, and the production process of, the image. Cf. *Remediation: Understanding New Media* (1999), pp. 31–44.

13 The rising number of publications on Light Art, and discussions about Light Art at international events on performance design (e.g. at World Stage Design 2013 – a conference moderated by prominent scholar and light designer Nick Moran on *The Aesthetics of Lighting*), indicate the increasing enthusiasm to explore these new (poetic) possibilities in light design for contemporary theatre.

14 Contemporary theatre, on the other hand, could accommodate this development in the medium of light as part of a broader change that it went through: liberation from the traditional hierarchy among media, the decline in the position of the text as the leading medium, the 'death of the character' (Fuchs), technological influences on aesthetics, rise in 'performativity' (Lehmann), influence of the digital culture on watching habits and growth in the cognitive capacity of theatre spectators, and more . . . (cf. the Introduction).

References

Aronson, A., *Postmodern Design* in *Looking into the Abyss: Essays on Scenography*, Ann Arbor, MI: University of Michigan Press, 4th edition, 2008 (first published in 2005).

Ball, D., *Backwards and Forwards: A Technical Manual for Reading Plays*, edited by Curtis L. Clark, Carbondale and Edwardsville, IL: Southern Illinois University Press, 1983.

Bar-Ya'akov, S., a review of the theatre performance *In the Solitude of Cotton Fields*, *Yedioth Ahronoth* daily newspaper, 17 March 2010 (translated from Hebrew by the author).

Baugh, C., *Theatre, Performance and Technology: The Development of Scenography in the Twentieth Century*, general editors: Graham Ley and Jane Milling, Basingstoke, UK and New York: Palgrave Macmillan, 2005.

Bolter, J. D. and Grusin, R., *Remediation: Understanding New Media*, Cambridge, MA and London: The MIT Press, 1999.

Donald, M., *Art and Cognitive Evolution* in Mark Turner (ed.), *The Artful Mind, Cognitive Science and the Riddle of Human Creativity*, New York: Oxford University Press, 2006.

Eco, U., *The Limits of Interpretation*, Bloomington and Indianapolis, IN: Indiana University Press, 1990.

Eco, U., *Semiotics and the Philosophy of Language*, London: Macmillan Press, 1984.

Eco, U., *A Theory of Semiotics*, Bloomington, IN and London: Indiana University Press, 1976.

Fischer-Lichte, E., *The Semiotics of Theater*, translated by Jeremy Gaines and Doris L. Jones, Bloomington and Indianapolis, IN: Indiana University Press, 1992.

Fuchs, E., *The Death of Character: Perspectives on Theatre after Modernism*, Bloomington and Indianapolis, IN: Indiana University Press, 1996.

Goren, T., a critique on the production of *In the Solitude of Cotton Fields* on the website *Habama* http://www.habama.co.il/Pages/Description.aspx?Subj=1&Area=1&ArticleID=12061 (last accessed 11 October, 2010).

Handelsaltz, M., a review on the theatre performance *In the Solitude of Cotton Fields*, *Ha'aretz* newspaper, Israel, 17 March 2010 (translated from Hebrew by the author).

Helbo, A., "Light and Performance: A Few Methodological Remarks", *Semiotica* 136-1/4 2001, edited by Richard John Harvey.

Hogan, P. C., *Cognitive Science, Literature, and the Arts: A Guide for Humanists*, London and New York: Routledge, 2003.

Holmberg, A., *The Theatre of Robert Wilson*, Cambridge: Cambridge University Press, first published 1996, reprinted 1998.

McConachie, B. and Hart, F. E., *Performance and Cognition: Theatre Studies and The Cognitive Turn*, edited by B. McConachie and F. E. Hart, London and New York: Routledge, 2006.

McKinney, J. and Butterworth, P., *The Cambridge Introduction to Scenography*, New York: Cambridge University Press, 2010 (first edition 2009).

Palmer, R., *The Lighting Art: The Aesthetics of Stage Lighting Design*, 2nd edition, Upper Saddle River, NJ: Prentice-Hall, Inc., 1998.

Palmer, S., *Light, Reading in Theatre Practice*, Basingstoke, UK: Palgrave Macmillan, 2013.

Peirce, C. S., *(1931–58) Collected Papers (CP)*, vol. 2, Cambridge, MA: Harvard University Press.

Peirce, C. S., *On a New List of Categories: Proceedings of the American Academy of Arts and Sciences* 7, CP 1551, 1868.

Pinker, S., *How the Mind Works*, New York: Allen Lane and The Penguin Press, 1997.

Ricoeur, P., "Mimesis and Representation", in *A Ricoeur Reader*, edited by M. J. Valdes, Toronto and Buffalo, NY: University of Toronto Press, 1991.

Shakespeare, W., *The Complete Works of William Shakespeare, Macbeth,* Act I, Scene I, London: Wordsworth Library Collection, 2007.

Solso, R. L., *The Psychology of Art and the Evolution of the Conscious Brain*, Cambridge, MA: The MIT Press, 2003.

Introduction to the performance analyses

In each of the following five chapters I present an analysis of a contemporary theatre performance, relating a phenomenological reflection on the experience of light to an analysis of the aesthetics, semiotics and poetics of light in that particular production. The purpose of these analyses is twofold: first, to demonstrate the validity and the usefulness of the new conceptual framework that I have developed in this study, taking five performances by prominent theatre-makers as test cases; and, second, to present five different performances that together provide a panoramic view of the state-of-the-art approaches to, and trends in, light design in contemporary post-dramatic theatre. I will provide an analytical insight into the creative work of diverse theatre-makers – light designers and directors – and their attitudes vis-à-vis the position of light design in the creative process of a contemporary theatre production.

Undoubtedly, there are many other prominent artists, an analysis of whose work could have greatly contributed to this book; unfortunately, however, there is no room for all of them here. I do not pretend to offer a complete overview of all the major contemporary performances, or to provide an encyclopaedic account of the most influential artists (directors and designers) of our time. Rather, I seek to present trends in the use of light that are original in the creation of both sensorial effects and representations, as well as to substantiate the conceptual framework as a valuable method for the analysis of light. The selection process of the performances for analysis involved many factors, such as the possibility of watching the performance live in the theatre, the intention to present a diversity of performances and their light designs, and the limit set to the number of performances that could reasonably be discussed in proportion to the entire study.

The five performances that will be analysed are (in their order of appearance):

Madama Butterfly by Giacomo Puccini – directed by Robert Wilson

On the Concept of the Face, Regarding the Son of God by Romeo Castellucci

Stifters Dinge by Heiner Goebbels

Rechnitz by Elfriede Jelinek – directed by Jossi Wieler

Peer Gynt by Henrik Ibsen – directed by David Zinder

The analysis, as explained in the previous chapter, consists of two stages in which the light on stage is thoroughly examined from a number of different perspectives. In the first stage I focus on *the aesthetics of the light-image*, its perceptual features, the technical description of what the image looks like and what lighting elements construct the light-image. This 'technical' report focuses on the light, but it also includes references to the effect of light on the spectator's perception, in conjunction with that particular light-image, of the scenography, the performance space, and the performers and their costumes. The second stage of the analysis takes a *phenomenological, as well as a semiotic and poetic perspective*. Here, I ponder upon the corporeal experience of light, and I analyse the *signs* that light creates. More in particular, I will focus on how these light signs are used to create a poetic dimension, engaging the spectator on a corporeal, emotional and conceptual level. The poetic dimension of light is analysed per light-image, with reference to the six different 'grounds of representation' that were elaborated in the previous chapter. The analysis of a limited number of remarkable light-images from each performance leads to the discussion of *the dramaturgy of light* of that performance. By 'dramaturgy of light' I refer to the orchestration of light processes throughout the performance, consisting of a combination of light concepts and their respective semiotic and poetic functions.

Chapter 5

Madama Butterfly

Music by Giacomo Puccini (1858–1924)

Libretto by Luigi Illica and Giuseppe Giacosa

Based on the play *Madame Butterfly* by David Belasco, after a story by John Luther Long

World premiere at the Teatro alla Scala, Milan, 1904

Revival of the 1993 production at L'Opéra National de Paris, Opéra Bastille, 2011

The artistic team

Stage Director, Scenography and Lighting Design: *Robert Wilson*
Musical Director: *Maurizio Benini*
Co-design Scenography: *Giuseppe Frigeni*
Co-design Lighting: *Heinrich Brunke*
Costumes: *Frida Parmeggiani*
Choreography: *Suzushi Hanayagi*
Dramaturgy: *Holm Keller*

Cast

Cio-Cio-San: *Micaela Carosi*
F.B. Pinkerton: *James Valenti*
Suzuki: *Enkelejda Shkosa*
Kate Pinkerton: *Anna Wall*
Sharpless: *Anthony Michaels-Moore*
Goro: *Carlo Bosi*
Prince Yamadori: *Vladimir Kapshuk*
Lo Zio Bonzo: *Scott Wilde*
Yakuside: *Jian-Hong Zhao*
Il Commissario Imperiale: *Slawomir Szychowiak*
L'Ufficiale del Registro: *Andrea Nelli*
Mother of Cio-Cio-San: *Ilona Krzywicka*
La Zia: *Vania Boneva*
La Cugina: *Catherine Hirt-Andre*
Il Figlio di Cio-Cio-San: *Theo Vandecasteele/Randi Razafijaonimanana*

Orchestra of L'Opéra National de Paris, 22 January 2011

Introduction

Robert Wilson has been one of the towering figures of contemporary theatre since the late 1960s. He is a pioneering visual artist, architect, sculptor and painter, and one of the most innovative theatre-makers among those who are associated with post-dramatic theatre. When the first experimental forms of Performance Art and Happenings emerged in the United States (to distinguish them from dramatic theatre) Wilson abandoned the linear and coherent story line and, instead, turned to a surrealistic, rhizome-like *'landscape theatre'* that was composed as a montage of non-narrative scenes, based on associative and elaborate formal relationships. In *Looking into the Abyss: Essays on Scenography*, Arnold Aronson writes: "Acknowledging the influence of Gertrude Stein, Wilson created literal landscapes or perhaps dreamscapes. Wilson's stage became a site for surrealistic images, phantasms, and repetitive movements [. . .] In Wilson, space and time coexist, but almost in opposition" (Aronson 2008, 109).

Wilson's creative work can be related to notions from the philosophy of postmodern art: in which the (modern) crisis in representing the sublime through formalism and minimalism has led to (postmodernist) attempts at representation through deconstructing of the stable image in favour of alternative, eclectic and fragmentary perspectives on the human condition. Especially in his early works, using deconstructed and conglomerated imagery Wilson explored the materials and media of art itself in western culture, including, for example: the sound and tempo of language, human movement, artificial lighting and perception of space, the use of non-professionals, sometimes disabled, performers, pastiche, absurd and other artistic qualities. These are but a few of the main notions that are relevant for opening discussion of Wilson's creation. His non-hierarchical use of light, scenography, music, performers, movement and text equally respects the various media as theatrical components that interact according to the 'orchestration' of the piece, rather than through the support of verbal narrative. Arthur Holmberg writes in *The Theatre of Robert Wilson* that "Moving theatre away from narrative toward lyric poetry, Wilson privileges formal patterns; he foregrounds spatial and temporal, not narrative, structure. By emphasizing artistic devices rather than story line, he veils narrative" (Holmberg 1998, 11).

With highly stylized design of lighting, scenography, costumes and make-up, Wilson made visual dimension of his theatre much more important than both textual meaning and the activity of human performers. So central and spectacular are the visual aspects of his work, that, in addition to directing, Wilson usually co-designs the lighting and the scenography for his performances, together with dedicated collaborators in their field of speciality. Stephan Di Benedetto writes in *Concepts in Spatial Dynamics*: "Where other playwrights provide a verbal narrative, Wilson uses the abstracted language of visual form to present a ballet of shape and space. Changing shapes, spaces and images flow by the spectators asking them to accept a visible journey filled with visual stimuli to goad their interest. The position of visible elements often is taken for granted, and so deserves scrutiny" (Di Benedetto 2000, 70). For more than five decades now, Wilson's dramaturgical and visual concepts have left their personal and imposing signature (uniquely identified with the artist) upon the theatre of the 20th and 21st centuries. No book on lighting design in contemporary theatre can be complete without reference to Wilson's style of lighting and the experience brought about by his aesthetics, semiotics and poetics of light.

Madama Butterfly is one of the world's most popular dramatic operas, featuring in the repertoire of most opera houses. The Paris production of *Madama Butterfly* (2011), directed by Wilson, is the only opera I have chosen to analyse in depth, among the five contemporary performances analysed in this study.[1] I include one contemporary opera performance in this book in order to examine the relations that lighting establishes with the music and the sung libretto as well – relations that are complex, occasionally surprising and unusual. It is interesting to examine how in this performance Wilson challenges the particular dramatic characteristics and psychology of the fictive characters in this opera with his post-dramatic, alienating theatrical style. The unity of space is disrupted and the temporal experience, too, is constantly disordered, while the dimensions of time and space on stage become different from those in the spectators' reality. Moreover, the performance relates to several of the highly intriguing issues typical of contemporary theatre *'beyond drama'*. It does so by generating a complex and strong aesthetic experience, contrasting the dominant presence of the medium of lighting with that of the performers, who restrain their physical and emotional expressions.

Another reason for choosing this particular opera production is Wilson's remark that the structuring of the piece in light was a fundamental phase in the creation process of the performance, and its development had already begun in the pre-production process (even before rehearsals started), and in the rehearsal room (prior to technical rehearsals in the theatre). Light was a part of the direction book. The lighting is integrated into the direction of the scenes from the very beginning, and is not 'added' as a final layer during the technical rehearsal preceding the premiere, as is the case in most commercial theatre productions. Wilson describes his way of working with lighting in the context of *Madama Butterfly*: "One of the first things I do in any rehearsal is to start with the light. Even if I am working in a rehearsal room I sketch with light. And usually the first thing I do is the countdown of the house lights going down and the first light cue – so I am thinking from the beginning with light". And later he notes: "So the piece is structured in light. And sometimes it goes against the music; sometimes it is just with the music. Sometimes the palette of the colours is very subtle – often it is. In this case, you have to be very careful, because this music can be too sweet".[2]

Wilson thus acknowledges the significance which the use of lighting has for him as early as at the beginning of the rehearsal process, suggesting a more creative and autonomous relation between the light and the music and the text/libretto, as well as between the light and the performers themselves. From the very beginning, the thinking about space must take into account the light that makes this space perceptible. Each spatial composition on stage consists of three layers: the predetermined space suggested by the scenography, the perceived space as defined by means of the light-image, and the positioning of the performers. Fundamental compositional choices include the relations between the human body and the space surrounding it, the optical qualities of the light reflected from the objects on stage, and intensity composition – differentiating light intensity and colour in different parts of the stage. Let us turn to an analysis of exemplary light-image from the production. I chose a single light-image that is in force while Butterfly first enters the space (Figures 5.2 and 5.3). I also examine the experience this image creates, its semiotics and poetics, against the background of the two previous light-images in the performance. The progression from a light-image similar to that in Figure 5.1, changing to another transitory light-image and later to the light-image in Figures 5.2 and 5.3, reflects some of the unique aesthetic qualities, the semiotic and poetic functions light has in this production.

Figure 5.1 Robert Wilson, *Madama Butterfly* (the Paris production), Act I. Pinkerton (left) in a conversation with marriage broker Goro (middle) before the wedding ceremony. Photo: © Cristophe Pelé/Opéra National de Paris

Figure 5.2 Robert Wilson, *Madama Butterfly* (the Paris production), Act I. Pinkerton (downstage), and Butterfly (upstage) while she makes her first appearance from upstage-right. Photo: Colette Masson/Roger-Violle/ArenaPAL

Figure 5.3 Robert Wilson, *Madama Butterfly* (the Paris production), Act I. Highlighted while entering, Butterfly (upstage right) wears broad white ribbons attached to her arms. Goro (mid-downstage) and the three chaperones (at upstage left) respond to Butterfly entering. Photo: Colette Masson/Roger-Viollet/ArenaPAL

The light-image of Butterfly's first entrance

In a dramatic work, any first entrance of a character onto the stage is much more than the mere physical appearance of the performer, or the joining of a character to the narrative course of events. The entrance of a character is anticipated by the way in which the playwright, or the librettist in this case, has built the text up to that point, and it usually leads to an escalation in the form of the dramatic conflict. Butterfly's first entrance is anticipated through the recitatives sung by Pinkerton (the American Naval officer), Sharpless (the American Consul) and Goro (the marriage broker) regarding the coming wedding and the expectation of Butterfly's arrival. Puccini wrote a clear transition between these recitatives into the leitmotif that identifies Butterfly throughout the opera, but first sung by the three chaperones just before being taken over by Butterfly. Let us take a look at how the light-image is constructed (aesthetics). Figures 5.2 and 5.3 take different perspectives and present different details on stage, while the colours and atmosphere in Figure 5.4 are closer to the light-image that prevailed the scene, although the photo shows a later moment in the scene.

Aesthetic analysis of the light-image

Seven lighting elements composed this light-image (Figures 5.2 and 5.3):

1   *Follow spots on Sharpless, Goro and Pinkerton* – Three follow spots, operated manually by lighting technicians from the front bridge of the house (above the audience), focus on the performers' heads and shoulders (Figure 5.2). Each follow spot illuminates one performer. On the floor, behind each performer, is a soft-edge spot of light with the shadow of his head in the middle, following the performer wherever he goes. As these follow spots have discharge lamps that belong to the gaslight category, the colour of the light they produce is cold white. Pinkerton's follow spot is more intense than those of Sharpless and Goro; he is highlighted in intensity and the contrast of light and shade makes his head seem to float in the rather dark surrounding space. All three performers remain partly in the shadow and their highlighted heads cast shadows on the floor behind them.

2   *A follow spot on Butterfly* – To distinguish her from the other performers' mysterious and fragmented appearance, a follow spot at a frontal angle illuminates Butterfly's entire body (Figure 5.3). Use of this lighting element and angle makes Butterfly the figure with the most complete visibility on the stage at this particular moment. She has almost no shadow in front (only behind her), rendering her appearance flat. Being the brightest object in the scene (wearing white, like Pinkerton), she is completely visible; her costume is highly reflective and thus she receives the most attention. The light source seems to have been hung on the portal bridge because the light hits the performer but does not reach the backdrop, and the shadow does not stretch far back. The light follows Butterfly as she treads slowly on the path from upstage right (the left side of the photo) toward the wooden square surface.

3   *Sidelights for the three chaperones standing upstage* – These sidelights are an interesting component in the light-image because they make us perceive the women as if sculpted, very plastic and full of contrast between the illuminated and the dark parts of their outfits (Figure 5.3). The sidelights illuminate the chaperones from

Figure 5.4 Robert Wilson, *Madama Butterfly* (the Amsterdam production), Act I. Pinkerton (stage-right), Butterfly (middle) and the three chaperones (at upstage left). Photo: Courtesy of the Dutch National Opera/Hans van den Bogaard

both sides of the stage, without hitting the backdrop or the floor. Although there are sidelights from both sides, the women partly cast shadows on each other and each is shadowed in the lower body. The women are only illuminated from the knees up. The lights that can generate such an optical quality are called profile spots, equipped with adjustable shutters that mask part of the output and shape the field of projection. The colour of the light is cold, non-saturated greyish-blue.

4   *Top light above the wooden surface* – This lighting element consists of several sources from above the wooden floor, all of which are in subtle and cold colour scale of grey, pale blue and dark lavender (Figure 5.4). The different hues of the light reflected from the wood create a painterly quality of depth and surface with a rich diversity of colours. There are different colours at different intensities, but the transition between them is very subtle. The downstage right area – where Pinkerton and Sharpless stand and look at Butterfly arriving – has the brightest tone and slightly warmer off-white colour. The costumes of the two men are softly illuminated by this lighting element, revealing part of the silhouette of the performers; and their shadows are cast on the wooden floor.

5   *The narrow horizontal platform lying between the wooden surface and stage left* – This lighting element emphasizes the horizontal architectural element downstage by greyish pale blue light with a glimpse of turquoise (Figure 5.4). It is produced using profile spots illuminating the platform from above, with the light cut exactly in the shape of the platform. This lighting/architectural element is 'mirrored' with the following last two lighting elements: *the blue horizontal 'stain' on the floor upstage* and *the blue horizon on the backdrop*.

6   *Blue horizontal 'stain' on the floor upstage* – On the dark stony plane upstage (just in front of Butterfly and the three chaperones), a long narrow horizontal area is 'painted' by dark blue light. This blue field stretches from stage left to right (Figure 5.4). The optical quality of this light is soft and its edges gradually vanish into black voids toward both down- and upstage. From a technical perspective, I assume that several lights with Fresnel lenses, masked by a set of barn doors, were used to generate this lighting element.

7   *Blue horizon on the backdrop* – Saturated, vibrant dark blue light, emanating from the floor behind, illuminates the lower part of the backdrop (Figure 5.4). It is so intensely blue that it recalls the works of Yves Klein with blue pigment powder, shiny 'pure' colour, as if radiating light from within. The intensity of the colour gradually decreases upwards on the backdrop, and the shadowed floor below (upstage) helps by creating a powerful contrast with the blue light. The softness of the blue light is achieved by the use of lights especially suited for illuminating backdrops and cycloramas, like fluorescent tubes or halogen Cyclorama lights. In front of the backdrop, which is a sort of plastic opera foil or a white cloth, there appears to be another black tulle fabric (gauze) that blurs the lighting on the backdrop. This lighting is positioned on the floor, just behind the backdrop, and is focused in the direction of both the backdrop and the auditorium.

Semiotic and poetic analysis of the light-image

Considering the lighting elements mentioned above, how are the aesthetic features of the light experienced or used as signs; what are the signs about; and how are the signs used in a poetic way?

Methodologically, I first examine whether the phenomenological experience and the semiotic function of light relate to the narrative and if so, how these aspects of narrative function as a ground of representation. In no way does the light-image strengthen the sense of fictive time or space of the narrative suggested by the libretto; rather, light disrupts their dramatic unities and coherence. According to this libretto, the scene happens in daytime at Pinkerton's new house in Japan. The lighting colours (cold blue) and low intensities contradict the information given by the text. The aesthetic features of the light-image – especially the blue horizon, the blue ground and the coloured light on the wooden parts – might well be interpreted as the conventional representation of night-time, had the production been directed according to the familiar conventions of the theatre of Realism. The formal characteristics of the lighting thus create a composition that avoids being an illustration of the signs already provided by the text, and deviates from the atmosphere of the music, not supporting the dramatic function of the music in 'telling' the story either. The previously warm space is altered by a blue scale of colours that contradicts the cultural convention of daytime in western theatre. The transition from the warm light-image (Figure 5.1) into the next image is also very rapid, thus deviating from the representation of nature as we spectators experience it in daily life. This is clearly a poetic configuration of the signs of light that invites the spectator to ponder its meaning. The light-image thus counters the description of the situation in the libretto, contrasts Butterfly's romantic leitmotif, and becomes a separate and independent source of meaning. Therefore, the semiotic function of this light-image does not seem to be grounded in *the narrative*.

The change from the warm light-image (Figure 5.1) into the one I analyse (Figures 5.2 and 5.3) brings about a new colour scale, a drop in the intensity and separation between the performers by means of very specific and selective illumination, differentiating the characters' visibility by light. Butterfly is the only one who glows in light and expresses true happiness, while the others, including her bridegroom and chaperones, are overshadowed. As the previous light-image changes into this one without any obvious reason, we try to find a settling one. By conjoining the various light-signs, we learn something new about the subconscious of the characters, which neither the music nor the libretto unveil as yet: light's aesthetic features generate tension with Butterfly's romantic libretto and the musical leitmotif when she first appears. Particularly significant is the contrast between Butterfly's bright and flat look and the shadowed appearance of the other characters in the gloomy, mysterious cold space. Indeed, the lighting does not function as a reflection upon Butterfly's present mental state. Instead, the experience of light functions as an unseen premonition of the miserable future that awaits her – a future that the spectators are already aware of, due to the confession by Pinkerton to Sharpless in the previous scene. Before their marriage ceremony, Butterfly and Pinkerton seem to be very excited and optimistic as they sing of their emotions and their mutual commitment. However, the spectators are well aware that the two have very different intentions concerning this marital relationship. The light-image reflects upon the mental state of the characters at the moment Butterfly enters the space, by changing the performers' visibility in a very explicit way, while the configuration of the light-signs assists in portraying the *shadows of doubt* in this marriage of convenience.

The light-image reflects upon the characters by anticipating their future situation and thus commenting with irony upon their temporary happiness in the present – as if the light and we addressees already share an anticipation and knowledge that the characters do not yet have themselves. In contrast to the stirring sweet music and the romantic content of the libretto, the light-image 'looks ahead' to Butterfly's agony that will follow this wedding, and to the opera's eventual tragic end. Light is used here to reflect upon and present *the duality of the moment*.

The transition from the previous warm light-image (Figure 5.1) to the current one (Figure 5.2) draws the attention of the spectators, i.e. it 'zooms in' exclusively onto the performers/characters. The transitory light-image of a wide open space, illuminated in greyish-turquoise colours, alters the characteristics of the space, and the following image attenuates the lighting intensity on stage and also highlights Butterfly, Pinkerton, Sharpless and Goro with follow spots. The lighting definitely draws the audience's attention to the characters in a very firm way, inviting the spectators to actively interpret the possible reasons for such a change in the performers' appearance, and to seek a better understanding of the characters' psyche. At this point the semiotic function of this light-image is, therefore, grounded in ***character***.

As its semiotics also refers to a subtextual level, based on a deeper analysis of the dramatic actions and themes that lie beneath the plot,, I suggest that this light-image also *mediates the dramaturgy of the verbal text into the medium of light*.

Butterfly's dramatic action is that of survival, in materialist terms: through marrying an American naval officer, she presumes she will secure her prosperity and love (in that order). Pinkerton's dramatic action, by contrast, is that of a 'colonizer': marrying *'a true American bride'* upon his return to the US remains his 'noble' wish, but for the time being (in Japan) he wants to spend some time with Butterfly. He formally marries her, but eventually regards her as a mistress rather than a wife. The central theme in this production of *Madama Butterfly* is that the moral decay of betrayal in love and self-deception leads to a destructive end. Hedonist Pinkerton proves to be disloyal to Butterfly from the very beginning, while the compliant Butterfly abandons her Japanese culture in order to secure a financially stable future. As both Butterfly and Pinkerton each see this marriage in such different terms, Wilson effectively indicates the gap between the two views through the light-image in this scene and in the preceding one. The emotional and moral difference between the two characters – at least in this production – drives them to a course that seals their fate. Light's aesthetics is used here to reflect on the theme of the opera. Butterfly glitters in white light and treads through a blue field of light behind her, so outstanding in her gloomy environment. Pinkerton and the other men gaze at her out of the dark areas of the stage, almost objectifying her. The overall image of the space and the visibility of the performers are charged with mystery and secrecy.

Before Butterfly's chaperones arrive, the lighting is similar to that in the earlier scene, as presented in Figure 5.1, representing a bright and warm countryside landscape on a sunny day. Once the ladies begin to sing offstage and enter upstage right near the backdrop, the lighting becomes colder and greyish and it turns bluer with Butterfly's entrance (Figure 5.3 and the colour of 5.4). The process suggested by the lighting, in relation to Butterfly's entrance, is that of darkening and 'cooling down' the space. The unusual use of colour conventions is also poetic – associating Butterfly's entrance with night-time, and with a dream-like fragmented space. The historical lighting convention of dimming light in line with the progression of the tragedy is ascribed to the theatre of the Renaissance (said to be first suggested by Renaissance theatre man Leone Hebreo de' Sommi). When Butterfly's musical leitmotif begins, orchestrated very gently and sweetly – and sung first by the chaperones – the previously warm and bright space turns cold and gloomy. When Butterfly herself follows and enters the space, it becomes even darker. Light's formal characteristics at this point create neither gaiety nor a festive mood, nor a romantic atmosphere for a lovely wedding ceremony. Butterfly seems to be unaware of the unstable qualities of her surroundings, unlike the spectators, who are aware of the friction in the situation on both narrative and aesthetic grounds. From a phenomenological perspective, the difference between the views of the two principals (Butterfly and Pinkerton) also manifests the distinction between *looking* at reality (perception) and *seeing* it (interpretation). Ironically, the contrast between the light-image and the scene, as the contrasting views of the two main characters, is beyond Butterfly's consciousness or cognitive capacities. But perhaps she (un-)consciously suppresses her doubts in the hope of a better future, as she often does in the absence of Pinkerton (during Acts II and III).

This light-image functions much like a 'soliloquy' delivered by the medium of light, as if a performative medium shares with the spectators a secret, ironic insight into the narrative. I would, therefore, suggest that the representation through this light-image is also grounded in the third category suggested by the conceptual framework: the *theme* and the *dramatic-action*.

Wilson designs Butterfly's entrance as a dream-like, surrealistic image within ambiguous and fragmented space. By illuminating her alone so brightly on the one hand, and leaving her in quite dark surroundings on the other, she appears to be almost floating above the black ground. Although the libretto indicates a unity of space that the characters inhabit, the lighting rejects and deconstructs the coherency of the space, redefining the look of each character in a different intensity, direction of light, and, most noticeably, the saturation of colour. The white light reflected from Butterfly's dress seems to detach her from the space, due to the sharp contrast of light and shade. With the long ribbons floating down from her wrists, the white Butterfly evokes associations of angelic purity – as if her light emanates from within, resembling the medieval representations of angels and martyrs, never portrayed with shadows. Contrasting with the other figures standing still and looking at her, Butterfly charges the scene with tension by her slow motion and suspending the passing of time.

By disrupting the coherency of the spatial dimension, the disappearing turquoise light from the ground, which was part of the previous light-image, also becomes significant. Not only is it highly effective in increasing the sense of visual depth, simulating an almost black void in the ground – but the emergence of this black void also lends spiritual and atmospheric qualities to the space. The use of this light-sign has a strong poetic effect, giving the space the magical, almost metaphysical quality of a landscape weightlessly floating, and disappearing while Butterfly arrives. In the present image, a dark 'royal blue' light shines on the lower part of the horizon behind a black skyline, but the colour is too saturated to be considered natural. This unnatural, highly saturated colour, together with the slow motion of Butterfly and the stillness of the other performers, charges the scene with a spiritual, almost ritual dimension. The three female chaperones, standing motionless upstage left, are illuminated in greyish light by high sidelights that reveal only their torsos, making them appear like statues. At the lower part of the stage, above the wooden surface, the three illuminated heads of the men seem to be almost disconnected from their shadowed male bodies.

The formal characteristics of the lighting mentioned above interact with the music and lend the scene a spiritual dimension and surrealistic and evocative qualities in a way not indicated by the libretto. Butterfly's musical leitmotif is challenged by the contrast that the lighting creates. The lighting and, no less importantly, the shadows in this light-image elaborate the multifaceted complexity of the scene and make it a more ambiguous and fascinating image, recalling the use of coloured light and shadows in the theatre of Romanticism to represent the deeper and darker part of the human soul.

The emotional effect of this light-image on the spectators, however, increases light's autonomy. As the scene features stirring music and a libretto that evoke tenderness and empathy, the surrealistic and painterly (almost two-dimensional) characteristics which the light lends the space, create tension and vagueness, even a sense of 'otherness'. The conjoining of all the media in the scene with this particular light-image slows down, even obstructs, the emotional effect of the music/text on the addressees. Due to the factors mentioned above, the reception of the scene as a whole becomes driven more by the conceptual approach, and less by an engagement with immediate emotions. This light-image assists in resisting the emotional empathy called for by the music, and in approaching the scene more critically.

Therefore, in view of its manipulative role on the addressees and its relation to the music and the libretto, the semiotic function of this light-image is also grounded in *atmosphere* or *emotion*.

The medium of light is strongly experienced as an active, ever-changing participant throughout the entire performance, although the lighting apparatuses remain concealed. The aesthetic features of this light-image are highly elaborate and consist of optical qualities with high precision, follow spot operation and numerous lighting elements. For example, through the fragmented highlighting of body parts, and the unusual visibility of the male performers/characters (Sharpless, Pinkerton and Goro), the spectators may become aware of the presence and dominance of the medium of light. The three men stand with their backs to the audience and turn into spectators themselves (by gazing at Butterfly entering). However, we can only see their highlighted heads illuminated by follow spots while the rest of their bodies remain shadowed.

Moreover, the transition into the present light-image (Figure 5.3) is quite short and takes only a few seconds – a highly sensed lighting change considering the difference between the warm (Figure 5.1) and this cooler light-image. The artificiality and temporality of stage lighting is enhanced and becomes even more noticeable because of the speed of the transition.

As if 'action painting' with light, Wilson recomposes the stage over and over again using a great number of light-images. In the present image, the shadowed areas on stage, the selective highlighting of figures in cold white gaslight (follow spots) or greyish-blue sidelights (the three women), and the royal blue in the background, create a very powerful combination of contrasted colours and illumination of *chiaroscuro* – far from anything that exists in daily reality. The lighting thus becomes more 'performative': because of the complexity in which they are (re)configured in this scene, the signs of light dominate, and draw attention to their own artificiality and sensory qualities.

The sensation of light, and the aesthetic pleasure one may gain from it, may raise questions about the possible meanings of this light-image, and about the role and meaning of the transition from the previous images to this one. The (self-)reference to the medium, the materials and the technology involved (i.e. hypermediacy) through the demonstration of light's unique qualities, increases the autonomy of light with regard to the text and enhances its poetic expression. The distinctive formal characteristics that comprise this light-image leave a vivid and memorable impression of light. Light facilitates an interesting new relation with the other media, for example by breaking the coherence of the scene and dividing it into separate visual sections. For the above reasons, the ground of the representational function (or meaning) of this light-image is also in the *sensation of light itself (hypermediacy* or *spectacularity)*, i.e. the medium of light celebrates its authoritative role and sensuous influence of its signs on the spectator.

Finally, I would like to suggest that the semiotic function of this light-image is *not* grounded in its capacity for *open meaning*. As elaborated in Chapter 4 (on the conceptual framework), a light-image whose semiotic function is grounded in *open meaning* suggests signs, or even semantic codes, that are as yet unknown to the addressee. In such cases, the sensory visual information, being a very primal stimulus influencing blood pressure, heartbeat and innate behavioural responses, is suggestive but in an ambiguous way. Light, thus, performs like a phantom and stimulates the spectator to generate an ongoing cognitive process, in an attempt to reach an interpretation of the suggested light-signs. Light, in other words, thereby arouses curiosity in the spectators to fill in the gaps of information in the scene with their own informed subjective interpretation. By doing so, the addressees try to interpret these ambiguous or empty signs in line with other, more simple signs and to test the validity of their interpretation in the broader context of the poetics of the performance ('performance-logic'). The less the text dominates our making of meaning in the theatre, the more liberty and openness there is for the experience of light itself, the bodily sensory stimulation and its cognitive effects.

Since the music and the narrative in this opera are so intimately interwoven around dramatic principles of psychology of characters and musical leitmotifs, and because of the dominance and clarity of the sung libretto, the range of possibilities for interpretation of light is narrowed. This is not the case in most of the original works that Wilson authors from scratch, without basing the performance on existing works or on coherent narrative plots. His early piece *Einstein on the Beach* (1976) or the more recent *The Life and Death of Marina Abramovic* (2012) could be taken as examples of performances in which the spectator faces an unclear, yet very carefully structured configuration of signs that can potentially receive as many interpretations as their interpreters. In *Signs of Performance*, Colin Counsell writes: "By filling the stage with objects/actions which seem to declare their own decidability, but which deny attempts to subsume them within a single interpretive discourse, Wilson both encourages interpretation and ultimately denies it. The result is a stage filled with iconographic components which, like genuine dream-images laden with a sense of potent, suggest their own symbolic status while refuting all attempts to discover what they are symbolic of" (Counsell 1996, 184–5). Although this light-image from *Madama Butterfly* is highly complex and elaborate, it is the concreteness of the narrative and its dramatic paradigm that restricts the hermeneutic possibilities of the experience of light: the corporeal, the emotional and the conceptual. The narrative functions as an obstacle to a more visually-based interpretation of the experience of the light-image. The strong presence of the text and the narrative limit the meaning potential of the light-image and its openness, thus limiting its autonomy. The *potential* of light to function as an autonomous 'character' in this performance also decreases. Therefore, I do not consider semiotics of this light-image to be grounded in *open meaning*.

The dramaturgy of light in *Madama Butterfly*

Three fundamental ideas can be distinguished in Wilson's dramaturgy for the lighting in *Madama Butterfly*, one of which has to do with the relation between light and narrative elements. The other two ideas relate to the unique interdisciplinary relationship between light and performers, the medial aspects of theatre lighting and the role light plays in this post-dramatic opera production:

1　*Light as a catalyst for action* – Against the background of Butterfly's constant *delay of action*, the lighting assists in embodying the sense of passing time and in metamorphosing the environment. Changing (light) conditions, which assist in emphasizing her stasis and passivity, pin Butterfly down as the locus of the tragic. For example, in relation to the fictional world of the narrative, at times light suggests a reference to the 'conventional' colours of day and night, or to the darkening horizon at nightfall.

　　However, light does not point merely to Butterfly's taking no stand against unstable conditions. Light also attracts attention to the state of spectatorship itself from a phenomenological perspective, through intentionally destabilizing the coherence of time and space and fragmenting them instead. Light shifts between supporting verisimilitude and being a more reflective and affective medium, by visually restructuring the stage-image and drawing attention to the performance's formal aspects. Wilson traps Butterfly and imprisons her in a square surface, the so-called 'home', surrounded by a dark, almost burnt-like terrain devoid even of vegetation (Figure 5.5). The simplified geometric wooden structure – the colonizer of the landscape – becomes a static cage for Butterfly. We watch her yearning for Pinkerton's return while letting her life pass by, and passively hoping that Pinkerton will decide to stay with her upon discovering that he has a child. In contrast to the rather stable and static ground level identified with Butterfly, the backdrop features a multitude of phenomena happening with light: vivid, bold and dynamic.[3] The large backdrop serves as a monumental canvas for the lighting's 'brush strokes' – consisting of long horizontal light-zones with soft edges – by which light leaves a deep impression of landscape seized by irresistible powers.

　　On the narrative level, another means by which the lighting constantly metamorphoses the space in colour, shape and dimensions, is the occasional disappearing of the entire stage into obscurity while only a single object – like a face or a hand – remains highlighted. This highlighting is a 'Wilsonean convention': leading the gaze of the spectator, much like film camerawork, using cuts, close-ups and zooming in or out. Such tremendous changes in visibility, when made suddenly and with high precision, tend to unbalance the spatial perception of the spectators, thus creating tension and directing their attention to particular objects on the stage (Palmer 1998, 62–73). These interventions of light in the image occur at several critical dramatic moments and, in a sense, they break the coherence of the scene and withhold the spectators from immersing into the magic of the performance. The side-effect of this 'device' is the visual phenomenon that is called the afterimage: the previous, fully illuminated stage image still 'echoes' in the brain for a few more seconds after its disappearance (Palmer 1998, 75–7). In the now darker lighting conditions, the reflection of the previously illuminated image (before its

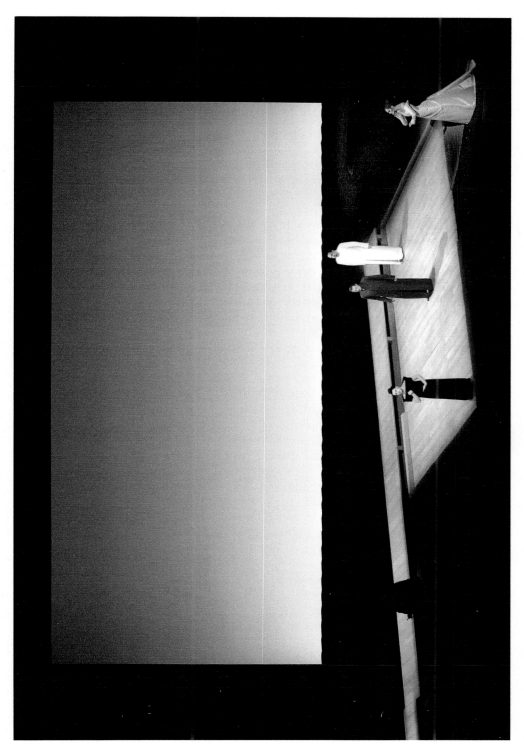

Figure 5.5 Robert Wilson, *Madama Butterfly* (the Paris production), Act III. Butterfly in black (downstage), Sharpless in gray (middle) and Mr. and Mrs. Pinkerton in the late scene in which Butterfly realizes that Pinkerton is remarried. Photo: © Cristophe Pelé/Opéra National de Paris

darkening) gradually vanishes, an effect caused by the instinctive widening of the iris in the eyes, intended to allow in more light and make spatial perception possible. Indeed, the transitions between light-images, when done in 'cut-time', leave the most remarkable impressions, disrupting the coherency of spatial reception of the spectators, and eliciting curiosity as to the reason for the change.

The second act of the opera emphasizes the state of immobility inside the house, in anticipating Pinkerton's arrival, while so much happens around it. The passivity chosen by Butterfly is contrasted to light's hectic activity taking place beyond. Harsh light transitions incite (if not Butterfly – then at least) the spectators to exchange a passive state of spectatorship into a more excited and alert one. The absurdity and contrast between her passivity and action around her lies at the core of Butterfly's tragic character.

2   *Fictive character: light vs performer* – In numerous scenes, a unique relationship can be found between the lighting and the performers. The performers themselves avoid imitating what they sing about and remain 'frozen' in a single gesture, whereas the lighting changes and may reflect the progression of the emotional or mental processes of the characters in the narrative. Light goes 'hand in hand' with the performers in representing the inner drama of the characters and their motivation to act. In such cases, part of the performers' domain is actually 'remediated' or taken over by the medium of light. I would like to consider the relation between the art of light and the art of acting in this performance against the background of post-dramatic theatre.

Wilson's work is immediately recognizable by its minimalism, the alienated appearance of its performers, and its visual qualities: the painterly and sculpture-like stasis or slow motion. Because of the distance and coldness that emanates from a performer, the audience is (quite paradoxically) motivated to 'investigate' its aura, soul and body. Wilson sees this enigmatic coldness and minimal emotional expression from the performers as an opportunity for the audience to reflect on what it sees. The (minimal) indications that the performers transmit concerning the situation remain open and do not refer to one particular representational form for a specific type of emotion, thus allowing each spectator to participate and relate to the situation more actively using her or his imagination.

Similarly to Brecht, Wilson asks the performers to keep themselves and their feelings separate from the text and the fictive character, and to refrain from portraying empathy or affection for the characters. Rather, the text is (re-)presented along with highly stylized gestures and choreographed body language, suggesting a critical approach to the text by posing a gesture against reciting the libretto. In order to avoid simply repeating the signs that the text already suggests, the performers' movements are minimal, slow or frozen, and occasionally reflect other aspects in the dramaturgy of the performance, create tension and thus enrich the possibilities for interpretation.

Like Brecht, Wilson incites the spectators-addressees to investigate and reflect upon the performance, to listen carefully to the music, to feel, and to use the highly stylized stage-images in order to imagine what is not represented. Wilson's minimalist choreography bears a high degree of openness regarding the human condition to which the movement can relate. Corporeal expression (excluding the voice) is stripped down to its core, to represent the 'inner world' of a fictive character, in terms of information the body may suggest. In this opera production, emotions are subdued and suggested through the physical restraints that the narrative imposes on the human, sculpture-like figures.

Before I connect the discussion about the work of the performer to that of the light, I need to elaborate a little more on the performers' inner tension created by Wilson's staging, and the opportunities it brings about for the poetics of light. Hegel differentiated between the sensory (the aesthetic experience, based on sensuality) and the *logos* (the conceptual meaning) – the former is the most beautiful and the latter is, philosophically, the highest in degree. According to him, Classical Greek sculptures of the mythological gods conveyed the most balanced relation between these two qualities by introducing both a pleasurable beauty and, at the same time, an inner agony. Kant calls this the *'sublime emotion'* – a pleasure deriving from, and despite, pain (Lyotard 2006, 23–4 and 31). As for the text, Greek tragedy itself is considered *logos*; however, its realization as a performance evokes a sensory experience. By representing a concept using a visual form, in our thinking, we identify the concept using one particular sign. Inevitably, we do not merely manifest the concept and limit its formal expression but, unnecessarily, by this shaping we also lessen or narrow the potential cognitive processes or hermeneutic activity that we are capable of making with the concept. Hegel considered that the aesthetic experience elicited by a representation could damage the capacity of the *logos*, or a concept.

As in any mimetic art, theatre performances also consist of complex, even deconstructive, relations between concept and form. For instance, when watching a performer playing a character, the performer's voice, his or her physical form, the individual interpretation of the text and other factors affect our reception of the spoken text. Tangible visual embodiment, therefore, threatens to overshadow the conceptual ideal. The sensuous precedes the logos, as the artefact loses some of the conceptual qualities and abstract dimensions while obtaining more 'pleasurable' qualities. Drama, as Lehmann quotes Hegel, "casts everything aside which in appearance does not conform to the true concept and only through this 'purification' brings about the ideal" (cited in Lehmann 2006, 42–4). While dramatic texts have always been written for the stage and the written work has always been complemented by a visual representation (the *logos* depended on the sensuous), drama has also brought about its own deconstruction of the ideal. Light – as suggestively as Wilson uses it – escapes concrete literal form. It contains drama of its own, next to the dramatic text. Light affects us both emotionally (subconscious) and on more aware levels by evoking feelings and conceptual thinking about signs.

Brecht's turning away from the effect of the *'suspension of disbelief'* and elaborate imagery, which has interested – and still does – the theatre of Realism, marked a new era with regard to the performance of dramatic texts in the theatre. Although Brecht still remained within the dramatic paradigm in terms of using characters, dramatic plot and conflicts, he raised the performance to a higher conceptual level and cognitive operation on the part of the addressees. Brecht did so by reducing the dominance of verisimilitude on stage and leaving more space for interpretation to the imagination of the spectators. However, the conflict between characters was still the backbone of the performance. Jane Collins and Andrew Nisbet note that, according to Lehmann, the conflict in contemporary theatre happens "'between bodies', whereas the post-dramatic process occurs 'with/on/to the body'" (Collins and Nisbet 2010, 234). In this respect, Wilson can be considered Brecht's progressive successor. However, in Wilson's theatre, the performers intentionally conceal much of their individual characteristics and enhance their sensory expression through a high degree of artificiality. In that sense, they submit themselves to serving a highly sensory representation, the aesthetics of which are so elaborate and distinct, while the textual dimension in the performance (the Hegelian 'logos') loses part of its impact.

Like Edward Gordon Craig, Wilson seeks to reach the basis and *the essence of the drama by the way of its presentation*, for which the performer is but one colour out of a broader palette of media engaged in the performance. Here with the term 'drama' I refer not only to the essence of the particular text (the libretto of *Madama Butterfly*), but also to the performative questions Wilson faces while adapting the dramatic text to function in a post-dramatic performance. Wilson masks the authentic individuality of his performers (like 'Über-Marionetten'), using heavy make-up, wigs, gloves, bodily deformations, a grotesque style of speech and strictly dictated body language.[4]

This idea is supported by the following statements given by the performers who worked with Wilson on this performance. Cheryl Barker, who played the main role of Butterfly (Cio-Cio-San) in both the Dutch and French productions of *Madama Butterfly*, mentioned in a video interview how difficult it was for her to restrain her emotions and corporeal movements while performing the role. The human presence on stage was so highly stylized and strictly contained that she was even uncertain about what she would be able to do through facial expression or merely through her eyes. Martin Thompson, who played the role of F.B. Pinkerton in the Dutch production, stated that through performing in such a reductive acting style "the thoughts are pure and direct". Using highly stylized 'performativity' the production enabled the focusing on what Wilson takes to be the core and the essential aspects in this drama, thus suggesting an alternative aesthetics to the theatre of Realism. Almost echoing Hegel on the *logos* and the sensory, Thompson commented: "You see just the thoughts. Just the way you move your hand, the way you move your head. It just means a very specific thing, not many things". The gestures of the performers are symbolic and Wilson is used to organizing them like hieroglyphics. He describes the working process during the direction of the opera: "I staged the entire piece silently first. The movements have to stand on their own. They [the performers – Y.A.] do not start with the music first; they start from the movement". Then Wilson states: "Some anthropologists believe that man was moving before he was speaking, and from movement, sounds came, raised to a higher vibration until language was formed".[5]

In this respect, Counsell notes:

> In a society where life is lived at a frenetic pace, where we are bombarded with media 'messages' and forced to share our personal, expressive space with others in congested public areas, this retreat into a private, contemplative world is for Wilson a necessity, a means of individual 'survival'. It is this view of contemporary existence and its problems which informs his work.
>
> (Counsell 1996, 180)

Each character has its own movement style, choreographed into a set of gestures, aimed at representing its inner intention and emotional situation, or being a critical reflection of the director upon the situation. It begs the question how much of the performers' own individual characteristics remains visible and come across in Wilson's work, when they function so completely as the director's 'Über-Marionetten', entirely choreographed, their faces obscured by full make-up and painted facial expressions.[6] Apart from their voices (which remain natural and authentic), the performers submit entirely to the formal characteristics of their bodies. The overall image of the performance functions as a representation of a hallucinatory or dream-like reality, fragmented and vibrant, and unexpectedly changing.

The relation obtained between the medium of light and the performers leads to interesting new perspectives and possibilities for experience and interpretation of the light, the music and the libretto. For example, light plays a dominant role in Butterfly and Pinkerton's last duet – which ends Act I – just after the marriage ceremony and the boycott by the priest, Bonzo. Pinkerton verbally expresses his sympathy for Butterfly's pain and she gradually takes comfort from her love for Pinkerton. However, their body gestures and facial mimicry do not indicate this according to the norms of daily behaviour. In fact, throughout this romantic duet, the two lovers do not touch or look at one another; they stand close to each other in a frontal position to the audience, frozen in gesture, as if they want to hold hands but cannot bridge the gap between them. As they sing, the lighting on the backdrop changes numerous times and creates images in bluish scales, reminiscent of Mark Rothko's vibrant colour paintings, representing several 'steps' or degrees in the emotions that the characters experience. A visual activity (of light) surrounds the performers and lighting transitions seem to connect with the characters and their narrative.

Light, in this production, is occasionally linked to the fictive characters' emotional state of mind, like the reddish-orange light-image that intrudes upon the marriage ceremony, connecting to Butterfly's shock upon Priest Bonzo's arrival. The presentation of dramatic action in *Madama Butterfly*, therefore, depends on the involvement of lighting technology as a core medium, sharing the role that was once reserved for the actors alone. Clearly, the dominant presence of lighting technology together with the rather static or slow minimal acting style creates a new relation between *light* and *performer*. The first medium partly mediates the role of the second, as Appia has noted: "Like an actor, light should be active".

3   *Performing light as* 'Force majeure' – As I experienced the performance of *Madama Butterfly* at the Paris Opera, the influence that the lighting had on visual perception, and the metamorphoses that the light exerts on the spatial dimension, were indeed breathtaking and ground-breaking. Light developed its own 'scenario' or 'plot' within the performance; moving together with the music or with the performers and sharing synchronized transition moments with one or several of the other media. Alternatively, at times, light deviated from the atmosphere of the music/libretto and made the spectators aware of their own state of spectatorship. The sequence of static images, in which text is recited or sung, calls to mind early cinema narration by means of soundtrack, still images, and subtitles, and its descendant – the comic strip. In *The Analysis of Performance Art: A Guide to its Theory*

and Practice, Anthony Howell writes the following about the experience of stasis while watching a performance:

> Stillness enables us a reading of the performance piece, which is more akin to the way we read a painting than the way we read a conventional play. When a still tableau is presented, the audience is not required to 'follow' the action. They read the scene at their own pace, and the eye travels as it wills, upwards, downwards, across in either direction. When we follow a drama, on the other hand, we are given little time to develop our own thoughts. Instead, we are the receivers of the piece. Our thoughts about it occur in its intervals or after the final curtain. In front of a painting, we develop our own thoughts, and this is an active form of contemplation which the canvas stimulates.
>
> (Howell 1999, 9–10)

By means of the frequency of the changes and by the duration of cross-fading between light-images, lighting-changes created another sense of progression in relation to the opera, and tempi parallel to that of the music. Soft and slow lighting transitions could act as 'transparent' agents, concealing the action of the medium and reducing the awareness of its operations by the spectators.

Cinematic music works in a slightly similar way by adding an acoustic layer to the film and subconsciously affecting the emotions of spectators, without always calling attention to the music itself. Cinematic music exists as part of the soundscape and is integrated with the narrative by retaining its 'transparency' and remaining in the background of the main object. Lighting too has the potential to be 'transparent' for most spectators, but to become noticeable when it does something above their threshold of sensitivity. When lighting transitions are slow and soft, one can hardly perceive the beginning and end of these changes. Wilson's quick lighting transitions, however, are extreme and easily perceived by most spectators, disturbing the coherence of time and space and dismissing any sense of verisimilitude. The atmosphere created by light is sometimes opposed to, or holding back the atmospheric effect of the music, though occasionally the two media act in harmony. The possible relations light builds with the libretto also change when the light contrasts the libretto's content or withdraws from taking a position in respect to the narrative.

The structure of this opera production in light, i.e. sequence of light-images, reflects upon the music and the narrative. The lighting designs does much more than simply illustrate the psychological processes undergone by the characters in the narrative, or escort and pose a counterpart to the musical structure of the opera. Rather, and independently from the other media, the lighting during the performance creates great stage gestures and develops a dominant 'visual score' to the piece. In many cases, lighting changes are motivated by something different from, or even external to, the narrative. The lighting establishes its own patterns of action, its temper and 'behaviour', but the changing moments of light as well as its forms of transition, remain occasionally ambiguous and apart from the spoken word and the narrative dimension. In the big and rather empty space, Butterfly seems to be dominated by the fate of a major force (light) as the monumental powers of nature surround and shake her environment through light's ever-changing characteristics (mostly noticeably on the backdrop). Sudden and drastic changes of light, affecting the spatial perception of the spectators, assist in expressing the vulnerability of the human being in its hyper-technological environment, determined by the theatre stage. So impressive is the effect of light that it seems as though the lighting 'dominates' the human performers. The dominance of light is well-expressed through the following statement by Tom Kamm, a set designer and collaborator of Wilson in the opera *the CIVIL wars*: "A set for Wilson is a canvas for the light to hit like paint" (Holmberg 1998, 121). Lehmann writes: "Wilson's painting with light reinforces the idea of a unity of natural processes and human occurrences . . . their undertakings seem to be occurring as in a dream and thus 'lose the name of action', as Hamlet says. They change into an occurrence" (Lehmann 2006, 80).

Wilson's lighting style and methods have, indeed, major consequences for the work of the performers. Clearly as opera singers they must follow the conductor. However, at the same time they must perform their 'choreographed score' and be in tune with the lighting to such an extent that a beam of light would single out a detail as small as their face or hand. The spectacular lighting acts as a phantom, exists in its own right, exhibiting self-conscious behaviour, whereas the performers' freedom of interpretation is highly restricted. Part of the emotional expressivity of the performance rests upon the dichotomy between the grand gestures and monumental transformation of the lighting as opposed to the stasis and self-restraint of the performers. Yet, the contrast between the two reinforces their respective strengths.

Notes

1   The 2011 production I watched at L'Opéra National de Paris, Opéra Bastille, is a reprise of the 1993 production, which was also restaged in 2002 by the Dutch Opera in *Het Muziektheater*, Amsterdam and by the Los Angeles Opera, California in 2004 and 2006.
2   Interview with Robert Wilson on his opera production of *Madama Butterfly* by Giacomo Puccini, De Nederlandse Opera, Amsterdam 2003. DVD recording by *Opus Arte* 2005.
3   Light also changes the look of other elements on the rest of the stage, albeit not to the same extent as it changes the backdrop.
4   In the Paris production of *Madama Butterfly*, for example, the Americans (Sharpless, F.B. Pinkerton, Kate Pinkerton and the child) are only slightly made up, while the Japanese characters are heavily covered by make-up, giving them a very cold and artificial appearance. Perhaps the racial and national distinction achieved by the stylizing make-up relates to the western colonial perspective, patronizing and categorizing the 'other', and labelling whoever is different.
5   Interview with Robert Wilson on his opera production of *Madama Butterfly* by Giacomo Puccini, De Nederlandse Opera, Amsterdam 2003. DVD recording by *Opus Arte* 2005.
6   In this production of *Madama Butterfly,* only the American men Flowless and Pinkerton, as well as the child, present a less artificial appearance than all the other performed characters.

References

Aronson, A., *Looking into the Abyss: Essays on Scenography*, Ann Arbor, MI: The University of Michigan Press, 2008 (first published in 2005).

Collins, J. and Nisbet, A., *Theatre and Performance Design: A Reader in Scenography*, Abingdon and New York: Routledge, 2010.

Counsell. C., *Signs of Performance: An Introduction to Twentieth Century Theatre*, London and New York: Routledge, 1996.

Di Benedetto, S., *Concepts in Spatial Dynamics: Robert Wilson's Dramaturgical Mechanics and their Relation to the Visible on stage*, published in *Theatrical Space and the Postmodern Stage*, edited by Irene Eynat-Confino and Eva Sormova, Prague: Prague Theatre Institute, 2000.

Eynat-Confino, I. and Sormova, E., *Theatrical Space and the Postmodern Stage*, Prague: Prague Theatre Institute, 2000.

Holmberg, A., *The Theatre of Robert Wilson*, Cambridge: Cambridge University Press, 2nd edition 1998 (first published in 1996).

Howell, A., *The Analysis of Performance Art: A Guide to its Theory and Practice*, Amsterdam: Harwood Academic Publisher, 1999.

Innes, C., *Edward Gordon Craig*, in the series: *Directors in Perspective*, Cambridge: Cambridge University Press, 1983.

Lehmann, H. T., *Postdramatic Theatre*, translated and foreword by K. Jürs-Munby, Abingdon and New York: Routledge, 2006.

Lyotard, J.-F., *Le Postmoderne explique aux enfants, Correspondance 1982–1985*, translated by Amotz Giladi, Tel Aviv: Resling Publishing, 2006.

Palmer, R. H., *The Lighting Art: The Aesthetics of Stage Lighting Design*, 2nd edition, Upper Saddle River, NJ: Prentice Hall Inc., 1998.

Chapter 6

On the Concept of the Face, Regarding the Son of God

By Romeo Castellucci
Socìetas Raffaello Sanzio

World premiere at the Theater der Welt, Essen, Germany, 17 July 2010

The artistic team

Concept, Direction, Set design, Light and Costumes: *Romeo Castellucci*

Music: *Scott Gibbons*

Performers: *Gianni Plazzi*
                Sergio Scarlatella
                Together with:
                Dario Boldrini
                Silvia Costa
                Silvano Voltolina

Co-production

Theater der Welt (Essen, Germany), de Singel internationale Kunstcampus (Antwerpen, Belgium), Théâtre National de Bretagne (Rennes, France), The Nationaltheatret (Oslo, Norway), Barbican London and SPILL Festival of Performance (the UK), Chekhov International Theatre festival (Moscow, Russia), Holland Festival (Amsterdam), Athens & Epidaurus Festival 2011 (Greece), GREC 2011 – Theatre festival Barcelona (Spain), Festival d'Avignon (France), International Theatre Festival DIALOG, Wroclaw (Poland), BITEF (International Theatre festival Belgrade), spielzeit'europa – Berliner Festspiele, Théâtre de la Ville (Paris, France), Romaeuropa Festival 2011, Theaterfestival SPIELART München (Germany), Le-Maillon, Théâtre de Strasbourg, Scène Européenne (France), TAP Théâtre Auditorium de Poitiers – Scène Nationale, Peak Performances at Montclair State University (USA).

Introduction

The production *On the Concept of the Face, Regarding the Son of God* (2010), by the acclaimed Italian theatre company *Socìetas Raffaello Sanzio*, is the second case presented in this study. Since the 1980s, this company has developed its unique personal signature and became a pivotal force in shaping contemporary theatre identity, as well as a subject of myriad theoretical and critical discourses in the state-of-the-art theatre studies. This highly complex performance by director and visual artist Romeo Castellucci presents a fascinating and extraordinary work of theatre, introducing a sophisticated approach to the notion of theatrical pretence and a twofold poetic use of technology, and examining the limits of representation. A fundamental feature in this production, as in other works by *Socìetas Raffaello Sanzio*, is the power of images to emotionally provoke the imagination and suspend disbelief, even though the spectators are simultaneously aware of the artificiality of the image they perceive. We see the image and its 'shadow' at one and the same time; our sight is disrupted by what we think we see, and we are left with a strong impression that what we witness is a reality and not a theatrical spectacle – no matter how bizarre, dangerous, unconventional or potentially out of control the performance may become. Light plays an important role in this endeavour, and the analysis of the two first light-images will elaborate on this phenomenon. Moreover, spoken language is almost absent from this performance, and the medium of light gains new opportunities for reflection on the artistic potential of theatre lighting in terms of its aesthetics, semiotics and poetics, the visceral corporeal experience, and the emotional and conceptual processes that light involves.

Beyond the post-dramatic nature of this performance (which will be elaborated upon later through the analysis of light), I found a special appeal in analysing a work by a director who also designs the light and the scenography for his own performance, based on such layered contemporary dramaturgy. Being both a director and a visual artist, Castellucci 'moulded' a fascinating non-conventional role for the light to perform by assimilating autonomous visual qualities and post-Brechtian light effects. The critical engagement with the thinking addressees is based on image and sound, not on the epic, and it goes beyond a sense of irony or reflection upon the stage presentation. It constantly addresses the artificiality of the theatrical event against the background of the 'realness' one experiences, and imagines. However, for the sake of those readers who have not seen this performance, I will first give a descriptive account of the scenography, the costumes and the course of action in the first scene, and indicate the ways in which these are used poetically, before starting the analysis of the light.

Scenography and costumes

From the very beginning, the scenography of *On the Concept of the Face, Regarding the Son of God* dichotomizes design and non-design, artificiality and reality or, as Joe Kelleher and Nicholas Ridout describe it, "a certain exposure of the 'reality of representation', working both with and against the spectacle at the same time, 'moving one way as your horse moves another'" (Castellucci, Castellucci, Guidi, Kelleher and Ridout 2009, 2). The technical zones of the theatre stage remain in sight, like seeing the skeleton of an organism through its surface, without the one resulting from or supporting the other. The choice to unveil the 'naked' stage space and accommodate the architecture of the building as an arbitrary precondition adds an element of 'risk'. There is partial loss of control by letting the unknown characteristics of a building influence the aesthetics of the performance, so that it appears different in every venue. This condition also helps Castellucci to intensify the impression of 'realness', as though avoiding pretence, and to increase the spectators' awareness of their own state of spectatorship.

Figure 6.1 The spectators enter the theatre with the preset of *On the Concept of the Face, Regarding the Son of God* at the background. Courtesy of International Theatre Forum TEART 2012 (Minsk, Belarus). Photo: Kiryl Synkou

Between its naked walls, the bare stage encompasses a broad 'island set' designed all in white, and a huge portrait of Christ in the distance upstage, printed in grey tones and occasionally illuminated by apricot tints. The portrait is a fragment from Antonello da Messina's *Christ Blessing* (1465). From the very first image, the scenography features a dichotomy of its frontal and rear planes: the enormous portrait of Christ painted in Renaissance style, as opposed to the modern interior with its minimal, functional and quite sterile, space (Figure 6.1). A black void lies between the two 'worlds'. Downstage right, two elegant white leather sofas, a low table in white and an off-white carpet suggest a living room (Figure 6.2). At stage front is a flat screen TV on a credenza, and behind the sofas stand a little palm tree and a clothes pole. In the centre stage area stands a little white dining table with shining silver legs, and two transparent plastic chairs, with a wheelchair nearby.

The wheelchair refers to the father's disability (Figure 6.2); his connection with the outside (contemporary) world is unstable and depends on devices such as: a wheelchair, his glasses, a headset and television that allows him to view a mediated reality. Ironically, the living room and dining area – both spaces designed along quite contemporary, minimalistic and functional lines – lack warmth. The father looks estranged in the aesthetics of the space, emphasizing a generation gap: Old Masters vs IKEA. He wears a white bathrobe and slippers, and a diaper. The son, by contrast, is dressed elegantly, wearing a fashionable suit with white shirt, a tie and dark leather shoes; however, for most of this scene his jacket is hung on the pole.

The third location is at stage left. The bedroom is suggested by a white double bed covered with white sheets, two pillows, and a chest of drawers in front of the bed. On the chest is a plastic bottle that attracts no particular attention until it is used as a theatrical apparatus to interrupt the coherence of theatrical representation – the father stains himself with excrement liquid. Behind the bed, a white square plate serves as a metonym for a bigger wall and indicates other invisible, yet fictive, spaces in the apartment. If the position of the TV-set on stage right prevents us from seeing the images on the TV, being like a black hole, the wall in stage left fills a similar function, namely, suggesting imagined off-stage spaces. The interior will be evacuated for the second of the scenes I am about to analyze, besides the bed.

The course of action – the opening scene

Upon entering the auditorium, even before taking a seat, one sees the TV light already strobing elements of the scenography. A flat TV screen is already turned on and flickering some bluish light – showing that the spectacle has begun prior to our arrival. We are, however, only able to see the backside of the display and sense the tempo of changing images through the brightness of the TV light in the dark environment. We, spectators, are put at a disadvantage, unable to perceive the images on the screen but can feel their existence. The houselights are on, the curtain is open, and the stage is barely visible (Figure 6.1). Two technicians in black uniforms escort an elderly performer (Gianni Plazzi as the father) into the space and seat him on the white sofa at stage right, in front of the television display.[1] The father sits on the sofa, and puts on his glasses and headphones. The son (Sergio Scarlatella) enters the space from behind the little wall at upstage left, wearing, as mentioned earlier, an elegant suit and a tie. The son prepares medicine for his father and seems to be in a rush to leave the 'apartment', perhaps to go to work. All of a sudden, the father feels his stomach churn and the son realizes what

Figure 6.2 Romeo Castellucci, *On the Concept of the Face, Regarding the Son of God.* Gianni Plazzi. Photo: Courtesy of Klaus Lefebvre

had just happened. This is the first time we are made aware of the father's lack of bowel control. The father cries with shame and apologizes; the son tries to relieve the father's discomfort and reassure him. A devoted son, he begins to undress and wash his father's body, dresses him again and cleans the sofa and carpet. The foul stench of excrement spreads gradually throughout the auditorium.

Briefly, the son, then, repositions the father on a plastic chair near the dining table at centre stage. Once more, the father is unable to restrain his bowels and the cycle of cleaning repeats itself (Figure 6.3). Eventually, the son escorts his father to the white bed, leaving him alone for a moment. The father, crying, takes a plastic gallon container full of liquid excrement and spreads its content over his own body and on the bed, in full light. Astonished by what he sees upon his return, the son embraces his father and the two weep together (Figure 6.4). Shortly thereafter, desperately, the son approaches the portrait of Christ at the back and stands as if kissing its huge lips; he then departs from the stage behind the canvas. The lighting fades out and the transition to the second section of the performance begins.

"Let the Little Children Come to Me" (Matthew 19:14): first light-image

The following analysis is of two interconnected light-images, which together constitute the scene involving the children throwing grenades at the painting of Christ. These images stand out as representative examples of the reductionist approach and the minimalistic aesthetics of light that Castellucci often adopts in his work, yet which are capable of developing rich and multilayered suggestive semiotics and poetics of light that open up a vast range of potential interpretations. I analyse these two paired light-images one after the other, focusing on their phenomenological effects and semiotic functions, as well as on the relationship between light and other media in the scene, in order to elucidate dramaturgical aspects of light in the performance. With this intention, I will now turn to describe what happened in the scene with the first light-image, highlighting its most relevant aspects for the analysis of light.

This scene opens on a rather gloomy stage. The father remains sitting, bent over on the bed, holding his head in his two hands and pretending to weep silently. In contrast with his acting, numerous stage technicians dressed in black enter the stage (again, as the piece started) to empty the space of its content, leaving only the portrait and the bed (with the father on it). The soundscape of a basketball bouncing and rubber soles squeaking on a parquet floor escalates, becoming more extreme and irritating. As the transition completes, the subdued lighting on the bed shifts into a dazzling light reflected from the white floor, and so the focus moves away from the father to the front plane of the stage. A child then enters the stage from stage right, carrying a school bag on one shoulder. He wears fashionable sporty clothes – cut-off trousers, T-shirt and a hat. Without hurrying, he wanders in the direction of centre downstage area and empties the contents of his bag. Several dozen hand grenades fall to the ground, producing the sound of heavy metallic objects. Nevertheless, the overall soundscape is that of a sports environment. The child gazes at the grenades on the floor for a short period, directing the spectators' attention to this particular spot.

The combined absurdity and horror produced by the spectacle of the child observing the grenades against the background of that soundscape lead to a high degree of tension,

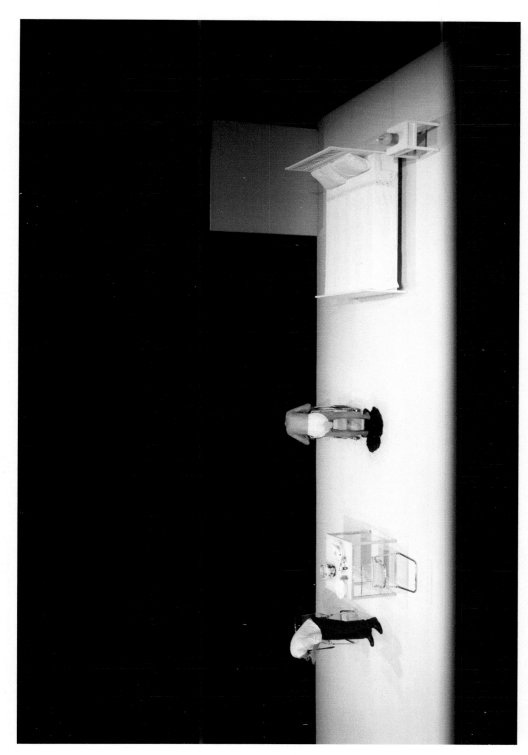

Figure 6.3 Romeo Castellucci, On the Concept of the Face, Regarding the Son of God. Sergio Scarlatella (left) and Gianni Plazzi (right). Photo: Yaron Abulafia

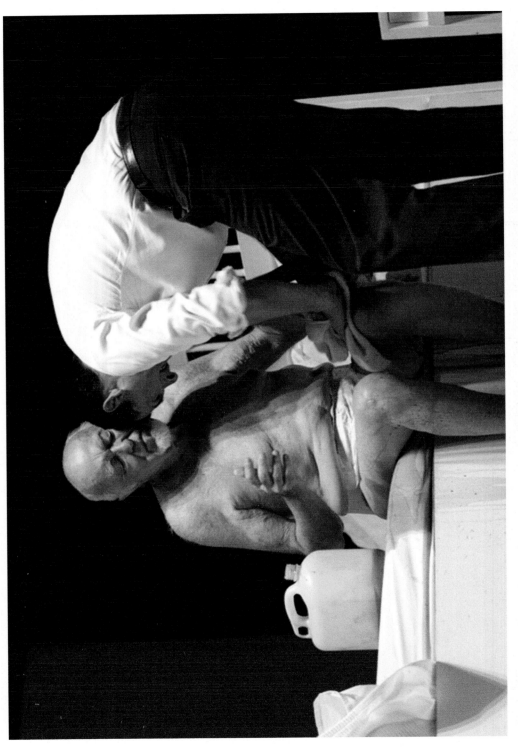

Figure 6.4 Romeo Castellucci, *On the Concept of the Face, Regarding the Son of God*. Gianni Plazzi (left) and Sergio Scarlatella (right). Courtesy of International Theatre Forum TEART 2012 (Minsk, Belarus). Photo: Kiryl Synkou

surprise, mystery and expectation among the audience. When I watched the piece, some of the spectators were on the edge of their seats while others tried to restrain their laughter. Suddenly, the child bends down to pick up one grenade from the floor, pulls out the trigger pin and throws it forcefully in the direction of the painting of Christ. An immense sound of explosion is heard when the grenade hits the canvas, evolving and distorting in time, but with no visual effect to accompany the sound. The portrait is not directly illuminated but is still visible to some extent. The boy 'bombs' the icon a few more times, and the sound is in synch with the striking of each grenade. Gradually, more boys and girls join in (Figure 6.5), reaching the number of 14 in total, all of them repeating the same action of bombarding the painted representation of Christ. The more grenades strike the wall, the more intensive and explosive the soundscape becomes, immersing the audience in the moment. Having described the scene, we can now analyse its first light-image.

Aesthetic analysis of the light-image

Two lighting elements composed this light-image (Figure 6.5):

1   *Front-of-house light (straight direction)* – Several halogen profile spots distribute a soft light and illuminate the stage from the bridge above the audience in the auditorium. The light-sources are in a pale greyish-blue hue that could be of either Lee 201#: *Full CT Blue* or *202#: Half CT Blue*. Usually, these lamps are focused on separate areas that merge into a complete frontal illumination of the stage, keeping the possibility of highlighting individual areas by means of differentiation in intensity. Due to the angle of the lighting bridge in relation to the stage floor, this lighting element can light the performers' faces from a quite 'natural' angle and create a fine and conventional visibility of the performers from the spectators' points of view. The optic qualities of this element are soft, evenly distributed and slightly cold, due to the use of this particular coloured filter that make the objects of illumination seem paler than their original colour. The individual light-areas have very soft edges, since their overlapping is invisible.

2   *Backlights* – Two groups of backlights, six in each flying bar, are used above the stage, as shown at the top of Figure 6.5. The front line of lamps illuminate the downstage plane while the back line is focused deeper, more up-stage. These light sources emphasize the silhouettes of the performers against the background of the portrait. Fresnel lenses on these light sources, distribute light with soft optics and coloured with a slightly cold filter, probably Lee 201#: *Full CT Blue*.

Semiotic and poetic analysis of the light-image

Considering the lighting elements mentioned above, how are the aesthetic features of the light experienced or used as signs; what are the signs about; and how are the signs used poetically?

In keeping with my conceptual framework, I first examine whether, and if so how, the phenomenological experience and the semiotic function of light relate to the narrative as a potential ground of representation. But before doing so, let us examine whether the

Figure 6.5 Romeo Castallucci, *On the Concept of the Face, Regarding the Son of God*. Several children and Gianni Plazzi (right). Photo: Courtesy of Christophe Raynaud de Lage

scene comprises any 'narrative', or narrative elements and some narrative structure. The relation between the first and second scenes reflects the dichotomy I noted earlier. The first scene (in which the son nurses his father) clearly has few narrative elements, although the minimal communication between father and son never becomes a real dialogue. The self-contradictory hyperrealistic acting with fairly silenced speech calls the spectators' attention to the nuances in the relationship between a father and his son by evoking emotions of empathy, compassion or thoughts about getting old. This intimate scene with its simple narrative plot consists of images and odour that are representative, and at times the stage representation rejects all pretence, as Gabriella Calchi Novati notes: "negation of representation through representation and the negation of theatre through theatre" (Novati 2009, 57). The case of the father spilling the liquid of excrement on him is one example of such negation (Figure 6.4). The children, and the light-image of that scene, continue in this vein and withdraw from any fictive pretence on the stage. Romeo Castellucci notes:

> . . . very often the theatre, the experience of theatre, needs some kind of literalness, some excessive form of reality. This excess of reality threatens on reality itself. And it is a reality that exceeds itself. The presence lies precisely, I think, in this, that the world that it creates is another world with other rules. It's often a very artificial world, a world of conception . . . And it is the presence of giving access to another reality by means of simulacrum or resemblance to the real that is often taken literally, and it is for this reason that it exceeds itself.
> (Castellucci, Castellucci, Guidi, Kelleher and Ridout 2009, 222)

And so the first scene suggests an "excessive form of reality" and the following scene with the children and grenades brings about a "very artificial world" with "other rules", ambiguous and repetitive, obviously lacking any narrative. The scene contains no verbal information whatsoever concerning fictive time or space. The confluence of dissociated contexts such as Christianity, sport games, military ammunition, and schoolchildren against the background of this light-image is also bewildering, making us wonder (and contemplate) what each of these contexts actually represents imaginatively. Moreover, what seems to be a violent act by the children, without any logical cause to its conduct, transposes the pivot of this 'childish game' (or conflict) from being a theatrical representation happening on stage into conflicting imaginative representations in the spectator's mind.

The uncertainty experienced by the spectators – while seeking out a narrative ground for meaning-making, or causal logic beneath what is happening – can only be 'solved' if they submit to their sensory experience and author their own 'narratives' and informed subjective interpretations. Like many unanswered questions with which the piece leaves the spectator to ponder upon, to contemplate and generate a settling meaning for, one can possibly relate to the social, political, existential/theological or psychological dimensions in the conflict between the youngsters and the portrait of Christ.

With this context in mind, and recalling the aesthetic features of the light-image, let us concentrate on the semiotics and poetics of light. It is a quite plain and simple, not decorative or elaborate image. Light, here, is somehow functional in allowing visual perception without manipulating our sight. Its slightly cold tone simply whitens the distribution of the light that usually turns somewhat yellowish when dimmed. In a sense, it is merely a colour correction to repair this 'distortion'. Consequently, the formal characteristics of the light bring into our perception the genuine colours of the performers' skin, and their costumes, without any significant modification. It is neither a fictive light nor emotionally suggestive. The absence of verbal text and the repetitive monotonous action of the youngsters, as inspirational and provoking as they are, do not offer a narrative, and the aesthetic features of the light do not emanate from a narrative, in terms of illustrating fictive light conditions of time and space. Therefore, the semiotic function of this light-image is not grounded in *a narrative*, as light's aesthetic features do not support or illustrate any narrative.

In this case light's formal characteristics do not reflect a mental situation in which a fictive character is portrayed. Let us examine whether the children can be considered 'characters' and whether the qualities of light embody the ground of *a character*. As mentioned before, by placing the children with their backs to the audience and positioning them as a crowd/chorus rather than individuals, Castellucci seems to prevent any identification with, or empathy toward, them. We can gather very little information about the members of this group, except for estimating their age and their socio-economic background through the clothing they wear. Not one of the children, whose sole action is to step on the stage and throw grenades at the portrait for no apparent reason, seems to perform a fictive character with a subjective psychological profile. Moreover the children are non-professional performers and their capability to portray a fictive character would therefore also be limited. All the children together are equivalent to one orchestrated chorus, acting in harmony and executing a performative task with no intention or pretence, 'here and now', as participants in a Happening event. Guidi notes in a conversation about pretence and illusion, in the context of iconic characters performed in mime, that "these figures are like keys because they are insufficient unto themselves . . . these are good inspirations, but no more" (Castellucci, Castellucci, Guidi, Kelleher and Ridout 2009, 221). The performative strength of the children against the icon of Christ is established, among other elements, upon their accumulation and insufficient characterization that allows us to consider them simply as a group of children and/or the representation of contemporary childhood. The light is so straight, plain, informative, and practical that it does not complement the characters by means of suggestive look by light. The light simply brings across their presence, in a neutral form. Since not even one single child/performer performs a fictive character with any psychological depth, I do not consider the light-image to reflect aspects of character. I would suggest, therefore, that the semiotic function of this light-image cannot be acknowledged as being grounded in *a character*.

As we know nothing about the children's motives for action, and since their monotonous action does not develop within the scene, there is no dramatic action in the conservative sense. Nevertheless, the repetitive activity reverberates within the spectator. It is the spectator who changes – and not the action performed. The plainness of the light, distributing evenly at high intensity, in my experience, does not become equivalent to a visual interpretation of a theme or dramatic action by means of light. The visual stimuli suggested by light itself are rather minimal, so that light is almost 'transparent' and 'invisible' in this scene.

Furthermore, the ambiguous qualities this scene consists of relate potentially to themes that span a variety of contexts, whose relevance and validity depend on the engagement of the individual spectator with the performance. With the aesthetics of light mentioned above, the light-image is 'neutral' in character, and follows the conventions of theatre lighting by which the focus is on the human performers. Nonetheless, the significance of this first light-image lies in preparing the spectators for the following light-image, surprising in its originality. The first image is more banal and conventional, while the second is exceptionally symbolic and manipulates our perception of both the space and the activity on the stage. Therefore, the aesthetic features of this first light-image reveal no remarkable characteristics in terms of lighting intensity or angle, of colour, dynamic aspects or optic qualities, and draw no special attention to the look of the children. Due to the above, the ground of the representational function (or meaning) of this light-image lies neither in *a theme* nor in *(dramatic) action*.

Light's aesthetic features – the plainness, colourless and high intensity that seems to flatten the image, in particular – escape atmosphere. The signs of light are not used to generate a supportive atmosphere and to reflect on what is happening in the scene, but merely used to create a neutral lucid visibility in the space, lacking distinctive character. Light is obviously not created out of a 'romantic' approach, to affect the emotions of the spectators through the use of colours or the interrelation of light and shade. Although the light-image takes a different route than this highly charged scene, it is not for the same reasons that Brecht often replaced the unified expression of media with multivocal, separate, and occasionally ironic relations. Here, the alienation between the light and activity on the stage does not create irony. Likewise, the encouragement of the spectators to become aware and critical shifts their attention from theatrical illusion towards the limits of representation. The light-image assists in disrupting theatrical pretence. Although we know that the young performers throw metal objects that only simulate grenades, yet, paradoxically, what we see triggers our imagination and we perceive as it were something real. This phenomenon is a central characteristic for the work of *Societas Raffaello Sanzio* and I will elaborate upon it in the later section about the dramaturgy of the performance. However, the fall into representation occurs retrospectively, in reverse order, when the next light-image comes to the fore with a strong emotional effect and atmosphere. I will elaborate on this 'theatrical mechanism' with respect to the next light-image. As for the first light-image discussed here, I do not consider its semiotic function to be grounded in *emotion* or *atmosphere*.

From my perspective, the semiotic function of this light-image is also not grounded in a *sensation of light*: *hypermediacy* (a deep impression from the presence of the medium) or *spectacularity* (a direct aesthetic pleasure). The aesthetic features of the light itself or the interaction the light-image has with the other media are too simple to evoke any light sensation. Additionally, the signs of light (providing clear visibility) do not display any explicit involvement of technology, as part of phenomenological experience and the poetic dimension of the image. The modesty and subtlety of the medium of light create no aesthetic pleasure originating directly from the light-image. The technology remains concealed and does not attract the spectators' awareness of the medium of light, whereas in the case of the following light-image, light calls for their attention. Consequently, the ground of the representational function (or meaning) of the discussed light-image does not lie in a *light sensation* of *hypermediacy* or *spectacularity*.

The last ground of representation against which this light-image should be examined is that of the *open meaning*. The light-image provides conventional illumination (general lighting) and exposes the space and performers in full visibility, while merely focusing on the children's position. As I explained thoroughly in Chapter 4 on the conceptual framework, light-images whose representation function is grounded in *open meaning* create a situation whereby we experience stimuli or signs of light as 'black holes in the picture'. These stimuli, or signs, in light cannot be easily understood as singular units or in relation to other elements of the performance, since we obtain no satisfying information from them. Yet the spectators sense the underlying associative force and the necessity to interpret the experience provided by the light. In such cases, the spectators are drawn to become active in filling in the gaps with their own imagination and draw connections between aesthetic pleasure and conceptual thinking to validate their interpretations; it recalls Roland Barthes's category of 'third meaning'.[2] Although I did not undergo this process in regard to the first light-image in this scene, I did during the transition to the following image, as discussed in detail in the next analysis. Its clarity and 'characterlessness' keep the first light-image devoid of ambiguity and mystery. This light-image was not intriguing enough to consider its semiotic function as grounded in open meaning. Therefore, the representation through this light-image was not grounded in ***open meaning***, since the image had (almost) no suggestive or ambivalent character.

"Let the Little Children Come to Me" (Matthew 19:14): second light-image

As the scene proceeds, all the children, without exception, face the portrait and continue throwing the grenades (Figure 6.6). The light changes, and the black space between the white floor and the portrait is illuminated, while the frontal light on the children fades out. The children remain lit by the backlights alone, and the grenades gradually accumulate on the floor. The old father stays seated on the bed, bent over with his head down. Obscuring his emotional reaction from the spectators, he covers his face with his hands, in what seems to be either silent weeping or the incapability to confront the dreadful sight. Once the last grenade is thrown, all the children casually pick up their bags, and leave the space together. The scene ends with the elderly man rising from the (possible death-) bed, making his way through a field sown with grenades and disappearing behind the portrait of Christ – as the light fades to complete darkness.

Aesthetic analysis of the light-image

One lighting element composes this light-image, partly included in the previously analysed image:

1   *Backlights* – An additional rear set of backlights illuminates the upstage black space between the children and the portrait of Christ, accompanying the set of backlights from the previous light-image that emphasize the children's silhouettes and cast their shadow on the white floor (Figure 6.6). The light from the additional sources literally hits the grenades as they fly towards the iconic portrait and descend. Occasionally, one can briefly perceive the grenades flying under the lights, intense and swift, resembling a barrage of hail. Since the light is from above, the grenades receive a glow on their upper part and a shadow below. All backlights are coloured with a slightly cold correction filter, probably Lee 201#: *Full CT Blue*. As mentioned before, these lamps feature Fresnel lenses, softening the optical quality of this light on the floor.

Figure 6.6 Romeo Castallucci, *On the Concept of the Face, Regarding the Son of God*. A group of children with Gianni Plazzi (right).
Photo: Yaron Abulafia

Semiotic and poetic analysis of the light-image

Considering the single lighting element mentioned above, how are the aesthetic features of the light experienced or used as signs; what are the signs about; and how are the signs used in a poetic way?

For the same reasons mentioned in the previous analysis, the phenomenological experience and semiotic function of this light-image is not grounded in *a narrative*. Clearly, the scene avoids presenting a narrative but portrays merely one major event related to the youngsters – they arrive, they throw the grenades, and they depart, leaving behind chaos. There is no suggestion of fictive space or time in which the situation takes place. There is, thus, no narrative to which the qualities of light may be related.

Light's aesthetic features – namely, the backlights silhouetting the boys and girls against the white floor, in the absence of any front light – are used as signs (in my experience) to reflect upon the children's mental state, or psyche, as personas. While viewing the performance, the sudden vanishing of the frontal light results in the anonymity of the children, feeling like losing them. The image of *shadowed children* throwing grenades is so suggestive and exhilarating because when the semi-darkness obscures their individual identities these children can imaginatively become anyone in their age – and this might hurt even more. It becomes easier to project one's own associations, ideas or emotions onto these shadowed child-figures. These unknown bodies evolve into *the idea of a character in the mind of the spectator*. We look at these silhouettes as if we were gazing at a black mirror. And even though the children do not pretend to undergo any mental process of revelation throughout the scene, so typical of fictive characters in dramatic plays, light itself does change through time and it influences our engagement toward the child-figures. As a result of this light-change (with the children as catalysts), light draws us, spectators, to look into our own abyss. Although Castellucci states that there is something resembling a childish game about this scene, for me, watching the shadowed children felt even more intriguing and horrific than watching them under full light in the previous light-image.[3]

Indeed, the children do not perform fictive characters (in the traditional sense), as none of them reflects a psychological profile of a character. In this scene, however, they nonetheless evoked in me empathy, anxiety, humour and regret. Bryoni Trezise refers to Jill Bennett's book *Empathic Vision*, and argues that "for Bennett, affect has a role in enabling a form of sensorial empathy toward the subject of trauma that works against the kinds of 'crude empathy' that merely offer 'feeling for another based on the assimilation of the other's experience of the self'" (Trezise 2012, 215). Perhaps the fact that we are not accustomed to watching such young boys and girls performing professional theatre, and definitely not 'performing war crimes', made their presence so effective and strong in my experience. Their sole activity in the scene is one of conflict – even if it is not a 'dramatic' one according to the Aristotelian *Poetics*. And the antagonist they confront is the portrait of Christ.

Ironically, this light-image makes the grenades more visible objects than the performers, when the latter are put in the dark. The exchange of attention reached by shifting the focus of the light from the performers onto the grenades – bouncing against the backdrop and rolling on the floor – intensifies the rebellious action of protagonists against the portrait of Christ as a symbolic act. It might be amusing to ponder who the 'heroes' of this scene are: the children or the grenades? Due to the emotional effect achieved by shadowing the youngsters and making them anonymous, the ground of the representational function (or meaning) of this light-image can be acknowledged as grounded in *character*; though not the dramatic kind.

Throughout the scene, the transition between the two light-images creates a *dramatizing effect*, albeit without any genuine dramatic action. Altering the look of the children intensifies the mystery around their action, and emphasizes the ambiguity around the concomitant danger and playfulness in which they act. Light gradually amplifies the overall experience of the scene and heightens its expressiveness, while the youngsters perform the same physical action monotonously, in fact. The *physical activity* (to distinguish it from a dramatic action) contains no progression and remains quite monotonous throughout the entire scene, without any evolution that could indicate a process of self-reflection by the children. It seems that the throwing of grenades at an iconic image is rather pointless and, likewise, the immersive soundscape of explosions does not trigger any emotion in the young children. One might wonder whether they are even aware of the danger inherent in their 'toys', and the reason for using them so. Castellucci is correct in noting the playfulness of the scene. Nevertheless, it is the structured, yet surprising, configuration of signs and contexts that creates rich poetics and makes the visual and acoustic dimensions of the scene so charged with associations for some of the audience, while outrageous for others. The signs of the light-image, being considered with the signs of the other media, constitute visual stimuli associated with the *theme* and the *action*.

The light-image alone makes the scene more radical and full of tension.[4] The aesthetic features of this light-image enrich the poetics of the scene by highlighting and intensifying the act of throwing grenades at the face of Christ while obscuring its executors. The bodies transform into *the idea of character in the mind of the spectator*, while struggling in a post-dramatic conflict. The electronically reworked soundscape of a bouncing basketball, with the splashing of the 'grenade hail' triggering pre-recorded sampled sounds of explosions, generate an ambivalent experience. On the one hand, aspects of playfulness, sportive liveliness, enthusiasm and a thrilling effect of speed and movement; on the other hand, the experience includes some degree of violence, depriving the youngsters of their individual features, and even the precocity of today's youth, the difficulty in protecting them from evil, depravity or – in tragic cases – abuse.

The space in between the protagonists (children) and antagonist (Christ) gains prominence as *the venue of their conflict*. The imaginary traces left by the grenades create a web in between the anonymous children and their objective. This space becomes a representative medium: between the pupils and the institution, between the followers and the shepherd, between sons and father, between Modernism and Classicism, and between 'action-painting' (of excrement on the floor) and the Old Masters portrait hanging upstage. In this space, grenades substitute textbooks inside schoolbags; the themes reflect rebellion against religious authority and private supervision (manifested by the huge observing eyes of Christ), and sociopolitical revolution of the young against the old order. Regarding the themes and the dramatized conflict noted previously, I would therefore consider the phenomenological experience and semiotic function of this light-image to be grounded in *theme* and (non-dramatic) *action*.

By bringing about the sense of loss of the children's identity – a highly theatrical effect in itself – the formal characteristics of this light-image are used to emphasize what we had been blind to earlier. The change from the previous image to this light-image may draw us, spectators, out of our comfort zone, for several reasons: in conjunction with the explosive sounds, the vanishing identity possibly becomes a light-sign for the loss of infant innocence, or worse – a sign of death. The violence, also manifested in the intense reflection of light from the white floor and the throwing of grenades, intensifies the emotional engagement with the scene, creating a disturbing and loud, even immersive, experience. There is something almost ritual in this repetitive pattern of violence followed by the children that, together with the silhouetting light, lends the scene a spiritual dimension, even without any connection to religious affiliation associated with Christianity.

The second light-image also manifests an artistic statement against a well-known lighting convention, by deliberately obscuring the children using backlight alone. This choice is clearly an outstanding deviation from a theatrical convention by which the focus is usually on the performers as the driving force of the scene, and, therefore, performers usually receive most of the illumination and attention. The strength of this light-image is in its indirect reference to the human condition: by picking up the grenades as they fly while leaving the children in shadow, the light assists in rejecting the kind of emotional empathy that the theatre of Realism encourages. Moreover, it is the transition from the previous, non-atmospheric and plain, light-image to this image that lets us fall into imaginative representation. In her essay, Trezise writes: "it seems that the very inversion of mechanics of representation generates a particular affective dimension through its process of self-negation" (Trezise 2012, 207). The first light-image 'informs' us with the artificiality of the presentation executed by the children, and yet the second light-image triggers our imagination to surrender the bewildering magic of theatre, closing one's eye to the mechanism of the image. On this note, Guidi states:

> In fact, the moment in which the techniques of the theatre are unmasked, according to a logic of dramaturgy that accept the disclosure of the technique of theatre, that is the moment that also achieves the maximum emotion . . . It's theatre, theatrical technique, and the theatre offers it as such . . . These are elements of the theatre which are not available to the cold and Brechtian mode because the epic mode has nothing to do with them. Because it is always a dramaturgy of the emotions. It is a dramaturgy that works on the nerves.
> (Castellucci, Castellucci, Guidi, Kelleher and Ridout 2009, 217)

By shifting our reception between what seems to be (performed) representation and the presentation (of the real), light creates an unstable atmosphere and evokes in us uncertain emotions toward the nature of what we experience in the performance. By confronting us with the shortcomings of our visual perception, i.e. with regard to our own manoeuvred field of vision that initially failed to detect details in the scene, light tantalizes us concerning the untrustworthiness of our incomplete sight and invalid experience. Therefore, the meaning (or the representational function) of the light-image is also grounded in *atmosphere* and *emotion*.

In spite of the simple aesthetic features of this light-image our attention to the medium of light increases. Light succeeds in doing so due to its liberation from the traditional hierarchy of media in the theatre, namely, the overturning of traditional lighting conventions with respect to the illumination of the performer. As already explained, without too complicated lighting equipment, the gradual reduction of frontal light and the decrease of visibility dominate a great deal of the scene. A major element in the semiotics of this light-image rests precisely on *the lack of light*, on the *'shadow of the image'*. Castellucci's choice to 'problematize' the visual perception of ongoing stage activity, and to reconstruct the image by means of light is no less than sensational in making light self-evident in our consciousness. It is the unconventional use of light that decisively directs the spectator's attention, provides aesthetic pleasure and launches an interpretive process concerning the significance of this lighting change. For the above reasons, I would argue, the ground of the representational function (or meaning) of the light-image also lies in the *sensation of light*. Two kinds of sensation: while *hyper-mediacy* relates to the dominant presence of the medium, *spectacularity* relates to the aesthetic pleasure one can gain from light.

The various grounds of representations I approached up to this point, in their unique ways, all indicate a tendency to erode some of the form in order to get closer to an underlying concept (the idea of a character, the loss of innocence or loss of life, the loss of confidence in visual perception and distinction between the illusory and the 'real'). This light-image is like an exercise of visual perception and reception – at the same time, honing these skills and, simultaneously, veiling them with imaginative representation in the mind of the addressee. The light causes the unity of space and time to collapse. Even though the ongoing physical activity of the children and the soundscape hold some coherency, the light transposes these elements away from their daily context. For these reasons, the 'black holes' that this light-image opens up in the scene cannot constitute one single answer – the experience is so poetic that the mind drifts from one association to another in search of a settling meaning. This is, therefore, an extraordinary example of a light-image the phenomenological experience and semiotic function of which is grounded in *open meaning*. Indeed, it is the light that enhances the tension and mystery throughout the scene, becoming far more spiritually and symbolically charged by tying a suggestive rhizome of relations between the various elements.[5] The light-image and its relationship with the other media are very intriguing and bear a suggestive character that remains ambiguous. Therefore, I would consider the representation through this light-image to be grounded in *open meaning*.

The Resurrection of the Face: the closure scene

The last analysis in this chapter will be dedicated to one light-image from the third and last scene of the performance. The scene begins with the father exiting the space and the light dimming to total darkness. After a while, once the spectators have become accustomed to their loss of any visual perception, immense gusts of wind, accompanied by a mesmerising soundscape of distorted shouting human voices, burst in at irregular intervals, striking the spectators' face and blowing their hair. A weak and soft light then slowly shines in and a glimpse of the portrait can be caught. The image is vague and seems to be squeezed downward – the width of the format remains the same, but its height is initially much smaller. This effect is achieved by the portrait's being slowly raised from the stage floor, until it is restored to its original setting. Two crossing lighting sources then illuminate the painting from the high stage balconies on the sides, one at a time, increasing and shifting in intensity and direction. Behind the canvas, the deliberate stretching movements of rope-climbers are revealed, as if a metamorphosis is taking place under the (printed image of the) skin. Light changes emphasize the sense of plasticity and three-dimensionality suddenly emerging from within the flat canvas. Soon after, dark stains appear dripping onto the canvas, as if these are drops of black ink, blood or faeces (from the first scene). These stains exude from the face through long rips or scratches, starting near the eyes – 'viscous tears of holy shit' (Figure 6.7).

In due course, the entire canvas becomes soaking wet from the dark liquid and the liquid erases the printed image, as if the face disappears. Some blinking strokes of white light flash from behind the canvas but the lighting sources themselves remain unclear. The rope-climbers tear the canvas entirely, as white neon letters integrated into a metal wall could be observed, just behind the portrait of Christ. Slowly, the text *You are my shepherd* becomes apparent (Figure 6.8), followed later by the emergence of the word '*not*' between the words, creating the statement *You are **not** my Shepherd*, perhaps denying or even denouncing the beginning of Psalm 23, originally: "*The Lord is my shepherd*" (Psalm 23, 1). Then, the image of Christ's portrait is restored in the form of lighting projection before the performance ends, and this light-image will constitute the third case for the analysis of light (Figure 6.9).

Aesthetic analysis of the light-image

This light-image consists of two lighting elements (Figure 6.9):

1   *Lighting in letterforms* – Behind the canvas with the portrait of Christ, a black wall stands and has cutouts in the shapes of letters, and neon or fluorescent tubes are installed just behind the cutouts. The cold white light in letterforms is reflected indirectly from what seems to be a white backdrop behind these cut outs.
2   *The projection of Christ in light* – When the portrait emerges after the canvas is torn, it is *an image of light*, projected on and reflected from the black wall. Importantly, it is not a print or paint, but *a coloured light* – like a slide projection produced by a video beamer from the auditorium.[6]

Semiotic and poetic analysis of the light-image

Considering the lighting element mentioned above, how are the aesthetic features of the light experienced or used as signs; what are the signs about; and how are the signs used poetically?

The light-signs in the scene are associated with two categories, from a semiotic perspective: a group of symbolic signs (letters), and an iconic sign (in form of light projection) that stands for the painting *Christ Blessing* by Italian Renaissance painter Antonello da Messina. To begin with, these light-signs that display graphically '*you are my shepherd*', rephrase the well-known verse "*The Lord is my Shepherd*" from Psalm 23 that is ascribed to King David. This psalm is associated with several narratives about belief and leadership from the Old and New Testaments. Interestingly, Psalm 23 is occasionally recited at Jewish and Christian funerals alike, and the ideas of human death and the Resurrection are definitely relevant to this performance. Likewise, the metanarrative of Christ underlies the entire performance in different degrees, due to the presence of the portrait. This narrative, however, echoes more explicitly through the last scene, with the portrait rising from the floor so 'dramatically' and the subsequent assault it suffers. The scene is nonetheless speechless; an English text is included, but no one is present to

Figure 6.7 Romeo Castallucci, *On the Concept of the Face, Regarding the Son of God*. Staining and distorting (from behind) the printed portrait of Christ in the last scene. Photo: Yaron Abulafia

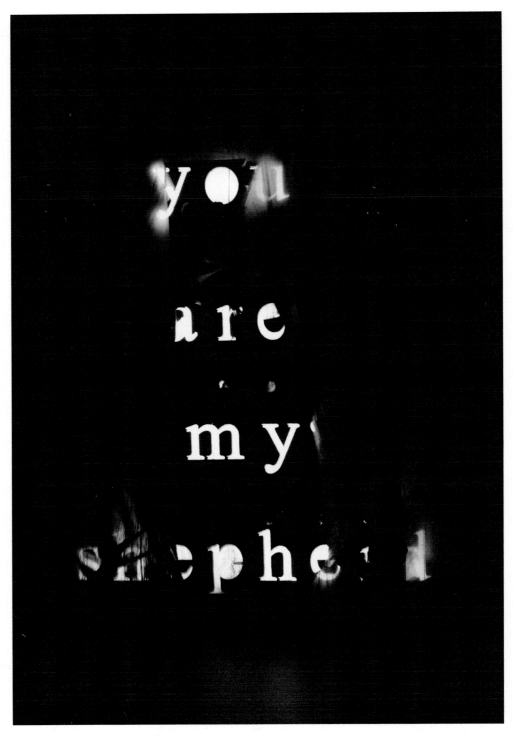

Figure 6.8 Romeo Castallucci, *On the Concept of the Face, Regarding the Son of God*. Tearing apart the already soaking wet canvas to reveal the neon letters in the last scene of the performance. Photo: Yaron Abulafia

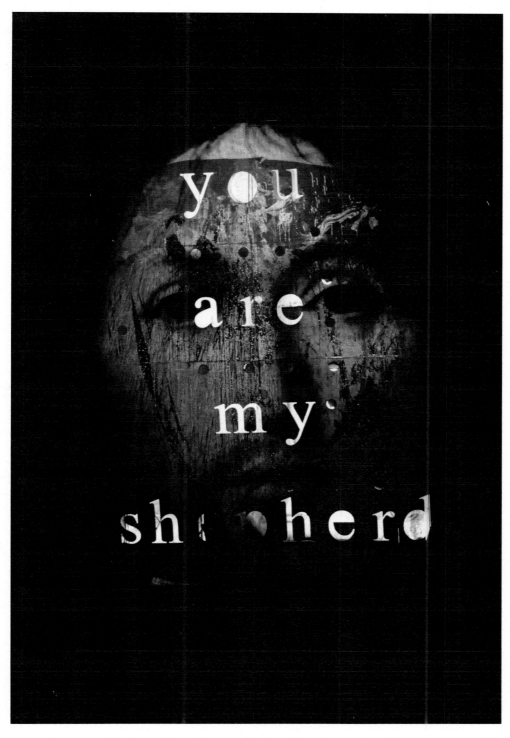

Figure 6.9 Romeo Castallucci, *On the Concept of the Face, Regarding the Son of God*. A projection of Antonello da Messina's portrait of *Christ Blessing*, after the soaked canvas was torn to reveal the neon letters *"you are my shepherd"*. Photo: Yaron Abulafia

utter it – the text turns into a visual representation and its underlying narrative remains unspoken.

In the absence of living beings/speakers, the medium of light steps into the role, so to speak, and graphically emits symbolic signs of the English language, recalling the most deeply embodied narrative of Western culture. The semiotic function of the light-image is, therefore, grounded in *the narrative* on two levels: not only are the qualities of light used as illustration of the text, taking artificial light shaped as symbolic signs of letterforms and words that relate to the narrative, but, on a more conceptual level, they also remediate and embody the narrative into the energy of light.

The second lighting element in this light-image – an iconic sign – is the projected portrait of da Messina's *Christ Blessing* onto the black wall, replicating the printed face in light. The spectators had witnessed the face rising from the stage floor at the beginning of the scene, after minutes of darkness and blowing winds that could be very well interpreted as an imaginative representation of the Resurrection. As the portrait re-emerges as a vision in light, followed by the staining and tearing of the canvas, and exposing the rephrased verse *'you are my shepherd'*, it calls to mind the idea of reincarnation. The iconic sign of the projected portrait-in-light is used to represent a recovered or *reincarnated image* of Christ in light, tied to the Christian narrative of the Resurrection. Therefore, in light of all the above, I consider the semiotic function of this light-image to be strongly grounded in **the narrative**.

Let us turn to the experience and meaning of light, with regard to ideas of *character* and a central *theme* or (non- or dramatic) *action*. Analysis of the light-image with reference to these three concepts integrated together becomes sensible in case of such a 'thematic character' as Christ. In this performance, the gradual development of Christ's character and the theme of the Resurrection are analogous to the evolution of the (concept of the) face from a material-based image into an image of light. From a physical perspective, the canvas absorbs some waves from the spectrum of light and reflects others, while the second image appears purely in light, seems more brilliant than the previous image and is combined with the lighting letters. Media transformation (from a solid substance into photons) and aesthetic transfiguration are used to represent a conceptual reflection of light upon the character. The sole text in the scene is *"you are my shepherd"* integrated into the face (Figure 6.9). The lighting letters within the face can be taken as a reflection upon the 'inner world' of the fictive character or its psychological state.

The two signs of light put together (letterforms and projection) are mutually reflecting and enrich interpretation possibilities. To mention but a few possible relations among many more: the symbolic signs of letters in light are engendered by, or emerge from, the stained portrait – in this case, the text substituted with the iconic image of Christ. Alternatively, the *form* of the face transforms into a *concept*, mediated into written language, and is now represented graphically in black and white. The reincarnation of the image in the 'sublime' light – recalling (cultural) memory of the face by means of light projection – complements the text. The destruction of the face is also the destruction of older aesthetics. Discarding the layer of the canvas might seek to provoke a prospect of self-salvation through the adoption of a new humanist position, rebuke of any institutional religious authority in favour of freethinking and existential ideas.

Unlike other scenes in the performance, the closing scene does not include any human performer, except for the hidden rope-climbers, dressed in black like puppeteers. Of all the scenes, this one is also the most colourful and saturated, fleeting, violent

and spectacular. With similarities to the disappearing children, the re-emerging face –
persistently reappearing as light after the abuse of its material representation – brings
back *the idea of a character* through empathy. One can consider this scene to be the
'Nietzschean requiem' of the performance, in which two characters or entities participate: one of which is the (imaginative) representation of Christ, whose narrative we all
know (perhaps the children did not); and the second is the individual spectator, who is
approached directly by the black stage with *"you are my shepherd"* in white letters. Just
before the light projection restores the face, the spectator can either read the verse but
envisage no shepherd, or understand the verse as a call for taking responsibility and
becoming a shepherd. After a while, the word *"not"* appears in the middle, to subvert
the previous meaning of the sentence. One can then read: *"you are not my shepherd"*, as a
refusal, opposition, anger, recognition by the spectator, or as the voice of inner doubts
one might have. The Nietzschean statement that *"God is dead"* can definitely be associated with the staining of the portrait of Christ and the disappearance of the face, and
also with the subversion of the verse by the appearance of light-signs in forms of letters. Due to all the above-mentioned, the representation through this light-image is
grounded in **character**, **theme** and (non-dramatic) **action**.

Various contrasting qualities in the aesthetics of this light-image bear a subliminal
tension that is central when experiencing this image., These include: the cold fluorescent tubes against mostly warm, peach-like, skin colour; the rigid graphic letter fonts,
laser cut, against the projection of a 'hand-made' portrait; and a product of enlightenment, industrial revolution and mechanical reproduction against the unique creation
of old-school, Old Master style. The visual qualities and the contexts of the two light-
signs (letters and portrait) are alien to each other and opposing one another, so that the
text seems to impose itself arbitrarily on the image (Figure 6.9).

The aesthetic contrast and conflicting signs mentioned above are used to intensify
the unsettling, inner tension within the image and within the spectator. Written language (entirely conceptual, symbolic signs) seems as if it was forcefully patched onto
the image of the face, originally painted in hand and expressing so much emotion. The
portrait – with a huge pair of eyes gazing back at the spectators – expresses sorrow,
deep compassion and understanding, and embodies the tragic human condition, the
melancholy and self-agony. However, the configuration of the iconic portrait with the
letter signs together creates a relationship of contrast and submission: firstly, the portrait is 'rejected' and ripped, then temporarily replaced by the text, and later, it returns
in greater vibrancy.

Discomfort and friction, therefore, lie at the core of this light-image, affecting the
transcendental realm of emotions and atmospheres through a sensorial or emotive experience, especially by means of light. This morbid image, which was generated almost
entirely by lighting, was emotionally moving, disturbing and dissonant; yet so compelling as to keep me observing, and examining its atmospheric and spiritual effects, as
well as its conceptual depth. Therefore, from my perspective, the ground of the representational function or meaning of this light-image also lies in **atmosphere** and **emotion**.

This last scene is carried out as a performative installation or 'theatre of devices', with
kinetic and metamorphosing scenographic elements, such as the canvas, letters in light
and the projection. It is accompanied with a soundscape of distorted human voices associated with a terrified crowd of people in pain, without any apparent speaker or speech
occurring. However, the way in which Castellucci composes the images in this part of

the scene is outstanding: light becomes the only visible medium and spatial perception is challenged when the stage is so dark that it becomes a 'non-space', and instead we perceive only a flat image on the back wall. The letters of light recall the works of light artist Bruce Nauman (1941–) and Joseph Kosuth (1945–), with neon tubes, shaped in forms of letters and figures. Although Castellucci conceals the lighting sources and the technological equipment behind the back wall (used as a masking for the light to go through the cutouts), the medium of light celebrates its authoritative role and the sensuous influence of its signs – the material of which the signs are made comes to the fore.

Taking into consideration the conceptual complexity that has already been presented in the analysis of this light-image, the signs of light become mostly prominent in a highly spectacular manner – as if the 'resurrection' of the portrait (projected in light) manifests the victory of light over darkness and the staining ink/blood/excrement. Clearly, the way in which light is employed here enhances the poetic dimension of the medium of light and that of the scene. Therefore, the sensorial experience and semiotic function of this light-image is also grounded in a *light sensation of spectacularity* (aesthetic pleasure) and *hypermediacy* (a deep impression from the presence of the medium).

Projected in light, the portrait is a light-sign whose meaning remains open and asks for our special attention. The portrait undergoes a symbolic transfiguration during the three scenes of *On the Concept of the Face, Regarding the Son of God*, and it is the pivot of 'open' meaning in the performance. Each scene in turn lends further significance to the image of the face, through the gradual evacuation of the space and the growing abstraction of the performance:

– In the first scene – that of 'The Father': the portrait remains on the whole ignored, until the father and son both howl together next to the white bed, resulting in the illumination of the portrait and the son leaving the father in favour of Christ (kissing its painted/printed lips).
– In the second scene – that of 'The Son': the face becomes the target for the grenades thrown by a group of children, and three light-images characterize and emphasize different aspects of the action: first, focusing on the children; then, moving away to the grenades and the medial space to the portrait; ending with highlighting the portrait of Christ gazing back at the children or at the spectators, or at both.
– In the third scene – that of 'the Holy Spirit': the portrait is destroyed, then restored or remediated by the medium of light, eventually creating a setting in which all the visual signs are merely signs of light.

As a light-sign, the projection of the face in light does not offer any clear instruction for interpretation. There is nonetheless a subliminal consistency and logical trace marked by visual dramaturgy, whereby the face in light is a 'successor' of the printed portrait. It is highly sensed that the artist has created an intentional framework in which the use of the sign follows certain underlying logic, perhaps unknown as yet, but reasonable. The portrait in light escapes the pinpointing of meaning, and it 'drifts' into complex areas, but not according to arbitrary choices. One has the opportunity to notice that the light-signs have no fixed position, their relations with the signs from other media are unstable and their context evolve in surprising ways. Whether one's view follows a causal or formal logic, the emergence of the projected portrait is an exciting sign that triggers the spectators to ponder its *openness of meaning* and complement the 'black holes' with informed subjective interpretation. I would, finally, suggest that the representation through this light-image is also grounded in ***open meaning***. The light-image is strikingly engaging and it evokes cognitive activity regarding the spiritual and conceptual dimensions of the scene and the light, in particular.

The dramaturgy of light in *On the Concept of the Face, Regarding the Son of God*

Three fundamental principles can be distinguished in the dramaturgy of the light in *On the Concept of the Face, Regarding the Son of God*:

1   *Light as a philosophical category* – Light helps us study the nature of our reality, negotiate and acquire knowledge about the conditions of our existence, since light generates 'illumination', in terms of clarification. From the beginning, without light there is no visual perception and the spatial dimension cannot be grasped. According to our instinctive, survival-related, emotive and associative cognitive patterns, the human brain distinguishes some phenomena or objects to be more urgent and worthy of attention than others. Light has the potential to tune our attention differentially. Light makes an impact on our perception of (staged) reality by exposing and highlighting different elements of the performance, resulting in a higher degree of attention and a deeper semiotic effort concerning those elements. Light constitutes a beautiful manipulation of the spectator, a pair of spectacles through which to look at the performance. It *recomposes* the visual perception of reality and affects how we prioritize our attention. As we have found earlier in this chapter, even when the same activity occurs and merely the light changes, perception is reworked and becomes more (self-) evident to the spectators. Light 'convinces' us to perceive and think in a certain way. Therefore, *light is an argument – it is rhetoric!*

   In the first section of the performance, for example, the lighting emphasizes the general direction in which the father and son will go – walking from the living room (audience left) through the table area (centre), and ending near the bed (audience right). However, the light does not follow the spacing of the performers on the stage wherever they are, as already noted, according to traditional conventions of theatre lighting design. The light foresees and anticipates the motion of the performers by highlighting areas and scenographic details prior to the performers' arrival. It precedes the performers and moves away from them. With the metamorphosis of the space, light lends significance and poetic expression to objects (such as pieces of furniture) by increasing their visibility, and without the performers actually using or reaching out to these objects. In this respect, light sets the space in motion, starting from the living room, where the noisy television displays the outside world, then it moves to the little dining table, and ends near the bed, where one escapes into the subconscious mind of dreams and imagination. It seems as though light pushes towards the bed the central action of the son cleansing his elderly father. Clearly, approaching the bed also signifies the degeneration of the old man and his withdrawal from the events of normal daily life (furthest away from the TV), moving desperately from one point to another, yearning for relief or rest (in peace).

Likewise, the light-images in the scene with the children previously analysed are shown to constitute another example of how a change of light that sets the space in motion can affect our perception and trigger a whole new cognitive process regarding the meaning we give to what we see, even though it is the same continuous activity. We reveal in that activity details anew simply because it is illuminated differently.

2   *Light as a spiritual category (toward the representation of the sublime)* — Ever since the emergence of the Classical Greek tragedy, the assimilation of mythical ingredients such as the transcendental realm of gods usually went hand in hand with the use of natural – and, later, artificial – light. Light was (and some lighting designers would say: still is) the most spectacular medium used to visually represent spirituality and sublimity. This convention originated, in particular, in the Christian medieval theatre, but gradually declined with the Renaissance, as the religious influence lost its central position in the theatre.

In *On the Concept of the Face, Regarding the Son of God* we find a unique and contemporary use of autonomous light, for the representation of highly complex cultural issues that both the theatre and visual arts have long been confronting: how to escape the corruption of a concept by giving it a representative form. Light Art also originated as a reaction to philosophical debates among visual artists, who aimed to escape the form and eventually dismissed the imitative image of reality and the pretence of light (in painting) for the sake of real light.[7] These artists adopted the medium of light and sought to create sensory, emotional and conceptual experiences primarily by means of artificial light. In the last scene, too, we find an aesthetics that is highly identified with ideas of various light-artists. In the previous scenes as well, light shows mysterious behaviour and autonomous character. It integrates with all the other media involved, but still remains dominant and follows a subliminal logic, or will of its own. Even the lack of light, in the minutes of blowing winds, provides a powerful immersive experience that becomes so meaningful in respect to the elderly man vanishing behind the portrait just before. These profound qualities of light allude to the imaginative representation of Christ, or to *our view* on what Christ represents for us, first through the medium of print and later through that of light.

3   *'Make-believe' and the boundaries of representation* — Although elements in Castellucci's theatre occasionally come close to Hyperrealism, it would be misleading to consider them as a 'naïve' representation of reality based on verisimilitude. Paradoxically, by pointing to the artificiality of the performance and presenting its pretence, the spectators know that whatever they perceive on the stage is genuine, but then they still fall into imaginative representations. The effect, however, is two-sided. On the one hand, the intimate and hyperrealistic performance of father and son – the first loses the control of his bowels and the latter cleans him – is compellingly emotional and creates empathy (thus, as effect of 'make-believe'). On the other hand, withstanding any theatrical illusion, the environment in which the scene is located manifests the artificial qualities of the situation: neutral non-atmospheric light reveals the bare theatre stage and its architecture. A more explicit example is the father spilling the liquid (we imagine to be excrement) on himself, by himself,

out of a plastic gallon near the bed; as if to remind us that what we see is not real (Figure 6.4). Such friction interrupts the emotional elevation, while making the theatrical event more believable, in the sense of genuine staged activity, happening 'here and now'. We know that the image is artificially constructed; yet, *we submit to the image **we imagine**.*

Castellucci himself states (and I assume he does so jokingly) that in his theatre there is "no magic . . . The work is not a work of imagination – I like more connection between things that belong to us".[8] However, on a more serious note, the theatre of *Socìetas Raffaello Sanzio* ardently examines the boundaries between the fictive (or illusionistic) representation of reality and the actual reality; or, in other words, how to present something 'true' (showing reality, in the broadest sense) in a place that is not the 'real' world (theatre). In his essay *Make-believe: Socìetas Raffaello Sanzio do theatre*, Ridout writes:

> This tendency to see the 'real' in the work of *Socìetas Raffaello Sanzio* is in fact an effect of the success of their theatrical pretending . . . The intensity of the encounter was produced by the fact that I had never seen anyone else taking the imitation game so seriously. It was as though no other theatre had considered that it might be possible to make representations that might be taken for the real thing; as though no one else believed that the theatre might be a kind of magic.
>
> (Ridout 2006, 177)

By means of vast production efforts and tremendous budgets, the almost hyperrealistic scenes encourage us to believe that all we see on the stage happens for real, as ambiguous, cruel or dangerous as it may seem. This 'realness' is enhanced by the participation of small children, babies or living animals, and situations consisting in actual danger and possible loss of control. Although stage and lighting technology often play a major role in the performances, Castellucci conceals a great deal of its complexity and reveals only what he can develop into a transcendental realm of *the poetics of the machine*. The mechanical and the animal, each in its own way, represent the poetry of the inhuman, and their usage is rhetorical in order to establish trust in the 'realness' of the presentation. Castellucci states that when engaging with a work of art, he wishes to become lost or confused, despite the risk inherent in such kinds of event: "Risk is to be lost in the piece, when I encounter an object of art".[9] Beyond the spectator's risk of 'failing to know something more' or failing to engage with the piece, there is also the artist's risk, of which Castellucci's work consists: the unexpected participation of babies, animals and the extensive pre-programmed stage machinery and technology of lighting, sound, video, flying bars, etc.

Aside of the risk in the process of representation, an effect of 'make-believe' is also achieved through the presentation of pain – a pivotal feature in the theatre of *Socìetas Raffaello Sanzio*. Not a pretended pain, as provided on the stage by image and sound, but the pain that the addressees themselves experience through seeing and hearing pain presented to them. Lehmann writes that post-dramatic theatre brought about "a transition from *represented pain* to *pain experienced in representation*" (Lehmann 2006, 166, italic in the original).[10] Seeing pain has a penetrating, almost immediate, visceral effect on the body of the beholder, resulting in a powerful emotional affect. The condition of pain presented by a performer, Trezise notes, "can articulate a conception of the remembering body in postmodernity that moves it beyond simple alignments between spectator sensation of, and empathic identification with, a suffering other" (Trezise 2012, 208).

Very delicate and accurate work of dramaturgy is required in order to blend different modes of representation in opposing directions, and to balance contradicting forces within the theatrical moment, giving away some literality while obscuring other stimuli/information. The power of the image in cognition, and its influence on our imagination, depends on the associations of the spectators and the semiotic drift in which they engage. The emotional effect on the spectator, writes Trezise, "is built out of a continuous collapse and rebuilding of relations between real and fake, sensation and spectacle" (Trezise 2012, 207). For example, the first light-image in the scene with the children takes 'an objective' position of showing the activity on stage without modifying it in perception. Light conducts an informative function, seems to merely enable visual perception. The following light-image, silhouetting the children, creates an artificial atmosphere and drastically affects our reception of the scene. If the first light-image is plain and seems to be lacking in artificiality, the second image is an example of pretence, 'performativity' and effect of dramatization.

Castellucci is quoted in *The Guardian,* stating about this performance: "Theatre is a very powerful form because it is very close to real life. Theatre is a black mirror of our existence" (O'Mahony 2011). A review by Matt Trueman gives an idea what degree the effects of immediacy and suspense of disbelief reach when the effects of pretence and the 'real' collide. Here, faeces and odour are used to complement the tragic effect of a declining man, but the piece of 'realness' that cannot be fabricated is the naked old body, concomitantly horrifying and humanizing the form of theatre. Trueman refers to the empathy spectators develop, since: "Each of us will be the son. Each of us will be the father". Concerned with the future, the horror "comes not from the shit, which we know to be synthetic, but the father's bottom. Weathered and limp, it is so out of shape that it's almost unrecognizable as a bottom. This eroded state of degradation awaits us all" (Trueman 2011).

Castellucci examines the influence of different types of representation on our corporeal experience by stimulating our senses and imagination in powerful and uncompromising ways. His poetics are engineered to wind around hyperrealistic pretence blended with 'exposure' of the underlying mechanism of the representation, trapping the spectator against the background of reality vs imagination. As this chapter presents, light plays a key role in this duality, fundamental and highly identified with the theatre of *Societas Raffaello Sanzio.*

Notes

1 Throughout the entire book, I indicate positions and sides of the stage according to the Anglo-Saxon system, taking the performers' point of view, which is opposite to what is common in most European theatres that relate to the spectators' perspective.

2 For elaboration, see in Chapter 3 and Chapter 4 of this study.

3 *Holland Festival 2011 – Meet the Artist:* Romeo Castellucci in a conversation with the audience, Schouwburg Amsterdam, the Netherlands, 11 June 2011.

4 The change in the scene is ascribed to the medium of light, since the physical activity persists in the same monotonous way, as well as the sound of explosions, and it is the light that modifies the way we perceive the children on stage.

5 The notion of 'rhizome' is put forward by Gilles Deleuze and Félix Guattari in *A Thousand Plateaus: Capitalism and Schizophrenia* (1989), and is referred to in the introduction to this book.

6 As already explained in the introduction to this study, I consider certain light outputs and effects that originate in video beamers as light and not as film, especially in the case of this portrait, when the projection could have been generated by a simple profile-spot lantern with a coloured glass gobo (like a projection slide for lighting). Perhaps the production chooses to use a video beamer as a potential distributer of a greater light intensity and for practical touring reasons. However, the image is static; it is not a work of film but a static coloured frontal projection of light. For the reasons mentioned above, I analyse this projection like any other light, without reservations.

7 For an elaboration of this subject, see Chapter 2.

8 Romeo Castellucci in a conversation moderated by Thea Brejzek in the Prague Quadrennial 2011, Prague, The Czech Republic, 16 June 2011.

9 Ibid.

10 Lehmann, H. T., *Postdramatic Theatre*, translated and foreword by K. Jürs-Munby, Abingdon & New York: Routledge, 2006.

References

Castellucci. C., Castellucci, R., Guidi, C., Kelleher, J. and Ridout. N., *The Theatre of Societas Raffaello Sanzio*, Abingdon and New York: Routledge, 2009 (first printed 2007).

Deleuze, G., and Guattari, F., *A Thousand Plateaus: Capitalism and Schizophrenia*, Minneapolis, MN: University of Minnesota Press, 1st edition, 1987.

Lehmann, H.T., *Postdramatic Theatre*, translated by Karen Jürs-Munby, Abingdon and New York: Routledge, 2006.

Novati, G. C., "Language under Attack: The Iconoclastic Theatre of *Società Raffaello Sanzio*", in *Theatre Research International*, 34, 1, 2009.

O'Mahony, J., *Romeo Castellucci: Christ . . . What is that Smell?*, Guardian.co.uk, Tuesday 19 April, 2011. http://www.guardian.co.uk/stage/2011/apr/19/romeo-castellucci-concept-face-son?INTCMP=SRCH (last accessed 7 November 2011).

Ridout, N., "Make-believe: *Società Raffaello Sanzio* do theatre", in *Contemporary Theatres in Europe: A critical companion*, edited by Joe Kelleher and Nicholas Ridout, Abingdon and New York: Routledge, 2006.

Trezise, B., "Spectatorship that Hurts: *Società Raffaello Sanzio* as Meta-affective Theatre of Memory", in *Theatre Research International*, 37, 3, 2012.

Trueman, M., "Carousel of Fantasies: Review: *On the Concept of the Face, Regarding the Son of God*", Romeo Castellucci, SPILL Festival, the Barbican, London, Monday 25 April, 2011. http://carouseloffantasies.blogspot.com/2011/04/review-on-concept-of-face-spill.html (last accessed 7 November 2011).

Chapter 7

Stifters Dinge (Stifter's Things)

By Heiner Goebbels

World premiere at Théâtre Vidy-Lausanne, 13 September 2007

The artistic team

Conception, music and direction: *Heiner Goebbels*
Set design, light and video: *Klaus Grünberg*
Collaboration to the music, programming: *Hubert Machnik*
Sound design: *Willi Bopp*
Assistant: *Matthias Mohr*

With the artistic and technical collaboration of the Théâtre de Vidy team

Stage manager: *Nicolas Bridel*
Robotics: *Thierry Kaltenrieder*
Light technicians: *Roby Carruba, Thierry Arnold*
Electricians: *Christophe Kehrli, Roger Monnard, David Perez*
Video: *Jérôme Vernez*
Sound: *Frédéric Morier*
Assistant stage manager: *Nicolas Pilet, Fabio Gaggetta*
Mechanical construction: *Stéphane Boulaz*
Table guitar construction: *Erik Zollikofer*
Construction of the set: *Thomas Beimowski, Hervé Arletti, Thuy Lor Van*
Props: *Georgie Gaudier, Eric Vuille*

Under the technical direction of *Michel Beuchat*

Co-production

Spielzeit'europa/Berliner Festspiele, Grand Théâtre de la Ville de Luxemburg, Schauspiel Frankfurt, T&M – Théâtre de Gennevilliers/CDN, Pour-cent culturel Migros, Teatro Stabile di Torino

Co-commission

Artangel London.

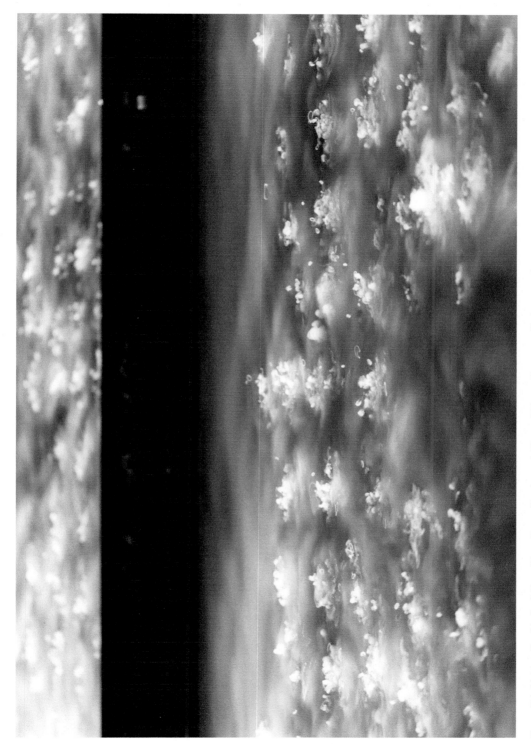

Figure 7.1 Heiner Goebbels, *Stifters Dinge*. Foggy 'landscape'. Photo: Wonge Bergmann/Ruhrtriennale

Introduction

One of the most inventive and versatile artists in the landscape of contemporary theatre is composer and theatre-maker Heiner Goebbels, whose work builds on non-hierarchical relations between media. This multimedial oeuvre crosses genres, moving to and from between music theatre, contemporary opera work, 'visual concerts', Performance Art and performative installation. Since the beginning of his musical career in the late 1970s, Goebbels composed soundtracks and music for numerous films, theatre and ballet productions. Since the early 1980s he has created a number of radio plays, where he explored how separate media such as music, sampled sound and verbal text could be brought in relation to one another without losing their respective integrity.

The poetics of Goebbels' work is fundamentally distinct from the Wagnerian Gesamtkunstwerk, where "everything is blended and works to the same end". In contrast, in Goebbels' work, as he states himself: " . . . lighting and words and music and sounds are all forms in themselves. What I am looking for is a polyphony of elements where everything keeps its integrity, like a 'voice' in a piece of polyphonic music. My role is to compose these voices into something new" (*The Telegraph*, 22 June 2012).

The distinctive function and the autonomous expression Goebbels gives each medium in the performance, together with his long-time collaborating scenographer and light designer Klaus Grünberg, are central in the discussion about light in contemporary theatre. Together they increase the addressees' awareness of the unique aesthetics of each medium, rather than fusing the experience of the various media in perception. Thus, media interrelate in Goebbels' music theatre in a manner that is very different from what is custom in the mainstream theatre of Realism. In the latter, for example, most of the time the visual and acoustic media (e.g. light, scenography, costumes and music) will support the medium of the verbal text by a 'doubling' of its signs. In contrast, Goebbels' theatre avoids pretence, fiction and the suspension of disbelief. He does not believe in 'representation' – in the sense of something pretending to be something else on stage. In an interview with John Tusa, Goebbels notes: "But I believe in a lot of emotional stage effects, which I also use in my pieces, but what I really try is to avoid the hierarchy of the elements, how they are used in conventional theatre".[1]

Goebbels treats the verbal text as performative material, one of several vehicles by which to stimulate the addressees, giving it no priority over other media at work. Before and beyond its conceptual content, the text's unique poetic effect also lies in its own musicality or, in other words, in *the sound of language*. Working with language as if it was music and emphasizing the sound of spoken or sung language connects to Goebbels' extensive use of sampled sound recordings. This is the case because "sampling allows for and suggests that anything can become material of an artistic process (echoing Adorno's concept of material) and shares, as an attitude and approach, significant territory with some of the discourses and practices of devising theatre" (Roesner 2014, 223).

Stifters Dinge (2007), the 'performative installation' or 'mechanical theatre performance' that I discuss in this chapter, excludes any human performer in favour of 'stage poetry' – a quality that emerges out of imagery, music and soundscape created with the use of robotics, machinery and stage technology. This work stands in an interesting relation to Edward Gordon Craig's well-known notion of the 'Über-Marionette', one interpretation of which was the exclusion of the living performer and its replacement by a highly capable marionette, but also to Adolphe Appia's ideas about music as the performance's driving force. The reminiscences of human presence and traces of the world of nature fleet between the ruins, the images and the words – giving rise to atmospheres, emotional effects and imaginative representations that the addressees create as a response to their individual experiences. When, as a result of exploring the forms arranged by the artist, the addressees ponder their own subjective experience – in complex and ambiguous works like *Stifters Dinge* much more than in the theatre of Realism – "each new experience creates neuronal pathways that forever change the brain" (Di Benedetto 2010, xii).

The space, a haunted 'garden' devoid of any living creature, is a highly elaborately engineered environment. It consists of a composite of sculpted trees without any foliage positioned between piano fragments and plastic piping overlooking shallow water pools, plastic containers and loudspeakers (Figure 7.2). The bare stage and its unveiled apparatuses become a receptive canvas for the imaginative representations one makes and projects onto it. The space produces its own soundscape using a rich variety of original instruments, noises and samples of recorded human voices singing and speaking in multiple languages from different periods and cultures. As Tadeusz Kantor noted: "It is possible to express life in art only through *the absence of* life, through an appeal to DEATH, through APPEARANCES, through EMPTINESS and the lack of a MESSAGE" [Kantor's emphasis] (Kantor and Kobialka 1993, 112).

The bringing together of different art-forms – theatre, Performance Art, installation, light, video, music, sound, prose (and even a philosophical debate) with diverse aesthetics of image, music, sound and text – into one performative event is central to this work. The ambiguous arrangement of forms (or signs) in different media in *Stifters Dinge* lends the verbal text a looser and more unstable position. It thus time and again calls for the examination of the text's features and the renegotiation of its potential meanings. When the text is so 'open' to multiple interpretations, the addressee is invited to generate information with regard to the text through the numerous other, simultaneous perspectives that are supplied.

Dramatic action is absent and a new 'drama' is created *in-between media*. It may result from media standing in counterpointed relations of contradiction, from the accumulative reflection of media upon each other, supporting each other's signs, or from media taking separate directions, thus establishing their autonomy. Both the absence of dramatic plot and the lack of characters increase our awareness of the aesthetics of the experience we gain while watching and listening. This audio-visual composition for five pianos and no pianist invites us to pay more attention to the nature of things, and to look at details which we habitually tend to disregard in the traditional theatre, where they become an illustrative support to the narrative.

Stifters Dinge invites us to take a mysterious 'journey' to distant past cultures, to an industrialized nature and an absent humanity, where a sequence of awe-evoking ambiguous atmospheres is meticulously created by light and water, mist and heavy smoke (Figure 7.1), kinetic sculptures and samples of recorded singing and spoken text. From the very beginning, once the spectators are seated, a mysterious sound, like that of a metronome with echo gradually changing its pitch, creates a sense of suspense. Video projections of organic forms in monochrome, slightly resembling the images of cells, move in slow motion (Figure 7.3). Two stagehands, black-clad and fully concentrated on their task, cover three rectangular surfaces with white powder before filling these areas with water. As soon as the two technicians leave, this industrial garden gradually awakens and unveils its own personification, as a living being.

Figure 7.2 Heiner Goebbels, *Stifters Dinge*. Pianos, trees, smoke and water. Photo: Mario Del Curto/ Théâtre Vidy-Lausanne

Figure 7.3 Heiner Goebbels, *Stifters Dinge*. Two stage technicians at work (during the beginning of the show), spreading the white powder. Photo: Wonge Bergmann/Ruhrtriennale

Light-image: *Waves of Light*

The first light-image I analyze lasts for about five minutes in a scene that features light reflections of water onto tulle screens to the sound of incantations for the winds ("Karuabu"), as recorded in 1905 by the Austrian ethnographer Rudolf Pöch in Papua New Guinea. At the beginning, the emerald-bluish light of video beamers hits the three flooded surfaces and generates a quite soft and dynamic reflection on the ceiling. As this happens, very slowly, four screens roll down in turn, starting with the most distant one. A male voice begins to sing in an unknown exotic language, reviving a forgotten tradition from the depths of more than one hundred years ago. Even without understanding the lyrics, the recording quality is archaic in terms of its sound. At stage right, one little loudspeaker 'stands out' and is highlighted with white LED light while it 'speaks out' the incantations. For a short time, before the tulle screens unroll and reveal the reflections, it is the brightest object that calls for our attention in a dark space.

After the four screens are unrolled, a single powerful, bright light bursts into the space from the back and sets the screens in vertical motion. It shines through the moving screens in the direction of the spectators. In accordance with the positions of the screens, light reflections from the water are subject to constant change (Figure 7.4). The constant metamorphosis of the images on the tulles caused by their vertical motion and intervals results in unexpected visual sequences – screens unveiling and shadowing one another, revealing reflections that are similar to a graphic seismograph, reminding one of the representation of a sound wave as seen in sound-editing software, or the energy of the wind moving the sails. The totality of the image might also suggest the sun reflecting in the sea. However, our experience is subject to simultaneously contrasting influences: we are caught by the imaginative representation of nature we generate out of the image yet, at the same time, we acknowledge the reality of the theatre, in which we perceive artificial lighting and scenographic elements in a performance space.

Aesthetic analysis of the light-image

Two lighting elements compose this light-image (Figure 7.4):

1 *Strong diffused light from upstage toward the spectators* – one lighting source is placed in quite a low position between the pianos and sculptured trees, facing the spectators. Such brightness is possibly the performance of 5kw halogen or 2.5kw HMI Fresnel (with a warm filter, in the second case). Whatever the type of bulb, the instant emitting and blocking of light previously performed makes it clear that a mechanical dimmer was placed in front of the lens, since light was switched on and off more quickly than a usual voltage-based dimmer enables.
2 *Cold white LED light on a loudspeaker* – a small LED unit attached to the top of the speaker illuminates its box/body and membranes. This cold light generates a soft and small field of illumination, and turns on whenever the very same loudspeaker emits sound or playbacks a speech.

Semiotic and poetic analysis of the light-image

Considering the lighting element mentioned above, how are the aesthetic features of the light experienced and/or used as signs; what are the signs about; and how are they used poetically?

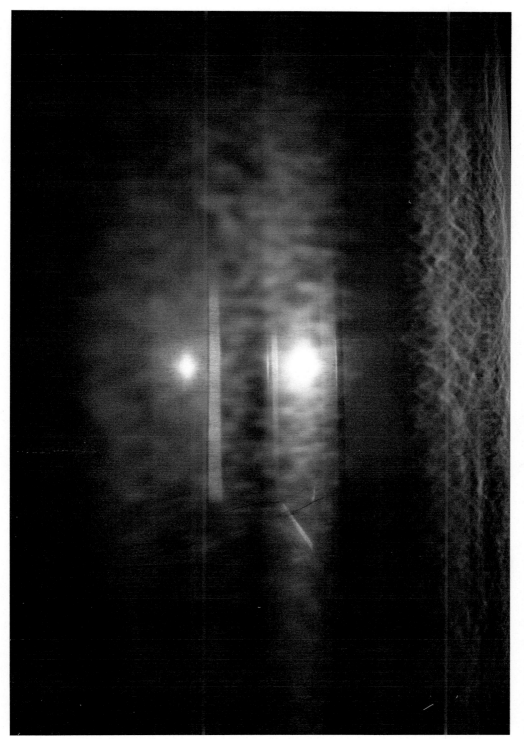

Figure 7.4 Heiner Goebbels, *Stifters Dinge*. Water reflections appear on tulle curtains. Photo: Mario Del Curto/Théâtre Vidy-Lausanne

In my conceptual framework, I first examine whether – and how – the phenomenological experience and the semiotic function of the light-image relate to *a narrative*, as a possible ground of representation. *Stifters Dinge* embodies no narrative in the classical sense. Its structure is highly fragmented and ambiguous. In each scene, the various media interrelate in different arrangements, interchanging leading and supporting roles, their relationship being constantly 'under construction', fleeting and complex, apparently following an internally authored 'poetic logic'. This poetic logic is not based upon causal thinking or the probability of events, which are both so fundamental in traditional narrative structures. And yet, even when the different media tread separate paths, there is poetic consistency and wholeness – the configuration of media as devised within the framework of one performance encourages the addressees to foster this assumption, thus supporting their efforts at interpretation. It invites them to constantly reassess the stimuli they register from image, sound, music and text, and based on this information, to make sense of them, and 'author' their own subjective narratives.

The light-image analysed here does not engage in simulating a fictive space and time. Even for those addressees who would recognize the incantations to the winds ("Karuabu"), the image cannot represent the time and space to which this recorded singing belongs. The perceptual features of the light-image – created mainly by the bright backlight that the water reflects onto the screens – do not illustrate, on the basis of verisimilitude, a situation in which we could imagine the absent singer. The aesthetics of light does not make the scene in any sense 'similar' to the text. Even though we identify water reflections they appear on moving canvases in the middle of an exposed black box theatre. That said, the light does bring about expressive qualities independent of the text/lyrics and the human voice and evokes a vast range of associations – some of which will be discussed later in this analysis. Therefore, in view of the above, the phenomenological experience and semiotic function of the light-image are not, this time, grounded in *narrative*.

The second ground of representation against which I examine the light-image is *character*. When the experience and the semiotic function of a light-image are grounded in *character*, light's formal characteristics are designed to reflect upon the 'inner world' of a fictive character and its mental condition, as derived from the written or verbal text. In *Stifters Dinge*, the absence of a performing human being who would become a subject for reference and identification for us makes us more attentive to the 'behaviour' of stage machines and to things we consider 'humane' in them, and by drawing analogies to human behaviour we seek to assign their work a meaning. In this wonderful scene in particular, due to its bewitching impact on the addressees, we can momentarily fall in with the magic of theatre and imagine the absent 'protagonist' to be somehow represented by the agency of the speaking voice. The light-image creates a 'stage effect' that does not directly complement or reflect a mental state of a character – instead, light fascinates us with its ongoing metamorphosis and renewal on the canvas.

In his essay "Human Stuff", Joe Kelleher writes about the process of unmasking the hero of the humanist drama in contemporary theatre. He notes the intention: ". . . as to expose the theatrical machinery itself as the means of production within which the human fiction is cooked up, and the stage meanwhile as the sort of place where actual humans (as well as non-humans, i.e. animals and things) find themselves lost or ill-fitting or overexposed" (Kelleher 2006, 25). To a certain extent, the experience of this light-image could be associated with a persona (the praying man whose trace we hear but don't see) due to the convention established throughout the performance that a loudspeaker is illuminated each time it emits the sound of human voice. By illuminating the loudspeaker 'in action', the apparatus is potentially personified and will be associated with the human voice it produces. Even in linguistic terms, the word 'speaker' stands homonymously for a human speaker and (as short) for loudspeaker. Whether the experience and semiotic function of this light-image are grounded in *character* or not, depends, therefore, on the imagination of the addressee – especially in a fragmented and ambiguous work such as *Stifters Dinge*. In my experience, however, *character* is not one of the grounds this light-image embodies.

Let us now examine whether the light-image embodies the third ground distinguished in the conceptual framework for the analysis of light: *dramatic action* or *theme*. When the experience and semiotic function of a light-image are grounded in *(dramatic) action* or *theme*, the aesthetics of light mediate the text's dramaturgical aspects, on the basis of an analysis of the subtext level. In *Stifters Dinge*, however, we find neither a dramatic text nor dramatic action – and human performers who could carry out an action are absent as well. In terms of associated themes, the mechanical transformation of the stage space evolves imaginatively into a metaphorical personification. We ourselves 'author' a narrative based on our interpretation of the interrelations between scenic elements of which we become aware. Searching for coherence, as we generally do when confronted with ambiguous signs, we suppose, for example, an invisible human presence which we consider is addressing us, although we miss a visual embodiment. Similarly, following our imagination, we may believe that we discover resemblances between the image of a singular light source and sparkling water reflections which the backlight creates on the canvases, and the look of a distant sunrise shining through the mist by the seaside. In my experience this phenomenon evokes socio-anthropological ruminations concerning the experience of nature in the contemporary world, all mediated so futuristically in *Stifters Dinge*. The representation of nature is obviously an imaginative representation that addressees construct on the basis of machinery, engines and robotics – not through verisimilitude and pretence.

That said, the open character of this work does not suggest any particular or concrete theme – it remains an 'open work', to use Umberto Eco's term. It is 'theatre of absence', as Goebbels himself characterized his work in the 2010 Cornell lecture: "Absence can be understood . . . as an empty centre: literally, as an empty centre stage, meaning the absence of a visually centralized focus, but also as the absence of what we call a clear 'theme' or message of a play" (Goebbels 2010). Any theme one finds in the work mirrors one's own individual reception process more than reflecting a previously established theme embodied by the aesthetics of this performance. The aesthetics of the image and the phenomena we experience in *Stifters Dinge* are so alienated from daily reality that the discussion of a theme might narrow down the sensory and phenomenological dimension of the experience in favour of an idea. In view of the above, the semiotic function and the experience of this light-image are grounded neither in *(dramatic) action* nor in a *theme*.

The following three grounds of representation in my conceptual framework – *atmosphere* or *emotion*, *sensation of light* and *open meaning* – are of particular relevance for the analysis of the light-image on which we focus in *Stifters Dinge*. A light-image embodying the ground *atmosphere* or *emotion* effectively stimulates primal sensory input. Light aesthetics is used to cast atmospheric and emotional effects upon its beholders, to highlight particular moments and selectively draw our attention to details in ways that help structure the experience of the piece in terms of its appearance.

A light-image the representational function of which is grounded in *atmosphere* or *emotion* affects our mood, heartbeat, blood pressure and perspiration – features some of which we become aware while remaining unconscious of others. The light-image under analysis definitely embodies the ground *atmosphere* or *emotion* by triggering the primal sensitivity we have for sunlight and for the presence of water in our habitat. Denis Dutton elaborates on these all-human, non-cultural inborn preferences in *The Art Instinct: Beauty, Pleasure and Human Evolution* (see also Chapter 3). The sensation of being illuminated throughout the canvases by the warm bright backlight – an image that resembles the sun and the sea – keeps us under the spell of light and lets us linger over memories of landscapes we recall (Figure 7.4). The seductive power and success of this image drawing us into the process of imaginative representation lies in recalling the most primeval natural elements that strongly affect our mood and eventually generate a sense of safety and calm.

The effectiveness of this light-image, in terms of the cognitive engineering of public behaviour, calls to mind Olafur Eliasson's famous installation in the Turbine Hall at Tate Modern, *The Weather Project* 2003 (see Figures 2.11 and 2.12). I wrote about Eliasson's artwork in greater detail in Chapter 2 and noted that Eliasson's image of the sun has caused many visitors to act out behavioural habits more suitable to the seaside than to an art institution. Under the chromatic orange light visitors sat and even laid down on the floor, enjoying the sensation of a gigantic illuminating LED circle they associated with the image of sunset. The highly saturated orange, warm-like light and the standard room temperature at the gallery cast the addressees in a sensory contrast. While the space was heated at normal room temperature, the public recognized the coloured light that often comes with physical warmth, and behaved accordingly. The relaxing attitude of many of the visitors relates to our primal instincts with regard to daylight and sun, providing us with warmth and a clear visibility that increases survival chances – light and the nearness to a water source are among substantial human preferences that affect our ideals of beauty.

The association of light with the sun, daylight and streaming water are embodied experiences on a primal sensory level – and the unconscious experience of water is present already prior to our birth. Monochromatically rendered, we catch a glimpse of a fabricated image of nature represented on stage with a certain degree of verisimilitude while being 'reminded' of the artificiality of the image by the moving canvases that roll irregularly up and down (Figure 7.4). Nevertheless, spectators find themselves fascinated by the constant renewal of the image and the space (as a result of the moving curtains) and by the opportunity to rediscover visual phenomena provided by the light and scenography. The light-image creates a stage effect, an atmospheric light that provokes emotional reactions independent of any narrative or text. It is due to the immediate engagement triggered by the diffused bright spot of light and water reflections. In view of the above, the semiotic function and phenomenological dimension of the light-image are grounded in *atmosphere* or *emotion*.

In line with the conceptual framework, the fifth ground I examine with regard to light-images is the *sensation of light itself*. When the semiotic function of a light-image is grounded in *light sensation*, the formal characteristics of light give rise to the following one or two qualities: *spectacularity* is based upon an aesthetic pleasure that we gain from the performance of 'skill and virtuosity' (Dutton, Ibid.) using light, and the appreciation we owe to the precision and craftsmanship involved in the making of the light-image. **Hypermediacy,** as a representational mode, reminds us of the medium, emphasizing the dominant presence of media and technology in our experience of an artefact (Bolter and Grusin 1999, 31–44). With regard to the analysis of light, hypermediacy refers to light's aesthetics boldly manifesting the medium at work, its materiality, and its practical functioning in the performance. The light-image exposes its constitutive elements and the *active presence* of the technology is clearly experienced.

In the light-image under analysis, the medium of light not only creates a sensational effect by illuminating the spectators so brightly and giving rise to associations related to the sun and the physical warmth of its light. Light also influences the dynamics between stage and audience, taking the addressees out of their comfort zone and turning their watching experience into something more communal, vulnerable, yet enchanting. Facing the audience, the fierce backlight pierces through the curtains and shines on the spectators, exposing them in their previously dark space. Although only a single light-image is present in this scene, the curtains that move and mask the light in different ways create an impression of an ever-changing imagery. Thus the very same light source creates a continuity of many different 'appearances', generating endlessly fascinating variations of landscapes as a result of subtracting light from the space using the screens. The high degree of precision with which the screens 'shape' and mask the light and shadows becomes especially evident when one screen moves in and stops exactly in such a position as to leave one single water wave visible on the canvas. Paradoxically, the more the light is obstructed, the more elaborate the images of water reflections appear, thus creating more imaginative depth on the canvas. Again, paradoxically, the shadows on the canvas bring clarity – the lack of light creates visibility! It is as if all the phenomena of light that we perceive come to the fore largely as a result of the shadows. Therefore, the interplay of light and shadow, as well as the illumination of the addressees, call for attention to the medium of light at work and produce a sensation based upon the experience of light itself. The light-image is therefore based on the ground of *light sensation*, exhibiting qualities of both **hypermediacy** and **spectacularity**.

The last ground I examine with regard to the light-image is **open meaning**. In the absence of human performers (and the vacuum that the two technicians leave after spreading the white grain and filling the water in the pools at the beginning of the show), light takes the centre of attention in this scene and plays a leading role. There are no human figures to occupy the space and set it into action, to give the space a human scale and give rise to emotional identification through fiction. The attention of the addressees is no longer drawn to performers and the absence of which provides freedom for discovery, and space for reflection on elements and media that in mainstream theatre are considered supportive, and therefore secondary to the acting of the performer. The medium of light here acts as the scene's driving force: setting its tempo and charging it with tension, movement and playfulness through visual perception. Light takes a step to the fore and no longer merely illuminates or supports another medium that is prior in hierarchy. Ambiguous and open with regard to meaning, and keeping a high degree of autonomy with regard to the music and the lyrics, it gives rise to imaginative uncertainty. In the context of this scene there is no one single final meaning to discover but, rather, an endless series of perspectives through which our experience of things can be examined.

In the theatre of objects without human performers, we are unable to approach the performance and predict the future events as we are used to do in the theatre of

Realism. In *Stifters Dinge*, images, sounds and music are all food for the imagination of the addressees, without any given meaning. Since the encounter with the piece suggests an engagement with an *'open work'*, to use Eco's notion, addressees are invited to experience visual and acoustic 'images', to ponder their aesthetics and find or construct connections between different stimuli in ways that will make sense for them, using their imagination. As the task of connecting different segments and generating subjective meanings is left to the addressees, they gain a degree of 'authorship' in relation to the piece.

In his Cornell lecture (2010), Goebbels quotes Helga Finter with reference to the recorded voices in *Stifters Dinge*, saying that the addressees perceive the voices as speaking to them. They connect what they see with what they hear, as Finter notes:

> in order then to formulate hypotheses about motivation and causality. His scopic desire stages what his invocatory desire [invokatorisches Begehren] is able to hear. In this way the perceptive intelligence of the spectator's own senses actively stages the performance when the spectator weaves and reads his own audiovisual text . . .
>
> (Goebbels 2010)

One's eagerness to discover motivation and causality by which to interpret visual phenomena can be relinquished in favour of the fascination with the autonomous qualities and mystery of light. In other words, an image that is haunting and alluring enough – even though its signs do not lead to a clear direction of interpretation – could cause an addressee to let go of a more conventional understanding. When the light-image embodies the ground ***open meaning***, light becomes a phantom performer with its own 'behaviour', its own logic and formal/conceptual reasoning. The signs of light are self-referential, almost narcissistically. The 'drama' is within *light itself*, and *in between the medium of light and the addressees*. This is definitely the case with this light-image. In view of the above, representation through this light-image is definitely grounded in ***open meaning***.

The dramaturgy of light in *Stifters Dinge*

Two fundamental ideas can be distinguished in Goebbels' dramaturgy for the lighting in *Stifters Dinge*, one of which has to do with the problematizing of visual perception. The other idea relates to the increased poetic potential of light within the polyphonic organization of media.

1   *Problematizing visual perception* – In various scenes, the performance challenges visual perception and unbalances the certainties we (spectators) have about our sight. The medium of light is both a means of obstruction and, through that, of discovering new and richer forms of visual information. One instance of this was introduced previously, in the analysis of the light-image that generated water reflections. Another valuable example is the scene in which Paolo Uccello's painting *Night Hunt* (circa 1460) is projected as light on the pianos in the back, but the spectators cannot 'perceive' the image of the painting (Figure 7.5).[2] Only when a bright plate enters the space and moves slowly into the projection field, details of the painting begin to be revealed (Figure 7.6).

Figure 7.5 Heiner Goebbels, *Stifters Dinge*. Paolo Uccello's painting *Night Hunt* (circa 1460) is projected on the pianos and water. Photo: Mario Del Curto/Théâtre Vidy-Lausanne

Figure 7.6 Heiner Goebbels, *Stifters Dinge*. Paolo Uccello's painting *Night Hunt* (circa 1460) is projected on the pianos and water. The white plate is on the left side of the pianos. Photo: Wonge Bergmann/Ruhrtriennale

The board 'travels' through space by means of a metal chain and two cogwheels – like the clouds and chariots in the theatre of the Renaissance. In fact, the spectators' visual perception of the projected content is dependent upon the presence, and the movement of the plate as a medium. Moreover, it is impossible to grasp the image of the projection in its entirety. Instead, one can follow the moving plate, see fragments of the painting and imagine or (re-)construct a total image.

Another example is found in the scene where the voice of Claude Lévi-Strauss is heard in an interview with Jacques Chancel, with Bach's *Italian Concert in F major* (BWV 971, 2nd movement) played simultaneously. Drops of water fall all over the three pools and a subtle warm light on two playing pianos and inside the plastic containers lend the space the inviting and pleasant atmosphere of an imagined interior where the conversation could have taken place (Figure 7.7). The conversation is about the human need for discovery and adventure in a global world already completely mapped and catalogued. Midway through the conversation, the light changes our perception of the space: the pianos disappear, the containers turn blue and the splashing drops get illuminated. But gradually, fewer and fewer drops fall while they appear as flashes of light from beneath the water's surface.

It is the light and the decreasing frequency of drops that make the image feel differently, as if its materiality is changing. The scene reinforces the work's exploration of visual perception, this time through the conflict of presence vs absence with regard to the speakers whose voices we hear. The absence of bodies provides space for new kinds of presence to arise and be noticed – both human and non-human. We become more attentive to performative elements – tangible and embodied elements or vectors of unknown energies – and their interrelations. Imaginatively, we become engaged with the absent image, with sounds or words that are out of reach and yet we experience their absence as intentionally composed and enchantingly troubling. Referring to his own work, Goebbels notes: "In such theatre the spectator is involved in a *drama of experience*, rather than looking at drama in which psychologically motivated relationships are represented by figures on stage. This is a *drama of perception*, a drama of one's senses . . . " (Goebbels 2010; emphases added).

The problematizing of visual perception in scenes with bodiless voices also involves a splitting up of the senses – separating the human voice from the sound-emitting body, and contrasting the experience of a human presence to that of voices devoid of any visual embodiment. The absence of a performer representing Lévi-Strauss or, in another scene, Malcolm X, enables the addressees to see things afresh and 'author' by and for themselves, imaginatively, a settling and satisfying representation. While looking for analogies between the aesthetics of light in conjunction with, for example, acoustic and musical stimuli, scenographic gestures and text-based content, the possibility to experience the light as a personified entity increases.

2   *Performing light within the polyphony of media* – Goebbels' work continuously de-synchronizes sensory faculties such as seeing and listening, avoiding the doubling of signs by the various media. Media tread different and separate paths, and their unique inputs are organized in dynamic rhizomatic structures rather than progressing in a single one-dimensional direction. The engagement with a work the structure of which is so complex calls for an exceedingly imaginative creativity and involvement of the addressees in the reception of the work. In *Stifters Dinge*, a

aber letztlich gibt es noch Chancen,
man muss nur jung sein...

Figure 7.7 Heiner Goebbels, *Stifters Dinge*. The space as it is seen during the early part of the interview with Claude Lévi-Strauss and Bach's *Italian Concert in F Major* (BWV 971, 2nd movement). Photo: Wonge Bergmann/Ruhrtriennale

powerful tension exists between the 'things' we perceive (see and hear on stage), and what we know about them on the one hand and, on the other, the imaginative representations we construct as a response to these perceived 'things'. The dramaturgy of light withdraws from the known lighting conventions of mainstream theatre such as, for instance: (1) creating a sense of continuity and/or changes of time and space between scenes; and (2) directing one's attention to *the centre* of the scene or (3) illuminating elements in the scene according to the hierarchy of media.

In *Stifters Dinge*, the progression from one scene to the next follows no narrative of any kind, and the 'centre' is not an embodied one but rather associative and imaginative, created mentally by the addressee. The reception of the work is more democratic and there is no division between central and peripheral; the traditional hierarchy of media, in which first the performer, and then the text precede over the visual and acoustic dimensions, is discarded. Light, in its turn, raises its game and develops an autonomous 'poetic behaviour' as if it would be a phantom 'performer', connected – and at times, not connected – to other events that happen in the space. One is free to undergo the experiential dimension of light and to decide about its semiotic function, according to one's subjective stance. Nevertheless, due to the ambiguity given with the organization of the media, there is no certainty, no way of knowing whether a light-image is providing signs intended by the author and, if so, what the meaning of these signs might be. Light, among the other media, is used as means to generate an artistic experience and not as the medium of a message.

In a conversation with Hans-Thies Lehmann, Goebbels notes:

> I am interested in a theatre that does not incessantly multiply signs but . . . I am interested in inventing a theatre where all the means that make up theatre do not just illustrate and duplicate each other but instead all maintain all their power but act together, and where one does not just rely on the conventional hierarchy of means. That means, for example, where light can be so strong that you suddenly only watch the light and forget the text, where a costume speaks its own language or where there is a distance between speaker and text and a tension between music and text.
>
> (Lehmann 2006, 86)

The move away from a linear progression through dramatic conflict and resolution towards what Gertrude Stein termed 'Landscape Play' brought about the possibility to structure a piece through a de-synchronization of media. The tendency in contemporary theatre that Elinor Fuchs coined 'Death of Character', too, increasingly encouraged the visual dimension in the theatre to flourish. As an artistic medium, light has a dominant influence on the imagination of the addressees, as we can sense in this performance, especially in the absence of fictive characters and/or human performers (Figure 7.8). It is so, since light is intimately linked to the emotion, feelings of empathy and (self-) reflection that addressees usually experience in relation to dramatic space and time in mainstream dramatic theatre, or to the living performer in post-dramatic contemporary performances. In *Stifters Dinge*, light develops its own unique visual language and calls attention to itself more effectively as the sensitivity of the addressee to small details and nuances is heightened. Some light-images seem to generate almost subconscious or 'transparent' phenomena of which one is not immediately or fully aware, such as

Figure 7.8 Heiner Goebbels, *Stifters Dinge*. Fog, light, pianos, trees and loudspeakers in the last scene. Photo: Wonge Bergmann/Ruhrtriennale

the slow colour changes that affect the hue and brightness within a projected painting during the reading of Adalbert Stifter's prose. The analysis of some of the light-images would allow us to trace the influences of ideas from the visual arts and Light Art in particular (Chapter 2) – the above analysis being a case in point. Other light-images emphasize the medium at work and reveal the poetic potential with which light can act, perform as a persona, or embody any of the grounds I introduced in Chapter 4: "A new conceptual framework for the analysis of light".

Notes

1   Heiner Goebbels in an interview with John Tusa, BBC, 3 March 2003.
2   Paulo Uccello, *Night Hunt*, circa 1460, 65 x 165cm, tempura on wood, side panel of a chest, Ashmolean Museum, Oxford.

References

Bolter, J. D. and Grusin, R., *Remediation: Understanding New Media*, Cambridge, MA and London: The MIT Press, 1999.

Delhalle, N., "Using Recorded Images for Political Purposes", in *Bastard or Playmate? Adapting Theatre, Mutating Media and Contemporary Performing Arts*, edited by Robrecht Vanderbeeken, Christal Stalpaert, David Depestel and Boris Debackere, Amsterdam: Amsterdam University Press, 2012.

Di Benedetto, S., *The Provocation of the Senses in Contemporary Theatre*, Abingdon and New York: Routledge, 2010.

Dutton, D., *The Art Instinct: Beauty, Pleasure and Human Evolution*, Oxford: Oxford University Press, 2009.

Fuchs, E., *The Death of Character: Perspectives on Theatre after Modernism*, Indianapolis: Indiana University Press, 1996.

Goebbels, H., *Aesthetics of Absence: Questioning Basic Assumptions in Performing Arts*, Cornell Lecture on Contemporary Aesthetics, 9 March 2010, at http://igcs.cornell.edu/files/2013/09/Goebbels-Cornell-Lecture18-1dnqe5j.pdf (last accessed 27 November 2014).

Kantor, T., and Kobialka, M., *A Journey Through Other Spaces: Essays and Manifestos, 1944–1990*, Berkeley, CA: University of California Press, 1993.

Kelleher, J., "Human Stuff", in *Contemporary Theatres in Europe*, edited by Joe Kelleher and Nicholas Ridout, Abingdon and New York: Routledge, 2006.

Lehmann, H. T., *Postdramatic Theatre*, translated and foreword by K. Jürs-Munby, Abingdon and New York: Routledge, 2006.

Roesner, D., *Musicality in Theatre: Music as Model, Method and Metaphor in Theatre-Making*, Farnham, UK and Burlington, VT: Ashgate Publishing Limited, 2014.

Till, N., "Investigating the Entrails: Post-operatic Music Theatre in Europe", in *Contemporary Theatres in Europe*, edited by Joe Kelleher and Nicholas Ridout, Abingdon and New York: Routledge, 2006.

Interviews

Heiner Goebbels in an interview with Ivan Hewett, *The Telegraph* (GB), 22 June, 2012. http://www.heiner goebbels.com/en/archive/texts/interviews/read/697 (last accessed 11 October 2012).

Heiner Goebbels in an interview with Roberto Rinaldi for *Alto Adige*, 3 December, 2008. http://www. heinergoebbels.com/en/archive/texts/interviews/read/452 (last accessed 12 October 2012).

Chapter 8

Rechnitz (Der Würgeengel)

By Elfriede Jelinek
Münchner Kammerspiele

World premiere at the Schauspielhaus München, Germany, 28 November 2008.

The artistic team

Director: *Jossi Wieler*
Scenography and costumes: *Anja Rabes*
Light: *Max Keller*
Music: *Wolfgang Siuda*
Dramaturgy: *Julia Lochte*

Performers: *Katja Bürkle*
            André Jung
            Hans Kremer
            Steven Scharf
            Hildegard Schmahl

Introduction

Towards the end of the Second World War, on the night between 24 and 25 March 1945, Countess Margit von Batthyány hosted a festive dinner for the aristocracy and the academic milieu in Rechnitz, a little town in Eastern Austria. The slaying of around 180 Jewish-Hungarian forced labourers by selected pro-Nazi guests was the highlight of the celebration, 'enhanced' by alcoholic intoxication and a brutish orgy. To date (2015), the remains of the victims have still not been found; nor have the Austrian authorities properly investigated the massacre. The city residents who knew about – or participated in – the crime have kept silent and refuse to reveal what actually happened, or to divulge where the victims were buried.

The production *Rechnitz* by the Münchner Kammerspiele (2008), directed by eminent opera and theatre director Jossi Wieler, is the fourth case study for the analysis of light on stage. This production is comprised of Elfriede Jelinek's fascinating and non-dramatic (prosaic) text, written in 'essayistic manner' and composed like a musical flow of multiple voices and counter-voices. The title refers to Luis Buñuel's film *The Exterminating Angel* (1962). The creative lighting design is by Max Keller, one of

Figure 8.1 Jossi Wieler, *Rechnitz*. Hans Kremer, Hildegard Schmahl, Steven Scharf, Katja Bürkle and André Jung. Photo: Courtesy of the Münchner Kammerspiele/ © Arno Declair

Europe's most prominent lighting designers of our time. Designing light for a complicated piece such as *Rechnitz* is indeed a challenging artistic endeavour. As this analysis will present, the relation between the light and such an ambiguous literary text brings about new experience of the work as a whole, and of light itself in particular. Let me first consider the structure, and some of the characteristics of the performance before proceeding to the analysis of light.

On the structure and characteristics of *Rechnitz*

Since Modernism, when artists sought new aesthetics and forms of expression, breaking with the dramatic paradigm and the conventions of 'realistic' theatre, the occasional use of literary works in contemporary theatre performances has increasingly become a trend. This search for new forms was shared by all the arts around the *fin de siècle*. According to Peter Szondi (1987), 'the crisis of drama' reflects the turning away from the dramatic framework of a well-made play, since the Aristotelian model became inapplicable when modern, and later postmodern, realities with their complexity and instable qualities were to be represented. Furthermore, Elinor Fuchs suggests that the concept of the psychologically elaborate fictive character loses its efficacy in contemporary theatre, while, instead, the position of the performer and its phenomenological impact on the performance is rising. As Hans-Thies Lehmann writes:

> performers in theatre want to transform not themselves but a situation and perhaps the audience. In other words, even in theatrical work oriented towards presence, the transformation and effect of catharsis remains (1) virtual, (2) voluntary, and (3) in the future. By contrast, the ideal of performance art is a process and moment that is (1) real, (2) emotionally compulsory, and (3) happening in the here and now.
>
> (Lehmann 2006, 138)

The production of *Rechnitz* reflects these ideas and specifically questions our capacity to revive, or re-present, the memory of past events in the present in captivating and tantalizing ways. Fictive characters are replaced by a group of spokesmen, messengers, or 'agents' of the text whose motivation for speaking remains obscure. Hajo Kurzenberger refers to the well-known convention of messengers in Greek tragedy, who had to transmit the incomprehensible and to stimulate the imagination of the addressees. This task is now undertaken by the Rechnitz-messengers in a contemporary, weird manner, since instead of bringing clarity they are, above all else, a source of doubt (Kurzenberger 2011, 135). Emotionally detached from the issues under discussion, they playfully assert different subjective conjectures as accurate and factual reports, and eventually contradict or shirk responsibility for what they say, claiming that they are merely the messengers. We can hardly follow any line of argument and causal course of thinking by listening to them. In a conversation with the audience at *The Cameri Theatre* in Tel Aviv, Israel, the actress Katja Bürkle stated the following:

> We do not play characters but perform the text of the messengers, there are many voices contained in one head that expresses movements of thought, many movements. Jossi and Julia considered how many expressing voices could possibly express the variety of thoughts of a whole society, men and women, of different ages.

There is an impression that the young countess speaks and within one minute – it becomes the old countess, or the servant. It changes frequently. We actually told tales, but through the words we kept the history distant from ourselves.

The emotional distance which the performers keep from historical events, through their radical 'reporting', seems to intensify with the moral and physical distance between the performers on stage 'far away', and us, the spectators in the dark auditorium. But here lies an ambivalence: in spite of the physical separation between stage and auditorium, the five performers persist in staring and addressing their speeches directly forward. Even when one of them is speaking, those who listen do not look at the speaker but instead continue gazing at the audience. On stage, the performers make almost no eye contact within one another; when this does happen, it seems to be meant only for checking the others' reaction or seeking confirmation and sense of solidarity. As a spectator, I recall how emotionally compelling and arresting they were and how demanding, making it seem almost impolite not to watch them constantly. The attempts of the performers to establish an immediate contact, and to embrace the public through kindness and an overly friendly attitude, caused feelings of unease, as if they were inviting us to become part of their group, or they wanted to share their secrets with us – something which of course never actually happens (Figure 8.1).

The plot of the written text is abstruse and spreads out in repetitive cycles to a wide range of subjects that emerge from the vast themes of the text. The plot progresses in different directions at one and the same time as the language used is condensed, associative and complex in meaning. Likewise, statements occasionally contradict each other and shift the meaning from side to side. The 'post-Brechtian' delivery of the text, cold and emotionally distant, encourages critical thinking as well as a drift from one idea to another. Therefore, the negotiation of meaning requires careful watching and attentive listening to all the nuances within image, action and speech altogether; the way an action is carried out and how a sentence is said are perhaps as important as what is actually being said. Working in collaboration, Jelinek and Wieler elevate each other's work, as Jelinek's words stimulate the imagination of the addressee and Wieler enriches the possibilities for interpretation through the sensorial dimensions of the play and behaviour of the performers. They also create paradoxes that remain unanswered (Kurzenberger 2011, 97–8). In most scenes, the various media (performers, light, scenography, costumes and music) interrelate critically or ironically, adding extra layers and possibilities for interpretation. For instance, the performers' physical actions on stage seldom support the text or the music. On the contrary, the image, the text and the music generate emotional experiences of shock and revulsion, of shame and embarrassment, sometimes laughter, thus creating relations of mutual irony that ask for critical reflection. In this respect, the actors are presumed to reach the greatest impact on the audience by contrasting the charm and lightness of their performance with the hair-raising content of their statements (Kurzenberger 2011, 136).

A range of possible memories, associations and questions flows from the kaleidoscopic conjoining of the media showing fragments of a changing reality in a wholly new light. The combination of the images on stage and the verbal text continuously arouses mind-provoking paradoxes that keep the addressees alert to the constantly evolving socio-political, historical and moral views. Wieler reminds us that the text was written not as a theatre play but rather as prose – the situation is not fictive and there are no characters in the conventional sense. According to Wieler, the creative team must have been very familiar with all the associated contexts that Jelinek brought into the written text before 'theatricalizing' it – like participating in an archaeological excavation into the depths of the text. Archaeology researches findings from the past, bits and pieces, and, by a process of collecting the fragments and learning about what was previously concealed, it connects the past with the present. The contemporary view of the past is, therefore, based on the possibility of restoring a piece of truth from the dust, and considering an interpretation that is based on the analysis of fragments from the past – there are still missing parts that the spectators complement in their own imagination. Furthermore, as archaeological research involves a selective process of separating findings from the general debris, the artistic team, likewise, must select what ideas to emphasize, and which parts of the complete text to perform. Dramaturge Julia Lochte disclosed that Jelinek herself approaches the collaboration in the theatre in a highly democratic manner; in a sense, the written text is an open work handed over to the theatre-makers, who create the performance, bringing the text into play.

The Shooting Scene: first light-image

The first light-image from *Rechnitz* that I analyse here appears during the scene of the shooting. For those readers who did not view the performance, I will first give a brief description of what happens in this scene: the five performers are seated inside narrow gaps within the walls, one behind the other, and seem to be breakfasting (or dining if this is to be associated with the festive dinner given by the countess) (Figure 8.2). One of the performers, André Jung declares that "these men were deposited in our hands in order that we will shoot them . . . moment, I see them! . . . To dispose of them, dispose, dispose, dispose . . . ". Throughout the speech, he meanders from one context to another, ranging from the act of mass killing, and practicing shooting as a privilege, to shooting under the influence of alcohol and associating it with sexual activity. In the course of presenting his ideas, the other performers continue eating boiled eggs and spitting out the eggshells all over the stage floor, in apathy and gluttony, shamelessly looking toward the spectators and back to their food. In Jewish tradition, salted boiled eggs are '*the*' typical food for the mourning period at the home of the deceased – an association that came to my mind while watching the performances in Tel Aviv.

As soon as Jung ends his speech, surprisingly, a long and intense sequence of gunshots catches both performers and audience as if under attack. The performers instinctively 'relocate' themselves by revolving the walls made of patterned woodwork with the red seats, sealing the openings in the two walls behind them (compare Figure 8.3 with Figure 8.4). They then take the red headphones and cover their ears – what appears to be an attempt to deny the shots and avoid the noise. Showing no interest or emotional reaction to what is occurring, they go on chewing the last morsels of food, tidy their nightdresses or nightgowns from time to time, and sit with crossed legs and folded arms. The light on the stage changes gradually throughout the scene, slowly, to the sound of the gunshots – as I will go on to describe in the aesthetic analysis below. The level of the houselights also increases.

Shortly after the last shot has sounded, performer Hans Kremer removes his headphones and, in an emotionally detached manner, declares laconically: "You have just

Figure 8.2 Jossi Wieler, *Rechnitz*. Hildegard Schmahl, André Jung, Katja Bürkle, Steven Scharf, and Hans Kremer. Photo: Courtesy of the Münchner Kammerspiele/ © Arno Declair

Figure 8.3 Jossi Wieler, *Rechnitz*. Hildegard Schmahl, André Jung, Steven Scharf, Katja Bürkle and Hans Kremer having a meal before the shooting scene.
Photo: Courtesy of the Münchner Kammerspiele/ © Arno Declair

listened now to the daily broadcast about the banality of evil". As Kremer completes his monologue, a variation of the musical theme from Carl Maria von Weber's opera *Der Freischütz* is played, this time in a more cheerful, folkloristic accordion version. The idea of listening to old music that is highly associated with the rise of nationalism in German music, ironically develops into a metonym for the massacre and more generally, one may recall the music played in Nazi concentration camps as well. From the beginning of the shooting, the light-image of the shooting scene (Figures 8.3 and 8.4) starts fading in and remains until the musical theme of *Der Freischütz* is played.

Aesthetic analysis of the light-image

Six lighting elements compose the light-image of the shooting scene (Figures 8.4 and 8.5):

1   *A green 'wash' of light on the upper walls* – A soft light, almost evenly distributed across the entire surface, illuminates the bright upper walls of the scenography in a highly saturated green colour (similar to Rosco's and E-colour's filter *089# Moss Green*). Each of the two walls is illuminated by separate light source, and a soft thin line of shadow is hung at the intersection of the walls. The light sources that generate this element are concealed at the sides of the proscenium arch, behind the portal, and the focusing is crossed – the light from the right hits the wall at stage left, and the light from the left hits the wall on the opposite side.[1] High up on the right wall hangs a reindeer skull. The green light casts its shadow on both walls, with two shadows at the same height as the object – an indication that the light sources and the reindeer are at similar heights. Above the green walls hovers a black empty space.

2   *A diagonal front-of-house light* – Two HMI Fresnels illuminate the stage from the auditorium's side-balconies and generate gaslight of a pale green hue. These two light sources, one at each side of the auditorium, are positioned about two metres above stage level at an angle of 45 degrees to the centre line. The low position of this lighting element at an unnatural angle flattens the plasticity of the performers' face and eliminates shadows, so the performers' look becomes rather erratic and hallucinatory. The optic qualities of this element are of an extremely cold light reminiscent of the white fluorescent tubes that distribute subtle and even illumination. Because the two sources generate a crossed illumination and each wooden wall is intensively lit by only one single HMI source, the light casts clear black shadows on the walls, one shadow for each performer (Figure 8.5 constitutes an excellent example).

3   *A single flattening front-of-house (head-on front light)* – Hung in the auditorium against the centre line in a rather low position in relation to the stage, this HMI Fresnel illuminates the entire stage and helps soften or 'fill-in' any shadows on the performers created by other lighting elements (see Figure 8.4). Inevitably, the side-effect of this lamp type and its proximity to the audience is the escape of some diffused ambient light spreading onto the spectators. The higher the intensity of this Fresnel lamp, the more visible the spectators are in the auditorium. Thus, due to the high intensity this lighting element has in this light-image, beyond its effect on stage, the field of vision expands and shifts the spectators' concentration from the stage to the presence of other spectators near them, and the entire state of spectatorship in a social situation.

Figure 8.4 Jossi Wieler, *Rechnitz*. A video frame of the shooting scene, showing the entire stage with Hildegard Schmahl, André Jung, Steven Scharf, Katja Bürkle and Hans Kremer. Video frame: Courtesy of the Münchner Kammerspiele

Figure 8.5 Jossi Wieler, *Rechnitz*. Hildegard Schmahl, André Jung, Steven Scharf, Katja Bürkle and Hans Kremer with headphones covering their ears in the shooting scene. Photo: Courtesy of the Münchner Kammerspiele/ © Arno Declair

4   *Top lights* – In this light-image, three top lights are used above the performers to enhance their silhouettes and increase the contrast between them and the walls behind. The colour of these light sources is slightly cold, using either E-Colour: *Full CT Blue 201#* or *Half CT Blue 202#*. Due to the soft optic quality of this element I assume that Fresnel lenses are employed. These top lights illuminate the stage floor and, due to their tungsten bulbs, slightly increase its warmth, as if to restrain the dominance of the cold pale greenish light that the HMI's produce.

5   *Second line of frontal light from the portal bridge* – The deeper plan of the stage floor, as well as the wooden walls, are illuminated by tungsten Fresnels from the bridge of the portal. These light sources are in either E-Colour: *Full CT Blue 201#* or *Half CT Blue 202#*. The light from this angle somewhat reduces the reflection created by the HMI Fresnels, and restores some vividness to the natural colour of the wood. This lighting element is mostly sensed on the wooden walls where the shadows of the performers appear, and also on the floor, but its influence is less dominant than the HMI gaslights.

6   *Auditorium light* – While this light-image prevails on stage, for nearly one minute the houselights in the auditorium are also turned on, the way they usually are before the beginning and after the end of a theatre performance. The houselights fade in while the sound of gunshots is played, and after the last shot is heard, the light fades out. The rising of this light surprises the spectators and reveals the auditorium in the middle of the performance.

Semiotic and poetic analysis of the light-image

Considering the lighting elements mentioned above, how are aesthetic features of light experienced or used as signs in this production; what are the signs about; and how are the signs used in a poetic way?

The brightness and harshness of light in a space increase a sense of openness, exposure and directness with regard to any visible object. This light-image generates a flat and bright look, especially of the performers. The combination of cold white HMI gaslight and warmer tungsten-based lighting, both used at unnatural angles, does not support the imagined representation of the historical time and place of the shooting in Rechnitz in 1945. Rather, light does something else here. While it avoids particularizing time and space, light creates *suspense* and *alienation from reality* that enrich the poetic dimension of this performance. Both light and spoken text distance the representation of reality from verisimilitude based on an imitation of the perceptual characteristics of reality – the light does so by means of the 'surrealistic' over-exposure and the unnatural lighting angles, and the text achieves the same goal by means of (1) its fragmentary nature (2) the unlikeliness of the events to happen and (3) the absence of any causal relations between them. The cumulative experience of this light-image with the almost static scene of shooting on stage and the houselights in the auditorium encourages the addressees to think critically of the theatrical presentation happening here and now rather than to dwell on a fictive situation.

Although the light prevents one to fall into the trap of fiction, two events potentially coincide in the scene. The first event unfolds within the stage and auditorium, shared here and now by the performers and spectators. The second event, recreated and imagined in the mind of the spectator, is the shooting of the Jewish forced labourers at Rechnitz. The narrative remains outside of the performance; we know what occurred in Rechnitz in 1945 and we use this as 'subtext' while watching and interpreting the performance. Addressees construct representations of traumatic experiences with which they could engage regarding the scene. We know that the actual shooting of the 180 forced labourers occurred at night, outdoors, but the light does not recreate this fictive/historical time and space. When examining this light-image in relation to the entire scene, the light shows a neutral and distant approach toward the physical activities of the performers, the soundscape and the spoken text. Therefore, in my perspective, the semiotic function of this light-image is not grounded in *the narrative*.

In line with our framework for the analysis of light, let us now examine whether the qualities of this light-image embody the ground of *a character*. As mentioned earlier, the text has been written like essayistic prose without any fictive character; it is more like a soundscape of multiple voices and counter-voices that encompasses diverse – and sometimes contradictory – opinions. Serving as 'post-Brechtian agents' of the text or the director, the performers give rise to a tapestry of subjective memories and drifting thoughts or imaginations but do not yet evolve here into elaborate round characters. The light-image, therefore, cannot be experienced as a visual reflection upon the psychological dimension of a character or the mental situation in which it acts. Even when weak traces of a character emerge for a short moment, contrasting voices and views unfold and disrupt the reception of the performers as coherent characters. For the reasons mentioned above, the imaginative representation achieved through this light-image is, again, not grounded in the second category proposed by the conceptual framework: *a character*.

Thematically, the performance invokes ideas regarding how we, three generations after the Second World War, are failing in accurately keeping the authentic memories of people who survived the Holocaust. Our cultural memory is constituted by mediated images and subjective reports. Indeed, knowledge is inevitably modified in any transmitting process, as any medium influences on the ways in which information is transmitted received. And so, the precision and validity of historical reports are put into question. This performance poses an ethical question regarding the authenticity of the information given by the reporters, but also concerning the degree of their involvement in the massacre. Did these messengers actually attend the extermination as witnesses, and, if so, did they seek a way to save peoples' lives or were they passive bystanders?

The uncertainty of cultural memory of history – in the lack of factual objective truth – seems to be one of the themes addressed in this scene (and other scenes too). For the addressees, being overwhelmed by a rhizome of various 'truths' contradicting each other, there is an urgent need for clarity. In this respect, the aesthetic features of the light-image, both on stage and in the auditorium, could be associated with the theme mentioned above. On stage, the visibility of the performers as constituted by various lighting elements emphasizes deviation from nature by light angles that invert shadows on the body and cold white colour that modifies the skin colour. This penetrating harsh light becomes significant when relating this to the evident context of death, as the performers appear to acquire a ghostlike appearance. In particular, the low frontal HMI light provides an extreme exposure of the performers 'reporters' by means of a flattening, gelid white light. Poetically, light is used here *to uncover the truth of evil* and unmask its shadows, by obliterating any sense of mystery.

Fading the houselights in during the shooting scene may also be related to the theme mentioned above. The houselights, which conventionally signify the distinction between gathering and performance time, slowly make the spectators increasingly visible and conscious of one another in their state of spectatorship, but also as a human landscape of passive spectators/silent witnesses. At this point, the performers not only address the audience verbally, but also watch the audience watching them. Dissolving boundaries between the stage and auditorium, between art and reality, between potential witnesses reporters and murderers proves to be a groundbreaking visual, emotional and conceptual experience. The light-image interweaves with the theme by calling to our mind, creatively, that we are not watching a representation of the massacre in Rechnitz; rather we are constructing an imaginative representation of it in our mind. In fact, as we listen to their provocative text – both vulgar and poetic in its own way – we are pushed out of our comfort zone under the examining eyes of all five 'reporters'. And the whistles of the bullets, like the performers' gazes at us, are penetrating. Spectators remain silent, passively seated, like the many people who have witnessed the horrors in the years of the Second World War and done nothing.

The ground of the representational function (or meaning) of this light-image, thus, lies in *a theme*, but **not** in **dramatic action**. In *Rechnitz*, we find performers backing off from taking any action, but reporting the actions of others (offstage). There is clearly an absence of dramatic action.

I would now like to examine the aesthetic characteristics of this light-image, their powerful atmospheric expression and emotional effect, in three separate channels:

1   A combination of frontal lights from different angles and types (HMI's, and halogen in pale blue) flattens and alienates the performers, by giving a marble-like coldness to their skin, in terms of tonality. This strange effect and somehow unsettling look is achieved mainly by using the cold white light (HMI Fresnels) that eliminates any shadow from the performers, making their eyes shine like glass, and evoking an antipathy towards them (Figure 8.5). Moreover, much of this harsh strong light is reflected back from the glittering lacquered wooden walls of the scenography onto the audience. Thus, the light makes the look of the performers and the scenography more jarring, or irritating, in the experience of the addressees. The space changes between a salon and a torture room/shooting room, with the red headphones used to silence the bullets' sound.

2   Saturated green light radiates from the upper bright walls, providing a 'vibrating' plain field of vivid coloured light contrasting with the concrete and particularized dark wood blocks below. The upper level of the space then displays very different qualities than these of the lower part – the abstract, spiritual and primary, against the practical, materialist and elaborate, respectively. This warm green light brings some playfulness and vividness against the pale and icy white light on the serious architectonic elements. Not only does this lighting element lend an ambiguous mood to the space, it also associates the sign of the colour green as an iconography of life and (in-)sanity. However, if one relates more to the narrative of the massacre in Rechnitz, the green light could also suggest a forest in which the aristocracy hunted animals – as a sport – and Jews – in an act of anti-Semitism. The green field of light becomes an atmospheric element that affects the emotion of the addressee either subconsciously or by interpreting the meaning of the colour as an imaginative representation.

3   The third component I consider is the unconventional lighting up of the auditorium throughout the scene and its effects on the spectators. In particular, this light
was a source of inconvenience and unrest for the spectators, turning them into
'gazed-at objects' by the performers and reversing the roles between lookers and
onlookers. The experience of this mutual observation and the exchange of staring
by performers and spectators alike are, nonetheless, exciting. Conventionally, after
the performance begins the houselights fade out until the end of the show. Here,
however, this sign is used differently, poetically, to confer another visual stimulus
upon the spectators that is the image of crowd of anonymous onlookers seen from
the back, organized in symmetric rows. The light 'hunts' (and 'haunts') us, the soli-
tary and nocturnal audience members; we are captured, paralyzed and silently 'put
on the spot'.

As noted in the chapter presenting the conceptual framework, the light-image – the
phenomenological experience and the semiotic function of which are grounded in
atmosphere or *emotion* – generates an expressive visual effect that emotionally manipulates the spectators or creates a pervading atmosphere that influences them corporeally.
As I have argued, these phenomena indeed occur with regard to this light-image. I
would, therefore, suggest that the ground of the meaning (or the representational function) of this light-image lies in *atmosphere* or *emotion*.

After having been seated nearly an hour in a dark auditorium, I remember how dominant and, for the first moments, disturbing the houselights were while they faded in.
These lights forcefully changed the spatial experience by restoring to one's perception
and consciousness both the theatre building and the situation of performance as a social
event. The strong presence of the medium of light made us aware to its functioning all
of a sudden, changing the 'default' condition of being free from public attention and
from being observed or disturbed by other people. This gesture was unconventional,
bringing a level of meta-theatricality and drawing attention to the important influence
of the medium on the watching experience, on emotion and imagination.

From a semiotic perspective, deviating from the theatrical convention by using the
houselights in the middle of the performance becomes significant and poetic, adding
to the possibilities of interpretation. Thus, the actual audience becomes the silent witnesses in the historical massacre, or, more radically, the light signals the end of the
killing game that went on in Rechnitz. The sensational experience of light calls to
mind the medium in operation in two possible ways: through *hypermediacy*, it relates
to a dominant presence of the medium, and through *spectacularity*, it relates to the
aesthetic pleasure and enjoyment one can gain from the light. In the case of this light-
image, the use of lighting technology on stage is not explicitly emphasized, yet the
dominance of the medium is experienced through the evident use of the houselights. I
would, therefore, consider the semiotic function of this light-image to be grounded in
the sensation of light through *hypermediacy*.

The green field of light in the upper part of the space is an outstanding and enigmatic element which has continuously triggered my imagination while pondering its
prospective meaning. It is a brilliant primary green, boldly vibrating as a mysterious
'hole' in the image, against the mostly elaborate and concrete physical space and 'realistic' costumes. This blank field of pure colour brings such different visual qualities
that, in my perception, it becomes an object in its own right beyond a simple green
illumination of the scenery. The light evokes a visual experience that is not dependent

upon verisimilitude. The light itself is the direct stimulus, as is the case with the Light Art. At will, the green field could also accept several interpretations with rather highly probable, narrative-related meanings I noted earlier, such as: the forest being a venue for hunting or liberation from the laws of civilization, the representation of (in-)sanity and the iconography of life. In contrast, apart from these ideas, the consistent existence of this light throughout a major part of the performance, and within the discussed scene as well, enriches the image with an enigmatic and ambiguous facet, the significance of which remains open for interpretation.

Thus, the attempt to construct an enduring interpretation of the green light involves 'drifting' mentally between various desires, emotional reactions, memories, and associations, while examining these against the background of cultural conventions and new information one gains from the performance. Experiencing this field of light may be oriented to: (1) the aesthetic level, derived from the formal characteristics of the light, (2) the phenomenological and pre-semiotic visceral/unconscious effect that the colour green has on the mind of spectators, evoking notions of relaxation or an association with nature. Additionally, one's experience might be: (3) conceptual semiotic, identifying a stimulus as a sign, leading to its interpretation in the poetic context. While watching this light-image in *Rechnitz*, I recalled in particular the work of artists in light such as James Turrell and Doug Wheeler, who use evenly plain light and vibrant illuminated surfaces. In *Rechnitz*, too, it seems that the (green) light reaches a high level of autonomy, re-establishing or redefining the relation between the light and other media. The representation is thus grounded in ***open meaning***, since the intriguing and suggestive visual qualities of the image remain ambiguous and constantly invite one to consider their function and significance.

The Town Residents: second light-image

The second light-image that I analyse from the production *Rechnitz* appears in the last section of the performance (Figure 8.7). For the readers unfamiliar with the performance, here is a brief description of the scene, which I refer to as '*The Town Residents*'.

A tune – the familiar musical leitmotif from the overture of the opera *Der Freischütz* (1821) by Carl Maria von Weber, this time in a light jazzy version – marks the transition into the new scene. *Der Freischütz* is considered to be the first German Romantic opera, liberated from the dominant influence of French and Italian operatic conventions. From a historical perspective, Weber's innovative adaptation of local folklore and national musical themes into the score, was intended to help in developing a national cultural identity, and later, a nationalist ethos, a reference that clearly connects the music of this particular opera with this theatre performance. In his essay *Investigating the Entrails: Post-operatic Music Theatre in Europe* Nicholas Till notes:

> Until the later eighteenth century opera meant in Germany, as anywhere else in Europe other than France, Italian Opera. The move to create a German-language opera emerged as an aspect of a developing German cultural identity in the later eighteenth century, and was, from the time of Mozart, combined with an interest in Greek tragedy as a precursor for the ideal of a communal national theatre in Germany, which became central to Wagner's construction of a myth of origin for his own operatic works.
>
> (Till 2006, 35)

Figure 8.6 Jossi Wieler, *Rechnitz*. Hildegard Schmahl, Steven Scharf, Katja Bürkle, André Jung and Hans Kremer. Photo: Courtesy of the Münchner Kammerspiele/ © Arno Declair

While the music plays, eleven revolving parts in the walls rotate slowly and remain open (Figure 8.6). Through the openings, a dark space beyond the walls is revealed, with white fluorescent tubes suspended in a row above paper targets for shooting practice. Hunting is relevant not only as a metaphor for the massacre in Rechnitz, but might also refer to the Nietzschean idea of the Übermensch, superior to all other living beings, also manifested through the skull of the reindeer (a noble animal) that hangs on the wall. After turning around, the walls reveal their rear side with white tiles instead of the patterned wood. The five performers then clear the space of dozens of fur jackets, scarves and a litter of grilled chicken leftovers (also manifestations of hunting in one way or another), and this is followed by a costume change (Figure 8.7). The performers' new outfits suggest a simpler and more mundane, even somewhat 'provincial' appearance in comparison with the initial outfits that were more official, aristocratic and meticulous. The change of costumes could also suggest the progression in time, starting with the festive dinner party, followed by the sleeping after the massacre and, here, concluding with the residents of Rechnitz concealing the deed.

After doing so, throughout the entire scene the performers stand still side-by-side in a line close to the wall with their arms held statically either behind or beside the body, or with their hands in their pockets, some of them with drooping shoulders. They are almost pushed back against the white wall, and they display less self-confidence than before (Figure 8.7). The performing is more restrained in this scene and the delivery of the performers is rather hesitant.

Aesthetic analysis of the light-image

The light-image consists of four lighting elements:

1   A *diagonal front-of-house light* – HMI Fresnels stand out as key light and illuminate the walls and the stage floor in a very cold, slightly pale greenish tint. This lighting element now distributes a higher intensity than in earlier scenes and it accentuates the whiteness of the tiles on the walls. Due to the low height at which these lighting sources are positioned, the performers look flat, somewhat similar to the effect that a strong camera flash has on a photo. This light-source reduces the plasticity of their bodies and faces, as well as casting clear black shadows onto the white tiles behind them.

2   *Top lights* – The same three top lights of the previous analysis also feature in this image. These tungsten light sources are coloured with a slightly cold filter of either E-Colour: *Full CT Blue 201#* or *Half CT Blue 202#* that change the yellowish tint of the light into a slightly colder and more neutral tone. The top lights highlight the performers' silhouettes, creating a contrast between their figures and the walls, and enhancing their look against the background of the reflecting white tiles.

3   *Flattening front-of-house (head-on front light)* – This lighting element functions as a soft fill light, and it consists of a number of lighting fixtures with halogen bulbs coloured in cold pale-bluish filter. In combination with the HMI diagonal front-of-house and the top lights, the range of colour temperatures of light is thus established on a scale slightly warmer than HMI colour.

4   *Green fluorescent tubes* – This lighting element consists of built-in green fluorescent tubes, which contour the upper edge of the wooden walls. Up until the last section

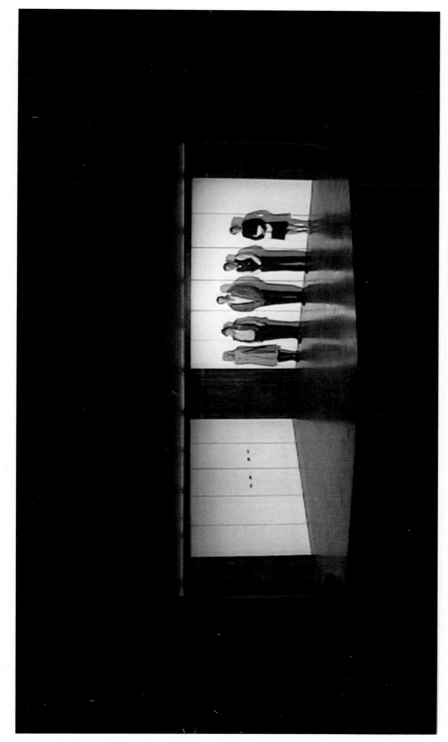

Figure 8.7 Jossi Wieler, *Rechnitz*. A video frame showing the entire stage with Hildegard Schmahl, André Jung, Steven Scharf, Hans Kremer and Katja Bürkle. Video frame: Courtesy of the Münchner Kammerspiele

of the performance there seems to be a synergy between the green tubes and the field of the green light, in changing proportions of intensity and vibrancy between the two elements, when most of the time they feature together. Once the transition into the current light-image is complete, for the first time we see the green fluorescent tubes on without the upper green field of light. Because the upper walls remain gloomy, these tubes now become an imaginary contour or an outline of the top edge – lower than the spectators perceived before – and so, the scenography appears to be more horizontal and compressed in perception. The deer's skull receives no direct light in this light-image (or in the images that follow).

Semiotic and poetic analysis of the light-image

Considering the lighting elements mentioned above, how are aesthetic features of light experienced or used as signs; what are the signs about; and how are they used in a poetic way?

The light does not suggest any illustrative reference to a specific space and time as derived from the text. That said, the text itself lacks any concrete description of time and space so in fact the light cannot illustrate any fictive light conditions based on information within the text. Thus, for the same reasons mentioned in the previous analysis, the semiotic function of this light-image is not grounded in *narrative*.

By means of pale cold light, which makes the skin appear white and lifeless, and due to the white background towards which they are pushed, the performers now look even whiter than in earlier scenes. The low position of the HMI light makes us perceive the performers' bodies as flat and casts their sharp shadows on the white tiles behind. In our perception, the space metamorphoses into a lower and closed venue, more silent and tense due to the light (compare Figure 8.7 with Figure 8.4).

Different stylizing of 'behaviour' and overall manner of reporting information also enhances the way we experience the performers in the scene. The body language becomes more static and suppressed, with expression coming mostly through the voice and face in an almost explanatory manner, sometimes apologetic, albeit still lacking emotion. The casual and intentionally banal costumes in this section effectively enhance a feeling of helplessness (Figure 8.7). The composition of the scene, with the performers' pushed against the wall like hunted beasts or victims, possibly suggests post-traumatic behaviour, but also resembles figures standing in a police line-up or facing a firing squad.

At this point, I would like to examine how a sense of compassion possibly influences the audience's reception of the performers as characters in the scene. As the scene unfolds, Steven Scharf approaches us with: "Lords of the land, please stop shooting for a moment. I know that it pleasures you, but . . . ". As a spectator, I associated the statement with the voice of the victims, and it also raised the question of whether the witnesses/reporters are guilty or innocent. It is not that the acting style in this section diverges from the playful, alienating and ambivalent attitude with which the performers constantly treat the text – rather, it is the image itself that suggests a subtler situation, and the text and light support that feeling. In my experience, for a brief moment, the five performers unite into one persona, a single fragile entity under attack. Schaft's standing with his hands hidden in the pockets of his raincoat, briefly looking left at two other performers – which otherwise happens only rarely during the performance (!) – and then begging to stop shooting when looking at the audience, is an instance in which the performers seem to have awaken from the horror and to yearn for some morality to re-emerge.

The aesthetics of this light-image – especially the pressing-flattening light, the light colour and its shadows – now conjoin with the other media. Together, they seem to indicate that a new stage has been reached in the human condition as represented on stage, emphasizing the state of captivity without any psychological dimension in the work of the performers. Although *Rechnitz* does not consist of well-rounded fictive characters in the Aristotelian sense (and their mental situation), this scene, in particular, evokes an emotional effect of identification and empathy toward the human performers, a fundamental feature in the audience's reception of fictional characters. Albeit for only a brief moment, the aesthetic features of the light-image assist in creating these effects. I thus consider the representational function (or meaning) of this light-image to be grounded in *a character*.

Although in *Rechnitz* there is neither a dramatic conflict nor a dramatic action with which the performers engage, we can discern a few central themes in the piece, such as, for example: *the instability that the memory of history suffers, its questionable validity* and *the problem of subjectivity and authenticity* in historical documentation of facts. The heavy shadow that floats above the space in this scene, replacing the green field of light, calls to mind a sense of absence or, in the historical context of Rechnitz, the themes of *covering and unveiling the truth* and *the concealment of guilt*. On the floor, the high intensity of the HMI front-of-house light in particular illuminates the performers, revealing every inch of their body as if they are under inspection or interrogation. In this respect, the light poetically implies both the concealment of the upper walls that had been previously lit green, and the pressing need for an uncovering of a truth by overexposing the messengers under extreme white light. The aesthetic features of this light-image, thus, have successfully mediated dramaturgical aspects of the performance into the medium of light. Concurrently, the semiotic function of this light-image is also grounded in *a theme*.

The colour composite, mainly consisting of the row of green fluorescent tubes and the cold white HMI light, creates an unpleasant, eerie image (Figure 8.7). Not only does the white light deprive any sense of vividness from colours in the space, but the rather strong reflection from the tiles on the walls also dazzles the spectators. I noted earlier how the light modifies our visual perception of the space, compressing it horizontally and so it seems to have become lower compared to the previous scenes. This light-image pulls the stage out of balance: under a continuous and horizontal thin line of green light two major white surfaces stand out, one vibrant and shiny, and against it the second – gloomier and almost greyish. The five performers stand stage left, 'packed' and fixed in position, emphasizing the diagonal line of the left-side wall, while the stage-right wall remains unoccupied. The formal characteristics of the light described above create a new environment with alienating atmosphere that that cannot but affect the spectators' emotional experience. Therefore, the experience of this light-image and its semiotic function in my opinion are also grounded in *atmosphere* or *emotion*.

The technological devices and the procedures involved in the creation of this light-image remain rather 'transparent' and concealed from the eyes of the spectators. Likewise, the mechanical aspects of lighting techniques do not in any way influence the characteristics of the signs of light. Nor does the light-image elevate the use of stage lighting as an apparatus into a poetic context. For these reasons, the meaning of this light-image is not grounded in *the sensation of light* – neither in *hypermediacy*, nor *spectacularity*. When the meaning of the light-image is grounded in **the sensation of light**, the medium of light demonstrates its authoritative role by increasing the materiality of the signs in light and creating a poetic dimension that rise from the technology used. As this is not the case here, the semiotic function of this light-image is not grounded in **the sensation of light**.

The last ground of representation against which I examine this light-image is that of **open meaning**. The aesthetic features of light, from this scene on, alter and recompose the scenography in our visual perception very differently than all that went on before. The light invites us to ponder the significance and reason for that change. It might be considered as an autonomous visual 'gesture' of light. Moreover, by intentionally avoiding any illustration of the spoken text and by taking a more interpretive position toward it, the autonomy of light from the text has had the potential to increase.

As I elaborate in the chapter presenting the conceptual framework, the autonomy of light is not so much the result of its being disconnected from the text or light's dynamic and increased visual activity, but rather of the *increased cognitive activity in the imagination of the addressee*. The cognitive process around the negotiation of open meaning is a reaction to the specific, unique visual experience one finds in a light-image. On the basis of my own professional experience, when the representational function of a light-image is grounded in **open meaning**, typical features in the reception process are: the fleeting meaning, the light experienced as 'phantom' in the performance and the drift from one possible meaning to another. As long as its relations with the other media constantly bring meaning into question, a light-image can still make us pursue light's autonomous and openness of meaning. I doubt whether this light-image consists of these abovementioned qualities, related to **open meaning**.

The dramaturgy of light in *Rechnitz*

Three fundamental approaches can be distinguished, underlying the dramaturgy of light in *Rechnitz* by the Münchner Kammerspiele:

1   *Thematic and atmospheric light in non-dramatic performance* – The production of *Rechnitz* constitutes a valuable example of lighting design in a non-dramatic, or post-dramatic environment, where literary work rather than a dramatic play functions as the 'engine' of the performance. When the spoken text is a dominant element, it is highly probable that the visual signs will be interpreted with reference to this text. At the beginning of this chapter, I discussed in some depth various aspects of the performance, such as the ambiguous and associative nature of the verbal text, the absence of fictive characters and dramatic conflict, and the audience being directly addressed in the monologues/speeches. The performers address their speech to the spectators – not to their colleagues on the stage – and the spectators are thus almost forced to become participants in the theatrical event. All speakers, no matter who, confront the addressees in the auditorium by staring constantly in their direction. I also described the immediacy that characterizes the way in which information is reported by the performers without the backing of a fictive situation being a motivation for the speech. In a rather post-Brechtian manner, there is no imitative representation of a fictive location or time in which the entire action can be situated.

Lighting designer Max Keller met with these conditions and created an appealing light design, sensitive and effective in both concept and form. The multidirectional flow of the text and its kaleidoscopic character challenge the artists and addressees to engage simultaneously with a broad range of associations. Taking an illustrative approach towards lighting design, while dealing with such a literary piece would not enable one to do justice with the complexity of the work and would surely narrow down the experience of the performance and limit the scope of potential interpretations. The poetics of light in *Rechnitz* is occasionally based upon informed subjective interpretation with reference to the subtext, as I suggested earlier in the two analyses. In addition, the poetic function of light in *Rechnitz* is often related to central ***themes*** in the dramaturgy or ***atmospheres*** that the light casts on the addressees. The dominant quality which the light brings is that of harsh illumination and exposure of the space in a way that often flattens the look of the performers.

2   *Light as a structuring authority* – Throughout the progression of the performance, the light helps us to distinguish two consecutive phases alongside the scenography and costumes. The first phase is from the beginning of the piece until the field of green light on the upper walls vanishes. The second phase starts when the white walls revolve and the costumes change and lasts until the end of the performance. In both phases, as it seems to me, there is a deliberate effort to create a sinister atmosphere and avoid any illustrative approach to the text. In the first stage the light shows us the space as high, open, highly illuminated and free to move about in, while in the second, we perceive the space as lower and broad, darker (up high on the walls and downstage), with the performers stuck to the white wall. The most outstanding difference, in light, between the two phases of the performance is the disappearance of the vibrant green light.

A careful examination, however, shows thirty to forty sequential light-images or lighting cues changing throughout the two-hour performance. Arranging seven different principal looks with diverse aesthetic characteristics, in each one of the seven sections the light-images bear an aesthetic resemblance to the 'principal type of look' to which it belongs. The main variance is atmospheric and it lies in the balance between the different illumination areas in the space, usually where the performers are present. Most light-images are thus variations, with slight modifications in intensity, of one of these 'principal appearances'.

The medium of light visually structures a series of atmospheres, disrupts the sense of plasticity and modifies, or remoulds, the perceived dimensions of the space. Most of the modifications from one light-image to the next, within a particular atmospheric section with one type of look, are those of minor changes of illumination areas. I therefore consider them as more functional changes of illumination, rather than as a development within the poetics of light. For example, when a light-image changes merely in order to resize an illumination area, in order to light a performer in a new area, the change is not necessarily made for poetic reasons. Nevertheless, the structuring of the piece in light-imagery of seven separate 'chapters', with each chapter possessing its own aesthetic features shared by all the light-images in that 'chapter', gives light a dominant formalist position in the performance. Such a visual condition as part of the development of light sometimes creates new interesting interrelations with the other media in the performance, leading to new perspectives. The structuring of the piece in different types of looks helps in creating a sense of movement, a certain tempo and renewal that could be clearly experienced. In this way, light suggests a separate and rather independent course of action, evolving simultaneously with the other media.

3   *Autonomy in relation to the text* – Three lighting elements used in *Rechnitz* set out a powerful phenomenological effect on the spectators and create a poetic dimension, liberated from the need to support the verbal text. The first element, as noted earlier in the analysis, is the striking and tantalizing houselights that are used to illuminate the spectators during the shooting scene. This lighting element is linked with the theme of preserving accurately the memory of the historical massacre while also calling to mind the notion of theatre as a social event for cultural reflection. Moreover, it poetically transforms the audience members into the silent and anonymous victims, or into witnesses/reporters, while the shooting sounds are played.

The second lighting element is the vibrant field of green light on the upper walls and the third element is the thin outline of green fluorescent tubes above the wooden walls. The green colour adds a sense of mystery and contrast into the space, due to the dissonance between the almost-spiritual entity of green light field and the quite severe material qualities of the scenography. In addition, the green colour raises questions about its meaning as it floats up high above the performers, and later, vanishes.

Throughout the entire performance, the medium of light shows a subtle 'behaviour' by very soft transitions. Mostly the lighting adheres to a simple and 'modest' aesthetics of light, is not sensational (not 'spectacular') and does not emphasize the presence of lighting technology. The use of pale colours, in particular, increases the effectiveness of the green lighting elements and the houselights so they become more significant and autonomous in relation to the text.

Note

1   Throughout the entire book, I indicate positions and sides of the stage according to the Anglo-Saxon system, taking the performers' point of view, which is the opposite of what is common in most European theatres, which relate to the spectators' view.

References

Fuchs, E., *The Death of Character: Perspectives on Theatre after Modernism*, Bloomington and Indianapolis, IN: Indiana University Press, 1996.

Kurzenberger, H., *Jossi Wieler – Theater*, Berlin and Köln: Alexander Verlag, 2011.

Lehmann, H.T., *Postdramatic Theatre*, translated and foreword by K. Jürs-Munby, Abingdon and New York: Routledge, 2006.

Szondi, P., *Theory of the Modern Drama*, Minneapolis, MN: University of Minnesota Press, 1987.

Till, N., "Investigating the Entrails: Post-operatic Music Theatre in Europe", in *Contemporary Theatres in Europe*, edited by Joe Kelleher and Nicholas Ridout, Abingdon and New York: Routledge, 2006.

Interviews

An after-show conversation between the artists and the public after the performance of *Rechnitz* at The Cameri Theatre in Tel-Aviv, Israel, 12 February 2011.

Chapter 9

Peer Gynt

By Henrik Ibsen
The Hungarian State Theatre of Cluj

Premiered at the Hungarian State Theatre of Cluj, Romania,
21 March 2008

The artistic team

Director: *David Zinder*
Scenography: *Miriam Guretzki*
Light: *Yaron Abulafia*
Costumes: *Carmencita Brojboiu*
Music: *Zsolt Lászlóffy*
Dramaturge: *Andras Visky*
Choreography: *Melinda Jakab*

Performers

Old Peer Gynt: *Zsolt Bogdán*
Young Peer Gynt: *Ferenc Sinkó*
Aase: *Emőke Kató*
Solveig: *Anikó Pethő*
Solveig's father, Monsieur Ballon, Huhu: *Lehel Salat*
Solveig's mother, troll, lunatic, thief, Solveig as old: *Csilla Albert*
Helga, troll child: *Hanna Salat*
The Button-moulder: *József Bíró*

Button-moulder-photographer, a strange passenger, a thin man: *Áron Dimény*
Ingrid, woman in green, Anitra: *Andrea Kali*
Bridegroom, troll interpreter, thief, Button-moulder's servant: *Balázs Bodolai*
The bridegroom's father, troll, Herr von Eberkopf, lunatic, cook: *Attila Orbán*
The bridegroom's mother, herdgirl, troll, female Arabic dancer, lunatic: *Enikő Györgyjakab*
Villager, herdgirl, troll, female Arabic dancer, lunatic: *Andrea Vindis*
Villager, herdgirl, troll, female Arabic dancer, lunatic: *Tünde Skovrán*
Villager, troll, steward, Begriffenfeldt: *Levente Molnár*
Dovre-master: *Ernő Galló*
Villager, troll, Mr. Cotton, King Apis: *Ervin Szűcs*
Villager, troll, Trumpeterstraale, Hussein, Button-moulder's servant: *Róbert Vass Laczkó*

Introduction

The production of *Peer Gynt* by the Hungarian State Theatre of Cluj-Napoca (2008) is the last 'test case' in this study. Of the five selected performances I analyse, *Peer Gynt* is perhaps the most traditionally 'dramatic' one. However, the staging of this dramatic work resulted in a performance that went far beyond the tradition of 'well-made-plays' with which *Peer Gynt* is associated. A highly elaborate visual dimension enriches and accompanies the production alongside the dominant text in the performance. In many ways, the adaptation of the original *Peer Gynt* text in this production expands the world of the text into a provocative and imaginative (re-)presentation of the play. It creates a sense of immediacy, of direct contact, among the spectators and the performers, within the visible architectonic space of the stage, and it concomitantly heightens the audience's awareness of the artificiality of the event, and of the state of 'performativity' (to use Lehmann's term). The light design for this production undoubtedly deviates from the dramatic course of the play, creating its own 'light-motifs' and 'behaviour' patterns with dominance and autonomy that characterizes its poetics.

The Hungarian State Theatre of Cluj-Napoca in Romania (with its artistic director Gábor Tompa) is currently one of Europe's most acclaimed repertory theatre companies and a member of the exclusive *Union of the Theatres of Europe* (UTE). An additional reason for choosing to write about this production is that *Peer Gynt*'s light design will serve in this section of the study as the only performance designed by the author-artist. In contrast to the other analysed productions, here I write about a piece in which I was involved as a collaborator, so I am able to provide insights in the artistic process and write about visual experiences or signs of light that I myself have created, and the realization of which I experienced in the theatre. For the sake of clarity, I should make it clear that I do not pretend to be able to write about *Peer Gynt* with the same critical distance I had while analysing the other productions. Instead, I will here use the conceptual framework as a reference and structure with which I write about the ideas I had concerning the functions of light I designed for *Peer Gynt*, the experience I and other spectators had while watching the performance, and the sensorial, emotional and conceptual dimensions of this light design.

About the adaptation of the play

Written by Henrik Ibsen, *Peer Gynt* had its world premiere at 1876. Inspired by a Nordic folk tale, Ibsen wrote this play in five acts, entirely in rhyme. It is a fascinating journey play, featuring the decadent life story of Peer Gynt in search of his 'true self' – a theme deeply associated with *fin de siècle* art and with Ibsen's biography at that point in his career as a playwright. The play bears philosophical and religious and mythical influences, manifested by dozens of diverse characters, some transcendental and some animal – nevertheless, it is full of wit, and occasionally nearly satirical.

For theatre director David Zinder the premise of this production is about 'becoming'. It is about an endless search for a kind of personal establishment, or accomplishment, which never happens. In this adaptation of the play, two performers double the role of Peer Gynt, playing young and old Peer – in several scenes both are simultaneously present – as if the scene we perceive is a flashback through the eyes of old Peer. Zinder notes:

Most of the play takes place, in a sense, from the end of the play, as old Peer is look-ing back on his life, so he appears in many places. He appears at the beginning of the play, he appears when Peer meets Solveig for the first time, he appears later in the Boyg scene – he is the Boyg [the old Peer – Y.A.]. And then, when Aase dies he is there with young Peer, together, because this is when the journey begins, this is when Peer leaves.[1]

The production also emphasizes the idea of documenting one's path in life, by add-ing the role of a photographer who takes photos of Peer in specific moments of moral decline throughout the performance, and later spreads these as evidence against Peer when the Button-moulder wants to punish him. According to Zinder, it is the:

> . . . concept of keeping a kind of record of your life, and trying to compare different stages of your life – is this the same person? Thus, the Button-moulder, who appears in the original text only in the third act, now has two forms: one is a photographer and one is the Button-moulder at the end. And he appeared right from the begin-ning, and he was taking photographs right from the beginning, and at the end of the play the photographs are actually on the stage . . . and this connects to the scene with Peer and removing the masks and trying to find out who he is underneath it all.

Beyond the addition of a photographer, the adaptation also includes Solveig in a num-ber of the key scenes in which Peer debases his morality, although Ibsen himself does not include Solveig in these scenes. Her presence, of which only we as spectators are aware, illuminates Peer in a critical light, calling to our attention the immorality of his deeds. I will elaborate on this idea both in the analyses of the light-images and when discussing the dramaturgy of light of this performance.

Every scenographic set constitutes a different relationship with light. Veteran thea-tre designer Miriam Guretzki describes the scenography as a cycle metamorphosing in relation to the different phases of the dramatic action. On the most basic sense, the four stages appearing above can be seen to correspond to Peer's *childhood*, *adolescence*, *wealthy midlife* and *declining years*. The inspiring ideas for the first set, Guretzki notes, were "a playground, a childish forest, in a way – a lap, a womb or internal parts of the body, something feminine and soft, a big presence of the mother". In order to immerse the spectators in the world of the performance, everyone sits on the theatre stage in close proximity to the performers, almost under the huge ceiling of the scenography. This nearness creates a sense of excitement and intimacy and a strong feeling of immediacy.

Peer disengages or actually ruins this phase in his life. In the performance, his destruction of the space brings about the next stage. Peer abandons the child's world of all possibilities where mother protects, in favour of the world of imagination where he meets the Trolls. With the Trolls, he tears down the red amorphous shapes, thus caus-ing the contents of these objects to spill out, turning the stage green. The red colour on the ground disappears and the ceiling becomes dark. The stage is now green, and covered with pieces of cloth, materials, bits of accessories of all kinds, shoes, purses – to mention but few. Beyond associating these green accessories with stolen objects that the Trolls might have taken from people, Guretzki envisages the second set as an imaginary forest, addressing the iconography of the colour green in western culture. Moreover,

Figure 9.1 David Zinder, *Peer Gynt* by Henrik Ibsen. The development of the scenography as the four maquettes show: the opening scene (Act 1), the Troll scene (Act 1), North Africa (Act 4), in the sea and back in Norway (Act 5). Photos: Courtesy of Dina Konson

conducting the greatest possible change in terms of colour and contrast of complementary colours (from red to green) also distances the representation of Peer's village from
his world of imagination with the Trolls, or the civilized law against the laws of nature.

With the third set, the sense of immediacy between the audience, the stage and the
performers increases even more. Guretzki describes the different aesthetic features of
the set:

> Again, very near the audience there was a mirror floor and a mirror wall, very frontal,
> very geometrical, very specific, not so amorphous. The main images were, first of all,
> to evoke a very different sensation, the idea of a material, sharp, clear, it's glass, it's
> dangerous, it's breakable, frontal, no perspective at all, materialistic, looks like a big
> piece of gold . . . in a way, the gold colour also suggested, for me, the desert.

The spectators are present in the space, sitting on stage near the performers, so that they
could have an almost tactile experience with the set. As a spectator myself, I could even
see the backside of the performers and other members of the audience reflected in this
mirror wall. Lots of light reflected all over the stage, disclosing also the technical areas.

For the last set, however, a more mysterious space was required, as Guretzki
comments:

> The third act [namely, the black set – Y.A.] was really a space for light and the
> elements were like obstacles for light . . . the image was, of course, ashes and some-
> how a return to the first and the second spaces – these are the village and the forest
> somehow . . . but there is 'nothing' [human] but remains and somehow obstacles
> for the light to illuminate through because it's a very spiritual and philosophical act
> and it had to be created by light.

A black variation of the green accessories from the second set with the Trolls reappears
in the fourth set upon Peer's return to Norway. With respect to the last act, Zinder
commented: "The third act [with the black set – Y.A.] could not possibly work without
this complex lighting because just the idea of this 'junk-sculpture' was not enough. It
had to be picked out in a very specific way, to make it work". The black set was, therefore, highly dependent on the interplay of light and shadow. But let us then delve into
the first analysis of light-image from this production of *Peer Gynt*.

Young Solveig and Aase Seek Peer: first light-image

Aesthetic analysis of the light-image

The light-image that appears in Figure 9.2 consists of three lighting elements:

1   *Cold sidelight for the downstage plane* (circled in blue in Figure 9.3) – Two sidelights
    from stage-right[2] outline the two actresses with a wide contour of cold, pale-bluish
    light (colour: LEE 201# *CT Blue*). This lighting element gives the skin and the cos-
    tume a greyish pale blue tone, like cloudy daylight under which any coloured outfit
    loses its vividness. In terms of the optical quality, these PC lenses beam quite a soft
    light, yet it remains directional and not diffused. Some light brushes the red stage

Figure 9.2 David Zinder, *Peer Gynt* by Henrik Ibsen, Act I. Anikó Pethő (left) as young Solveig with Emőke Kató (right) as Aase. Photo: Courtesy of © István Biró/The Hungarian Theatre of Cluj

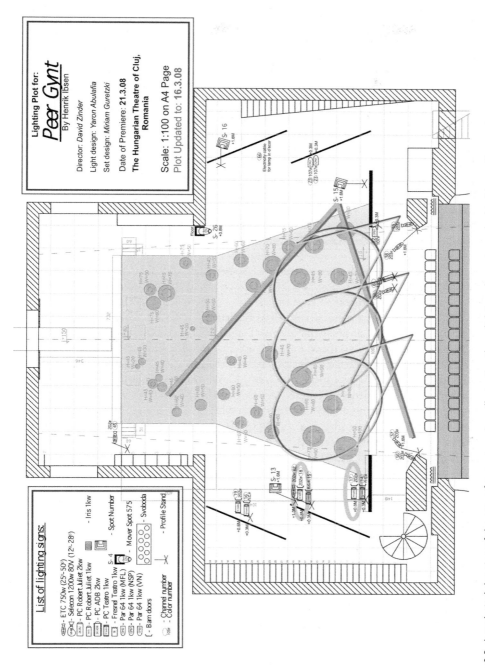

Figure 9.3 A technical drawing of the stage from a top view, illustrating three lighting elements marked in blue, yellow and orange

floor, cooling its original colour. The lamps are positioned on metal pipes visible to the spectators at approximately 80 cm above the ground and their 'hot spots' are above floor level.

2   A *diagonal front-of-house* (three yellow beams in Figure 9.3) – This lighting element consists of several PC lanterns hung above the right side of the audience area and next to the right portal. A relatively small area at centre downstage is illuminated by soft directional light in a very pale orange hue that modifies the default colour of the halogen bulb and makes it slightly warmer (colour: LEE 223# *Eighth CT Orange*). The lighting angle helps emphasize the plasticity of the body and create light and shade on it. It casts the shadows of the two actresses on the floor, and although the general light intensity is rather low, the shadows move clearly in cor-respondence with that lighting angle. The shadows are not completely black and sharp due to some ambient light produced by the sidelights, softening and lower-ing the contrast in relation to the surrounding. In terms of intensity, the front-of-house is secondary to the sidelights; the 'fronts' fill-in a bit of the shadows that the sidelights create.

3   *Orange-yellowish sidelight* (right side of Figure 9.3) – One source of discharge lamp with a colour mixing system illuminates the stage with saturated orange-yellowish light from stage left. Its wide lens creates a much softer and more diffused optical quality than the previous elements (PC's), softening the shadows on the stage floor. This lighting fixture is located in the open wings of the stage, visible to most of the spectators, with no attempt to hide it.

The proportions between the three lighting elements create intimate and soft light-space and emphasize the actresses against the background of their dimmed surrounding, helping to draw audience attention to the performers. The pale orange frontal light decreases the expressiveness and saturation of the orange light com-ing from the side. The contrast of colours gives rise to an expressive plasticity of both performers using cold, pale greyish-blue from one side and saturated yellow-orange light from the other. Occasionally, when the actresses move, coloured shad-ows appear on the costumes. Throughout almost the entire scene, Anikó Pethő who plays young Solveig, stands in the stage-right area and is mesmerized by Peer's mother, Aase played mainly downstage by Emőke Kató. Consequently, when the two ladies face each other in a dialogue, Solveig's appearance is warmly character-ized while Aase seems more pale blue.

Semiotic and poetic analysis of the light-image

Considering the lighting elements mentioned above, how are the aesthetic features of the light experienced or used as signs; what are the signs about; and how are they used poetically?

According to my conceptual framework, I will first examine whether, and how, the phenomenological experience and the semiotic function of light relate to the narra-tive, as ground of representation. The light clearly avoids being solely an illustrative approach to the text and ignores the details of fictive time and space, as given by the verbal text. As she chases Peer in the mountains, Aase states: "Everything spites me with a vengeance – Sky and water and these wicked mountains! Fog pouring out of the sky to confound him, the water luring him in to drown him" (Ibsen 1980, 43). The text here gives us an indication of what the fictive environment looks like: assuming that foggy weather diffuses the light and turns it grey, while it dims the vividness of any coloured object and blurs one's shadow. The light-image, however, in no way derives from or illustrates the light conditions of the fictive location as described in the text. It does not support the fiction by creating an illusion of specific time or space. Therefore, the representational function of the light-image does not lie in **the narrative**.

By means of colour contrast, I sought to differentiate between the two characters and reflect upon the mental state of each of them. Ashamed and agitated with Peer after Ingrid's kidnapping, Aase has her face illuminated in pale blue, as opposed to Solveig, whose face is lit in orange. The colour difference expresses their inner moods and draws a distinction between their states of mind regarding Peer's offence. Aase's brownish costume absorbs most of the orange light that hits her, but Solveig's white dress strongly reflects it (Figure 9.2). The lively orange light – having such an unnatural and saturated hue – signifies Solveig's high qualities and virtues. Solveig's light caresses both the figures in the scene and could be taken as a sign to Solveig's gaiety and encouragement for Aase or of her love and tolerance for Peer. In contrast to Aase, Solveig unhesitatingly accepts Peer's sin of betrayal with compassion, love and forgiveness. The opposing colours in this light-image thus represent the *dichotomy of the two women in Peer's life* and their different perspectives on the situation.

Representing this dichotomy between Aase and Solveig using light and colour is *interpretive and complementary to the verbal text*. The configuration of the light-signs (colours, small light-space, and a dark environment for the performers – among other things) adds unique expressive qualities that go beyond a mere supporting of the spoken text. The artificial aesthetics of the image (in terms of its non-verisimilitude) and, in particular, the orange light adds the scene a reflective dimension. For the reasons mentioned above, the phenomenological experience and the semiotic function of this light-image are definitely grounded in **character**.

The relationship between Peer and Solveig embodies a fundamentally religious theme in the play that has relevance for this light-image. The idea that even after living so long in betrayal one may be given the opportunity to get back to the right path is represented through Peer's revealing his 'true self' in the winter of his life. Solveig's role is that of an allegorical character and her almost-saintly purity complements Peer's impulsive behaviour, in a sort of Yin and Yang interplay. In his book *Peer Gynt and Ghosts, Text and Performance*, the Norwegian author Asbjørn Aarseth notes:

> Thus Solveig should not be interpreted as the portrait of an uncommonly patient Norwegian girl, but rather in terms of a religious and moral allegory, as a personification of divine grace, or, to be more specific in relation to the concept of the two parts of the self, as Peer's higher self, the centre of his spiritual identity.
>
> (Aarseth 1989, 46)

Consequently, the well-known Byzantine visual semiotic conventions, representing the Christian saints with a warm golden light, in absence of any shadow, were for me an important source of inspiration for the light-images featuring Solveig. The aesthetic features – constantly using yellow-orange light in this and other light-images – create a poetic dimension that is connected to her role as *a personification of a religious thought*. She becomes a brilliant source of illumination and is the highlight point in the space.

By conjoining these light-signs to the play, the medium of light mediates dramaturgical aspects of the verbal text and portrays these, or 'translates' them into new forms, suggesting a visual experience through light. The semiotic function of this light-image is, thus, grounded in *a theme* embodying its qualities.

I turn now to the question of whether the light-image refers to a dramatic action in the scene, and, if so, how. Both Aase and Solveig are secondary characters that illuminate aspects in Peer's personality, since neither are elaborated in great detail. As an allegorical character with neither motivation to act, nor dramatic conflict in the play, Solveig lacks full dramatic status. Her dramatic function in the play can be interpreted in terms of various staging possibilities. As this interpretation has important consequences for the understanding of Peer, Solveig is central in the shaping of the dramaturgy and visual dimension of any *Peer Gynt* production. Some interpretations have referred to Peer and Solveig as two allegorical characters that together constitute one self: Peer – the 'lower' animalistic or materialistic self, and Solveig – the higher spiritual or intellectual existence. Solveig's reaction in the encounter with Peer during the last scene of the play is unbelievable, when Peer returns and old Solveig does not confront him with questions about his life-long disappearance. Instead of accusing him, without hesitation and full of unconditional compassion, she says: *"You've made my whole life a beautiful song. Bless you now that you've come at last!"* (Ibsen 1980, 207–8). Her endless patience does not really make any sense, and a fictional character choosing passivity instead of conflict excludes a dramatic action; nor does it create dramatic tension. Consequently, as there is none, the representation in the light-image cannot be grounded in the ***dramatic action***.

The light-image, however, supports the atmosphere and the mood of the written scene by creating an intimate space with soft light on a rather small part of the stage floor. It regulates the proportions between the space perceived and the two performers, offering the possibility for dense mise-en-scène in which the performers remain visible. Likewise, the light strengthens the dramatic elements in the scene by means of a significant colour contrast. Nevertheless, employing all the features mentioned above, the atmosphere created by light in this scene, and the emotional effect it suggests, are still deeply influenced by the interpretation of the text.

While designing this light-image, I intended to affect the spectators' emotions by creating an atmospheric image. I realized that the effectiveness of the light-image depended upon the audience's projecting its own interpretation of the text on the light. Much of the experience of this light-image is gained through the spectators' empathy with respect to the characters' emotions. I suspect that our visual experience becomes more conceptually oriented when it is related to a spoken text; thus, the capacity of our imagination to experience and interpret the image according to its aesthetics in its own right is narrowed down because of the text. The experience of light on a more primal level is suppressed by conceptual thinking – visual information and language seem to compete, to a certain extent, for the imagination of the addressees. For example, experiencing a sequence of body movements and imagining their meaning while watching contemporary dance, will be surely influenced by a simultaneous delivery of text – in the absence of text, one will give even more attention to the visual qualities in the performance of the movement. Without any verbal text, we can check the relevance of our interpretation, when exploring the aesthetics of the movements even more thoroughly. In search of causal relation between events, it is very probable that (what we consider as) the signs of light will be identified with the emotions and the thoughts that we imagine the fictive characters to have. Because the text is so central in this scene, and because the light-signs are experienced with respect to the spoken text, from my perspective the representation through this light-image was not grounded in *atmosphere* or *emotion*. The image is not complex enough to directly affect the spectators' emotions, or to bypass, let alone to suppress the meaning that the addressees generate by listening to the text.

Thematically, this *Peer Gynt* production sought to expose its theatrical pretence, attending to the artificiality that inevitably plays a role in any representation process. This theme is of course connected to Peer's exploration of his true self. And so, all the lamps, metal stands, cables, ropes, flying bars and stage-tower remain visible to the spectators as a part of the space. The architecture of the stage encompasses the island-set and serves as a contrasting counterpart to the theatricality of the scenery – simultaneously presenting reality and fiction on the stage. In an interview with Zinder, he notes:

> You can see the machinery of theatre, just beyond, you can see the lighting, you can see the bars, we can see the ladders we can see the black walls . . . It was an island set in a sense that if you are looking only at what's happening, what's the action of the play, then you are in this kind of a fantasy world; but if you open up just a little bit – you are in a theatre. So that reflects, back and forth.

However, the distribution of visible light sources from both sides of the stage did not attract special attention regarding the technical processes involved in the creation of the visual experience or the signs of light. The lighting system did not engender a high degree of awareness in the spectators of the technical aspects involved in the construction of this light-image. The involvement of lighting technology in the visual experience was not emphasized; nor did light as a medium did create a poetic dimension that is based on an aesthetic pleasure. The semiotic function of this light-image was therefore not grounded in the *sensation of light itself*, neither *hypermediacy* (a deep impression derived from the presence of the medium) nor in *spectacularity* (derived from a strong direct aesthetic pleasure).

The final ground of representation against which I will examine this light-image is that of *open meaning*. In the chapter on the conceptual framework for light analysis, I explained that open meaning constitutes a complex situation, caused by insufficient information, or guidance, provided by other media, on how to experience and interpret what the light is doing to us. Consequently, in such a case, the addressees increasingly relate to their own personal memories and knowledge, drawing analogies, drifting among associations, and constructing imaginative representations. In fact, they contemplate and validate information regarding the light – information that the light artist intentionally did not include in the image. The 'openness of meaning' I refer to is different from the general characteristics of any artwork; it is *a constructed openness that the artist incorporates into the piece intentionally*. It is part of the poetics of the piece, originating in the piece's syntactic and pragmatic dimensions, and only later influences its semantics – in other words, the 'openness' in the meaning of light derives from the ways in which signs of light and other media are organized together and relate each other, and the changing relation between the signs and their user, namely, the addressee. This openness leads to a plurality of 'keys' for interpretation, since it liberates different individuals to act on and participate in the creative/constructive process that the piece initiates by remaining somehow 'incomplete' itself . . .

Open meaning also recalls Roland Barthes's notion of 'obtuse' or 'third meaning', pointing to a connotation of the image that is fleeting, and infinite in its possibilities for interpretation, residing in the imagination of the interpreter. It is a very poetic understanding, as "the obtuse meaning appears to extend outside culture, knowledge, information; analytically, there is something derisory about it" (Barthes 1977, 55). Perhaps the only way for a spectator to determine, in this case, whether a certain interpretation is relevant, acceptable and satisfactory lies in the degree of coherence that is found between the ensuing ideas that emerge in the interpretation process. The prospect of successfully constructing a settling and logical meaning with light-images that call for open meaning relies on the individuality of the addressees and their individual experiences; however, the challenge may encourage an exchange of opinions among the audience around the shared, unique and personal artistic experiences.

As I stressed earlier, the vague experience an audience has of the light-image and its signification under consideration here, even when considering the light in relation to the other media, creates a void of meaning as an aspect of the poetics of light. Yet the light and its relations with the other media appear to be carefully constructed, to initiate and constitute a subliminal creative presence of light in the piece, acting like a phantom.

A light-image the semiotic function of which is grounded in *open meaning* is, in a sense, an open work the spectator has to negotiate its significance with. In the case of the current light-image, and perhaps because of the dominant position of the spoken text in the scene, the light-signs do not evolve into an autonomous visual stimulus (of light) that launches a semiotic drift. Therefore, the light-image does not constitute a representation grounded in *open meaning*.

Peer Nurses Aase on her Deathbed: second light-image

We find the second light-image that I analyse from this production of *Peer Gynt* throughout the entire scene of Aase's death, just after Peer and Solveig have laid the foundations for their new home. Each of the photos above shows the stage, in the same scene, but from a different point of view, whereas the drawing features an overview of the performers' positions.

Aesthetic analysis of the light-image

Five lighting elements composed this light-image:

1   *Cold sidelight for the downstage plane* – Already introduced in great detail in the analysis of the previous light-image, the same cold pale blue light (created by PC fixtures with LEE 201# *CT Blue* filter) illuminates the downstage area where Aase is seen lying and Peer Gynt nursing her. The high-intensity distribution of the sidelight in this image produces a look and plasticity differing from those in the previously analysed image. Here, a shaft of pale bluish-grey light outlines the performers' silhouettes in a gloomily dimmed space. With reference to the scenography at this point in the performance, the green colour already swamps the red one; the space that was once red, soft and round is now a mass of green objects (it has been transformed by the Trolls). The sidelight almost decolourizes the green objects on the floor and the costumes of the performers, making the vividness of their colours fade. This lighting element serves as the key light for Aase and young Peer, charging

the performers' bodies with expressiveness and enhancing their plasticity. These sidelights partly illuminate Solveig as she stands downstage left, behind the two-way golden mirror board. One can see Solveig (Figures 9.4 and 9.5) lit more softly than Aase and young Peer (in Figure 9.6), as if Solveig fades away, because of her distance from the light sources and because the two-way mirror subtracts from the light reflected back from her into our eyes.

2   A *diagonal front-of-house* – Also featured in the previous analysed light-image, the diagonal front-of-house forms a rather small, lit area of about 3m diameter on the floor, where young Peer nurses Aase before she takes her last breath. The light-space has soft and diffused edges on the cluttered floor, and it is just sufficient to allow the supine performer to occupy most of the lit space. As opposed to the sidelights, this light is slightly warmer, having a pale tone of straw colour (LEE 223# *Eighth CT Orange*). This is a complementary lighting element in the visibility of young Peer and Aase, secondary to the dominant sidelights – Figure 9.6 demonstrates the difference of intensities between the (colder) sidelight and the (warmer) frontal light that comes from the upper right side of the photo.

3   *Flattening steel-blue front-of-house* – This lighting element consists of two Par 64 cans with CP 60 bulb ('very narrow'), directed downstage, in an almost flattening angle in relation to Aase's position. In the current light-image, this element is used with very subtle intensity to increase colour contrast between the warm and cold in Aase and young Peer. One can see the steel-blue hue on the blanket covering Aase in Figure 9.6. The sidelight, however, remains the most dominant lighting source on the two performers.

4   *Low and flat orange backlight* – This lighting element is used only within this light-image and constitutes, for me, its pivotal part and most significant poetic expression. A highly saturated orange backlight emanates from behind the golden mirror board, about one meter above the floor (Figure 9.7). To create this element, I used a moving light spot to project an orange light beam and illuminate Solveig from behind while casting her shadow, surrounded by a golden aura, onto the mirror. The light beam casts a shadow in the form of the performer's head and torso in the mirror, within a circular shape of saturated orange light. From the back of the mirror some light is reflected onto the performer's face, giving her skin a golden tint. Some light is also reflected from the back of the mirror to the dark backdrop, also 'conveying' Solveig's shadow onto the backdrop, thereby duplicating the shadow and magnifying it (see Figures 9.4, 9.5 and 9.7). Light and shadow instantly echo on the backdrop any movement of the actress behind the mirror. The two-way mirror reduces to a certain degree Solveig's visibility, giving the actress a more distant and somehow flattened look reminiscent of an old photograph, lacking colour contrast. Near the backdrop, caressed by Solveig's circular reflection of orange light, old Peer stands silently, gazing at Aase and young Peer (Figure 9.5). Both Peers wear the same brown woollen coat, dark trousers and shirt. The light and shade of young Solveig caresses old Peer up-stage.

5   *Shinbuster (low sidelight) for old Peer* – A touch of light from the upstage right floor illuminates old Peer's silhouette near the backdrop. He is half-illuminated, half in shadow. The colour of this lighting element is LEE 202# *Half CT Blue*, a little warmer than the sidelights on Aase and young Peer. The level of light intensity on old Peer is very low, enhancing a sense of depth and making him appear distant from the downstage plane.

Figure 9.4 David Zinder, *Peer Gynt* by Henrik Ibsen. Anikó Pethő as young Solveig during Aase's death scene. Photo: Courtesy of © István Biró/The Hungarian Theatre of Cluj

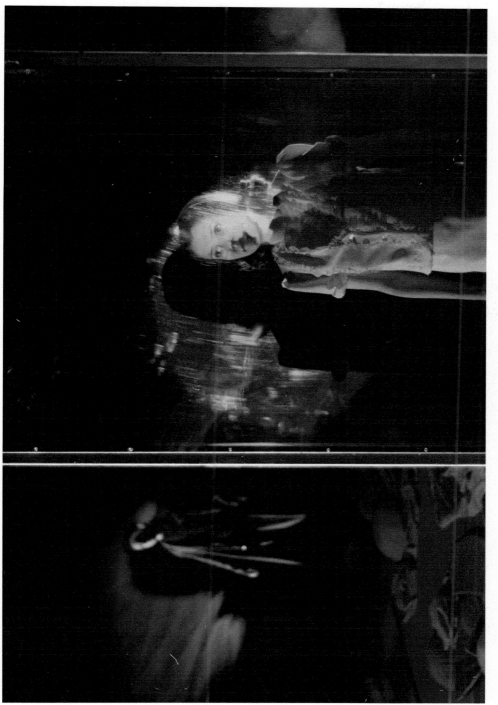

Figure 9.5 David Zinder, *Peer Gynt* by Henrik Ibsen. Zsolt Bogdán as Old Peer and Anikó Pethő as young Solveig during Aase'st death scene. Photo: Courtesy of © István Biró/The Hungarian Theatre of Cluj

Figure 9.6 David Zinder, *Peer Gynt* by Henrik Ibsen. Emőke Kató as Aase and Ferenc Sinko as Young Peer during Aase's death scene. Photo: Courtesy of © István Biró/The Hungarian Theatre of Cluj

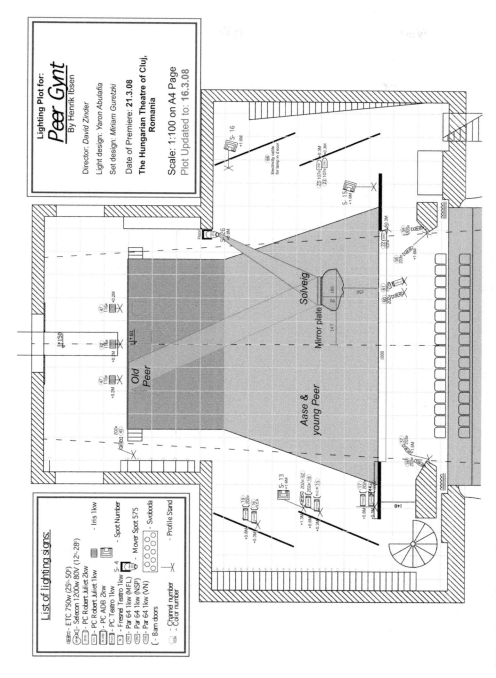

Figure 9.7 A technical drawing, illustrating the reflection from the mirror to the backdrop at the end of Act I

Semiotic and poetic analysis

Considering the lighting elements mentioned above, how are the aesthetic features of the light experienced or used as signs; what are the signs about; and how are the signs used in a poetic way?

The light-image does not support the fiction (fictive light conditions), but rather suggests new possible interrelations between light, space, human body, and word in ways that expand and elaborate upon our watching experience. As mentioned above, the light composes three separate light-spaces with various visual qualities for characters that represent different spiritual levels (dying Aase with young Peer, 'iconic' Solveig, and old Peer gazing). Although in the text the scene occurs in Aase's home with only Peer being present, here on stage the different characters are simultaneously present but within different subjective time frames. The light does not illustrate the space of the event as described in the play. Instead, the aesthetic features of light go beyond reinforcing a verisimilar representation of time and space. This light-image consists of visual stimuli, or signs, external to the written play, creating an image that stretches our imagination far beyond the original textual description of the situation. The ground of the meaning of this light-image must therefore be found in other grounds of representation than that of *narrative*.

The conglomerate of three separate, yet intimately tied spaces of light constitutes a composition in which the relationships between Aase and young Peer, Solveig, and old Peer become most suggestive and significant. By adding Solveig and old Peer to the scene, functioning as on-stage spectators, Zinder deviates from the realistic paradigm of the play and elaborates it by giving a form to the subconsciousness of the characters. The various signs of light – the cold greyish light with a tint of steel blue on dying Aase, the fragmented illumination of Solveig in orange light, with her shadow reflected onto old Peer and the backdrop – altogether disclose something of the emotions, memories and confusion that Peer might be painfully experiencing during his mother's demise and the parting of his beloved.

The characterization in light enriches the poetic dimension of this intimate scene with reference to both young and old Peer's states of mind. The reflective role of light is amplified by the distinction between various degrees of presence (presence in fictive reality or as a memory), and of time and space, giving each character a different visual quality. It is uncertain whether Solveig gazes inward to herself or forward through the golden mirror toward the audience. Is she actually present in this scene, or is she just there as a memory of one of the two Peers? Does Solveig's stasis behind the golden frame, recalling a sacred medieval icon, relate to Aase's death? It is up to the audience to decide whether or not she is aware of what is happening on the other side of the space.

As for old Peer, should we see the scene through him looking back on his own life? Or are we witnesses of the experience of young Peer? Perhaps old Peer and Solveig are reliving the situation in a moment of self-reflection, as two parts of one single identity? Therefore, I would suggest that the representation via this light-image is grounded in the second category offered by the conceptual framework, namely: *character*.

In the analysis of the previous light-image, I elaborated on the theme of Peer's search for identity and the higher part of his 'self', and noted Solveig is an allegorical and complementing character that represents transcendent virtues and values. The current light-image again reinforces this theme by creating two, or even three, visual qualities and kinds of looks for the performers. The first is the most straightforward and 'neutral'

formal characteristics, features Peer nursing the dying Aase (Figure 9.6). The second look (of Solveig) is more enigmatic and sensuous, created by a soft grey silhouette and a crisp saturated orange backlight that casts her shadow on the mirrored plate and partly illuminating her front by reflection (Figure 9.4). The third, caused by the reflection of the same orange light from the mirror onto the backdrop, features a little more than a contour of old Peer, standing in the midst of a dying out 'sun' marked by the shadow of Solveig's head (Figure 9.5). The last two appearances that are foreign to the original written scene, relate to one another in terms of colour and shadows and are more ambiguous and suggestive than the first one.

The dichotomy in this light-image between the different aesthetic features and two degrees of 'presence' in the scene *mediates aspects of the dramaturgy of the play through the medium of light*. The aura of light and the radiating golden image through a brilliant mirror, lend Solveig an appearance that could be referring either to Byzantine iconicity or to an eternal celestial element. Contrary to Solveig, young Peer faces the temporality of life, first – through Aase's death, and later – when encountering the Button-moulder who demands Peer's life. In addition, light is also used to reflect upon Solveig's unconditional love and compassion for Peer. While the light metamorphoses Solveig into an iconic statue with an increased vibrancy of light, old Peer declines in a fading sunset as he gazes, perhaps retrospectively, at his mother's death, and at himself as a young man bereft of direction. The religious symbolism of this light-image originates in the 'dramatic' psychological dimension of the characters, and then evolves into a subjective visual interpretation on the subtextual level. Therefore, the representation through the light-image is also grounded in *theme* and *dramatic action*.

The eye of the spectator can leap and flow among three highlighted locations in the gloomy space. The irregular and distinctive ways in which Solveig and old Peer are illuminated give both performers unique looks that relate to a mystical quality of the dim surrounding. The light and the moving shadows made me feel as if the space were haunted and full of tension. Taking the role of a key light, the orange backlight sparks into a rich and ambiguous composition consisting of the reflection of irregularly patterned light and shadows from the mirror, and two silhouettes of Solveig appearing simultaneously in the space.

Inevitably, the light-image and the verbal text in the scene are interconnected; however, the strength and efficacy of the image achieve more than merely providing a visual support for the text. Instead, and more importantly, the light here constitutes an extended *autonomous sensorial and emotional experience* that goes *beyond* the text. The simultaneous use of signs: the *chiaroscuro* effect of light and shade, the golden 'sun' reflection, the mysterious shadows, and Aase lying on her deathbed to the sound of quite dissonant music, all this gave the light an emotional, poetic expression grounded in *emotion* and *atmosphere*.

The aesthetic features of this light-image do not emphasize the presence of the medium of light itself, but rather conceal its 'finger-prints'. When the ground of meaning (or the representational function) of a light-image is in *light sensation*, 'the medium is the message'. The medium then becomes the primary driving force in the creation of a poetic experience. Either through *spectacularity* that relates to the aesthetic pleasure one can gain from light, or through *hypermediacy* that relates to a dominant presence of the medium, *light sensation* appears; either because the technology is interpreted as an imaginative representation of the human condition, or because the 'working machine' evolves to acquire a degree of a living poetry. This light-image dealt with here has none of these qualities; therefore, its semiotic function is not grounded in the *sensation of light itself*.

In spite of the suggestive character of the image and its appealing aesthetic features – in particular, the illumination of old Peer through Solveig – the dominance of the spoken text in the scene narrows down the chances of drifting away in an open process of interpretation, based upon the visual experience as such. The power of speech in a work like *Peer Gynt*, where the text is so central, determines for a great deal the experience and meaning addressees find, or imagine to find, in visual signs. It is so since the presence of text helps us to constantly validate the relevance of our interpretation for the visual stimuli.

A light-image of which the semiotic function is grounded in ***open meaning*** invites the spectator to investigate for him- or herself what the signs of light are about and how they are used to create a poetic expression. It is up to the spectators to complement the (missing) information, and construct an informed subjective, yet settling and logical, interpretation for the 'holes' in the piece, based on their experience of the given complex of signs. In such a case, as with most contemporary artworks, a greater involvement from the addressee is required in engaging with the 'incomplete' artefact that awaits its completion by the addressee, generating meaning subjectively and autonomously. When considering the relation between a light-image and other media, the light keeps a degree of ambiguity and openness that remain unsolved. Nevertheless, it has a sort of allure that invites the addressee not to give up pondering its poetic function. So, this vagueness is not for its own sake but is instead a carefully constructed enigma, generating a feeling that the meaning is subliminally present and not yet known. It is up to the spectators to decide what to do; if, and how, to relate to the sensorial stimuli and work towards an interpretation. The experience and the semiotic function of the current light-image are not grounded in ***open meaning*** – the sixth and last of the grounds of representation presented by the new conceptual framework.

The dramaturgy of light in *Peer Gynt*

The dramaturgy of light refers to the aesthetics and poetics reflecting our ideas concerning the artistic function of light in the piece and its 'behaviour' throughout the performance, its structure, its tempo, and its relations with the other media, in short. Four fundamental principles can be distinguished within the dramaturgy of light in this production of *Peer Gynt*:

1   *The position of light and its relation to the verbal text* – Most of the light-images, and the 'light-motifs' in particular, remain remote from an illustrative approach to the spoken text; while striving for a certain degree of autonomy from the verbal text, the relation of the light to the narrative is complementary and enriching. The aesthetic features of light were to create and emphasize an atmospheric experience or sensory effect for the addressees throughout the performance, calling attention to the characteristics of light itself. Although our point of departure was the written play itself, I considered the narrative as an open domain, from which to spread out into my own subjective interpretation of the situations in which the characters of the play function. From the start of the artistic process of this production, the light was designed to develop a strong visual expression, and this was taken into consideration when certain artistic choices for other media had to be made. For example, the designer Guretzki states the following regarding her use of materials in relation to the light:

I always think in a very different way, or the ideas come from the nature of the team, from the collaborators, the other artists. It's a very different process and a very different vocabulary each time. I think that, for us, this work was based on working with light – it was made for light. The spaces were designed for light and took into consideration that there is the potential of light to create those changes, both technically even and also the iconography, the ideas. The light had its very detailed and particular 'text' that was written on those 'back-grounds', in a way, of those sets.

To give one final critical perspective on the aesthetics and poetics of light that we created in this *Peer Gynt* production, I quote a fragment from an article that was published in the Romanian journal *Ziarul de duminică* entitled *Painting with light*, by the author Luminita Batali:

A presentation where the light, which embraces the characters and the scene, while it visually emphasizes the moments of the action, unifies the creation of Ibsen dramatically but also with deep lyricism.

It is a first class visual binder, which sustains the aesthetic identity of the performance throughout all the scenes.

The light-design . . . is very technical and of a high professionalism, and it also has poetical vibrations. Beside the actors, the light comments in a unique way on the complex states of mind of the characters. It is thus fantastic how the light follows Solveig's (Anikó Pethő) face until they form a unity – an aureole that is external, but reflects mainly internal light. In its chromatic avatars (red, an ethereal and mysterious blue, golden yellow, flashes and rays piercing the darkness) light seems to be caressing the characters, recreating dynamically the visual context of the drama. The lighting obtains, thanks to Yaron Abulafia's vision, a unique musicality, by expressing emotions in a flexible and lyrical way, but also in a transfiguration related to the cathartic essence of authentic theatre.

(Batali 2008)

2   *Light and the sense of materiality and spatiality* – An integral aspect in the dramaturgy of light is to affect our visual perception and change our sensing of materiality in space and the transformation of spatial dimensions in the perception of the spectators. The light for each act is designed with a different set of aesthetic features, largely using lighting elements prepared exclusively for the relevant act. The light-images in the first act mostly display soft optic qualities with warm pastel colours in scales of straw and pink ranging to red-magenta, apart from the orange light that 'brushes' the space upon Solveig's emergence. The light manipulates our vision and makes the space look higher and deeper than it actually is, scaling the human figures down in perception to match Peer's childish perspective. The palette then changes into green, turquoise and blue with a glimpse of flesh colour, since Peer encounters the Trolls and start questioning the destiny of his life. The darker scale of saturated blue-green stretches the character of the space in mysterious and eerie directions, as the chaotic floor seems like an endless deserted field of human remains, again, due to the light.

In contrast to the first two sets where softness prevails, the third set manifests stringency and utilizes extreme brightness that reveals the performers from all sides – the golden mirror discloses even their side turned away from the audience.

The light-images leave almost no mystery in the space; using rigid shafts of warm halogen lights (Svoboda lamps), the space achieves a sense of openness but also emptiness and lack of depth. The second act is the warmest, not only in terms of light tones, but also in the actual heat that the lighting setup generates (according to the play this act takes place in North Africa). The light-images in the second act create a strong sense of direct contact with the stage and the performers, almost an immersive experience, as a result of the image of spectators and performers merging in the mirror and the strong reflections of light onto the technical working areas on stage that often remain invisible to the audience.

In the fourth set, the light-images are almost completely monochromatic, with some slight pale-bluish tones. In the first scenes of this act, one cannot perceive the entire stage since the light picks out of the darkness merely certain performers or certain attributes of the scenography, so the space is imagined to be rather endless. Later on, upon the return to Norway, the monochromatic cold pale light unveils an environment full of black accessories (like the green objects of the Trolls). Coloured light restores vividness to the space only in the final scene of the performance, when Peer meets Solveig, now old, and her 'characterizing' orange light blooms back into the space – now a little paler than before.

3   *Solveig's 'light-motifs'* – This has been elaborated upon already in the earlier analysis of the two light-images. I developed the idea from a short line at the end of the play, describing old Solveig awaiting Peer in their now completed home, seated next to the window with a candle.[3] Calling to mind her allegorical character and Christian references, Solveig proves again her noble virtues of unconditional love and compassion by forgiving Peer his lifelong treachery. In this production, I use the candlelight as a motif to metamorphose the space into a warm scale of flame-like colours with the emergence of Solveig as if she herself radiates the light. This quality relates to Solveig when she is actually present in the scene, as written by Ibsen. Alternatively, pale blue light illuminates Solveig when her appearances deviate from the original play, *reflecting a memory, or the subconscious*, of Peer, of the audience, or both. In those additional appearances, when Solveig is a memory or a critical counterpoint to Peer, Peer's integrity and moral values are at stake. The contrast between the pale blue and the warm light helps to enhance the effect of Solveig's physical presence and moral nobility, and to call to mind, by means of coloured light, Solveig's almost sacred devotion.

4   *Active light and the mysterious passenger* – The beginning of the last act features an introduction by dynamic narrow 'pillars' of white light moving in a hazy environment, entering one by one, at intervals, into the dark space and occasionally striking elements of the set. This one-minute-long choreography of light-beams, moving slowly along sinuous paths and drifting between the sculptured black roots of the scenography, becomes the locus of attention and central object of observation at that time. It is only the fourth (sequent) beam that reveals young Solveig standing at the dark horizon, and, later, the fifth and final beam finds old Peer standing downstage; and so the scene starts. Peer is pinned down to a small and very specific light emanating from the floor while the rest of the space remains absolutely dark. Light in motion evolves here into a phantom vision and, after vanishing from the space, its effect remains subliminal. As theatre director Zinder notes with regard to this sequence:

Figure 9.8 David Zinder, *Peer Gynt* by Henrik Ibsen, Act V. Áron Dimény (left) as the Mysterious Passenger and Zsolt Bogdán (right) as Old Peer. Photo: Courtesy of © István Biró/the Hungarian Theatre of Cluj

This was like a prelude – the moving lights. Very thin beams of light moving. And then this became a prelude to the use of the same effect, particularly on the boat with the strange passenger. Because of the nature of the light, and the fact that it's so highly focused, and because it moved silently as if it had a life of its own, it's eerie, it's very strange and it created the right kind of atmosphere for this very powerful last act.

In a later scene when the mysterious passenger arrives and stops near Peer, the previous five light-beams move across the black roots in the space and flow towards Peer (Figure 9.8). When the mysterious passenger is about to leave, the narrow white light-beams flow away in various directions and he simply disappears behind the scenery of black roots. These light-beams, which create the overture of the fifth act, manifest the living and active, almost behavioural qualities of light. They establish a vague, magical atmosphere with a hint of menace. Light constitutes an aspect of the characteristics of the mysterious passenger in all his encounters with Peer, as a light-motif or as personification of light.

Notes

1 Unless mentioned otherwise, all quotations in this chapter are of personal communication with the artists.
2 I use UK and US stage terminology regarding position on stage and orientation of right and left (taken from the performer's perspective).
3 Aarseth writes in *Peer Gynt and Ghosts, Text and Performance* that the name Solveig means in Norwegian 'the way toward the sun' or 'the woman of the sun'; where Aarseth considers Solveig to be a saintly character.

References

Aarseth, A., *Peer Gynt and Ghosts, Text and Performance*, London: Macmillan Education, 1989.
Barthes, R., *Image, Music, Text*, Essays selected and translated by Stephen Heath, London: Fontana Press, 1977.
Batali, L., "Painting with Light", *Ziarul de duminică*, Romania, 9 May 2008.
Ibsen, H., *Peer Gynt*, translated and introduced by Rolf Fjelde, 2nd edition, Minneapolis, MN: University of Minnesota Press, 1980.

Epilogue

Figure 10.1 Yaron Abulafia, *Letter off*. Directed and designed by Yaron Abulafia, Grand Theatre Groningen, the Netherlands, 2007. Photo: Courtesy of Karel Zwaneveld

The emergence of Light Art as a visual art-form is no less than a revolutionary landmark in the development of the medium of light. Light has now arrived at its *artistic maturity*.

We, as theatre artists, cannot turn a blind eye to the myriad opportunities with which Light Art has provided the contemporary theatre. Ever since the 1960s, artists in light have been pondering phenomenological and conceptual issues, reflecting on state-of-the-art creative views, some of which I introduced in Chapter 2. The most respected museums, as well as alternative avant-garde exhibition-spaces, have gradually acknowledged the importance of light as an artistic medium, and nowadays exhibit works of light just as concert halls accommodate works of music. In the theatre, light clearly plays an equal role within a well-balanced collective performance of media. The post-dramatic turn has encouraged an *experience of multipolarity*, in which each medium maintains its *artistic integrity*, while constituting a part in a whole that is greater than the 'sum of its parts'.

The growing autonomy of light in contemporary theatre is a characteristic of *creative collaboration* in the deepest possible sense. It stems from a collective effort in exploiting the diversity and maximizing the expressive potential of each medium, and 'orchestrating' all the media simultaneously, in a non-hierarchical order. In this spirit, scenographer and director Pamela Howard, OBE, introduced the term 'artist in light' at the *World Stage Design* in 2013, for those visual artists whose medium in the theatre is light. To distinguish art from craft, artists in light are dedicated to participating as full partners in the extensive research and in the creative process of the artistic team, while concurrently exploring how *to embody their ideas in the form of design*. As creative artists, they offer 'bridges' to ideas concerning the human condition, and strive to awaken the emotions, memories and thoughts of the audience for whom the work is targeted. Artists in light will initiate and propose an *interpretive visual dramaturgy* that will greatly enrich the production, in imaginative ways that are unique to light.

The route of theatre lighting towards autonomy proceeds through two sectors: the *educational* and the *professional*. If we aim to extend the boundaries of the medium and to challenge the art of light to evolve, light design students in leading education institutes should be encouraged to practice their artistic research skills and learn how to communicate their ideas to the creative team. These students need to be mentored as individual artists-in-the-making, able to generate superb complex visual experiences that coexist with the narrative (if there is any). In theatre studies today the different disciplines, such as light design, scenography and directing often remain separate. Students, respectively, do not interact or learn about each other's discipline sufficiently, so that the focus remains solely on the text without examining how the disciplines might work together and explore how the story might be visually broadened and heightened. How inspired future theatre would be if student-directors were to acquire a *visual education* along with their experience with actors/performers and texts. And how much richer and innovative could the work of upcoming directors, scenographers and artists in light become, if universities and drama schools would integrate *collective courses in visual dramaturgy* and *the corporeal influence of images*, for these students altogether! Let us give the theatre-makers of the future a broader, up-to-date, palette of theatrical means with which *to cognitively affect the addressees*.

In the professional theatre, the main constraint for designing light, in particular, is time. The financial restraints become increasingly problematic. Most productions are unable to book a theatre house, a large technical crew, and a large lighting setup for

Figure 10.2 Anton Chekhov, *The Seagull.* Adapted and directed by Ira Avneri, light and projections by Yaron Abulafia, stage and costumes design by Dina Konson, Tmuna Theatre, Tel Aviv, Israel, 2013. Photo: Courtesy of Yaron Abulafia

Figure 10.3 Itzik Galili, *Romance Inverse*. Light by Yaron Abulafia, costumes by Natasja Lansen, National Dance Company Wales, the UK, 2010. Photo: Courtesy of Roy Campbell-Moore

Figure 10.4 Yaron Abulafia, *Letter off-*. Directed and designed by Yaron Abulafia, Grand Theatre Groningen, the Netherlands, 2007. Photo: Courtesy of Karel Zwaneveld

more than just a few days in order to practically realize and rehearse with the design. While working in one of the world's most distinguished ballet companies, the technical director told me that light designers would normally get only five hours on set to design a full-length story ballet. And this case was with a *national* company with significant financial resources. On the other hand, Robert Wilson often dedicates a number of weeks exclusively to the light design on stage. These extremes actually reflect different *artistic priorities* and an uncompromising eagerness to work with light creatively. Since light is so fundamental for a theatre-maker, ways to devote more time and money to the light design should be examined thoroughly. And if it is impossible to prolong lighting time, the creative process with respect to light must nonetheless start long in advance — even though, of course, one can really see the light at work only in the theatre itself, in the presence of the scenography, performers, and possibly also video, musicians and other production elements. In detailed preparatory table work, artists in light, directors and choreographers can elucidate the intended functions for each light-image, explore the aesthetics and the transition moments, and even simulate lighting, to a certain extent, by means of sketching and computer rendering. A dedicated creative collaboration between artists who engage deeply in a long research process could lead to unexpected routes to explore, and more original, inspiring views that could enrich the production dramaturgically. *The autonomous expression of light* could give rise to surprisingly powerful and captivating experiences, both emotionally and conceptually, if carefully constructed and integrated in detail with all the other media.

Light should radiate its illuminating qualities — corporeally, emotionally, conceptually and spiritually.

The multifaceted nature of the contemporary performance clearly fosters the poetic elevation of light, whether in opera, theatre or dance — it doesn't matter where you create, but with whom.

Glossary

Down and upstage   Downstage is at, or toward, the front part of a stage, near the auditorium. Upstage is toward, or at, the part of a stage furthest from the audience. The use of the names upstage and downstage for different stage areas originated from the raked stage, where stages were built with an angle to improve the sightlines of the spectators, and the visibility of the performers and the stage floor from the first rows of the auditorium.

Follow spot   This powerful lighting source, also known as a spotlight, projects a bright and narrow beam of light onto the performance space. A follow spot operator directs the beam and highlights the performer on stage. This lighting element is found occasionally in Classical ballets, musicals, and presentations and at times in operas.

Front of house   As opposed to the stage and backstage, front of house (FOH) is the auditorium and foyer. With regard to lighting, FOH stands for any lighting unit that is fixed in front of the proscenium arch and illuminates the stage from the bridges above the audience, or from the circles and side balconies.

Gobo   Gobo is a steel or glass template slotted inside a lighting source called 'profile spot' to obtain a projection image of almost any type of artwork. In the case of a steel Gobo, an artwork is cut out of the steel, allowing light to pass through. A glass gobo can be associated with a photographic slide put into the lighting source. Gobos shape emitted light in the forms of texture, patterns, structures, icons, letters and coloured images. The name Gobo derives from the phrase '*Goes Before Optics*'.

Moving light   This refers to motorized lighting fixtures that can change their focus, colour, optics, and other features because of mechanical abilities that are programmed and controlled from the lighting board. A moving light is a versatile and multi-function robotized luminaire designed to replace multiple conventional, static lighting sources.

Proscenium arch/portal bridge   The proscenium is the area surrounding the stage opening and the proscenium arch is the arch above this area. In many theatres, the upper part of the arch, which is above the opening of the stage, is built as a bridge equipped with lighting units, offering access for lighting technicians and stagehands. The portal bridge provides one of the most important lighting angles to illuminate the upstage areas from.

Shinbuster   This type of lighting angle is occasionally used in ballet, contemporary dance and theatrical performances, where it is necessary to illuminate the body but not the stage floor. Profile spots are most commonly used as shinbusters, since their elaborate optics can provide a sharp field of illumination with minimum light spill onto the floor. The lighting sources are fixed very low, near to the floor, and the light beam is cut parallel to the stage.

Stage left and right   In North American and British theatre this refers to the actor's sides when facing the spectators. In other European countries, by contrast the sides of the stage are named according to the director's perspective – that is, how the audience perceives the stage.

Index